A Field Guide to the Ferns

and Their Related Families
of Northeastern and Central North America

THE PETERSON FIELD GUIDE SERIES

EDITED BY ROGER TORY PETERSON

THE PETERSON FIELD GUIDE SERIES

A Field Guide to the Ferns

and Their Related Families
of Northeastern and Central North America
with a section on species also found
in the British Isles and Western Europe

BY BOUGHTON COBB

Illustrated by Laura Louise Foster

HOUGHTON MIFFLIN COMPANY BOSTON

To
EDITH
from whom I learned
that vision begins in
the ecology of imagination

Editor's Note

THE FERNS are a very satisfactory group if you would like to master one of the fields of natural science. The number of flowering plants in the northeastern and midland states runs into the thousands — too many for anyone but a professional botanist to really master. On the other hand, there are only a hundred or so ferns. A man, if he puts himself to it, can know them all, the common ones and the rarities, and then go on to explore the biology of these fascinating plants.

This was the reason that Boughton Cobb, busy business executive with a lifetime interest in the outdoors, selected the Pteridophytes, to which he would devote the years ahead. His father was an architect, and he himself majored in art and architecture until he went into the service in World War I. This background, he believes, probably gave him his strong feeling for the ferns, which he describes as "the perfect examples of the architectonic design found in all plants." Important too were his early years on the farm, where, a member of a large family, he was put in charge of a younger brother, with whom he spent long days in the fields and woods. By necessity he became a tutor, interpreting the ways of nature in as brief and graphic a form as possible.

This book, the tenth in the Field Guide Series, spans the interests of both the beginner and the expert. Comparative silhouettes make learning the ferns easy indeed; the full-page renderings (every one from a living plant) by Laura Louise Foster give further details and are very satisfying for their sensitive beauty alone; and small anatomical drawings instruct the more advanced student. In addition to the species discussions, a chapter tells of the place in the plant kingdom of ferns and their allies and another chapter, by the late Dr. Theodor Just, an international authority on paleobotany, deals with the ferns of the past. Gardeners, particularly those who have wildflower gardens, will welcome the hints on maintaining native ferns. Mr. Cobb's own fern garden, a 20 x 30 foot "picture garden" built on a limestone ledge in Falls Village, Connecticut, includes virtually every fern of the northeastern states.

In most wooded sections in the Northeast or Middle West, fifteen or twenty species of ferns can be found quite easily in a morning. A dozen more can usually be found without too much trouble by exploring a little farther afield. These are the common widespread species. The others are more local, particularly the limestone species. Like many of the mushrooms, many ferns are found both in Europe and in North America. In fact, almost half of the ferns described in this book are also found in Britain and western Europe, as Mr. Cobb shows in his comparative check-lists.

Mr. Cobb, a graduate of Harvard University and a student of the Columbia School of Architecture from 1915 to 1917, is a life member of the American Fern Society and a member of many other botanical, horticultural, and scientific societies. He has collected and observed ferns intensively from Florida to Quebec and from California to Vancouver Island, as well as in parts of Puerto Rico, the British Isles, and Italy.

The artist, Laura Louise Foster, has brought to the fine drawings in this Field Guide a lifelong interest in nature. She possesses an unusual ability to observe and portray plant life with the delicate precision which satisfies both scientific and aesthetic standards. Her husband, a well-known horticulturist, naturalist, and teacher in Connecticut, has contributed the section on ferns in the garden.

The artful integration of text and illustration has resulted in a Field Guide that will be a pleasure to possess and a joy to use.

ROGER TORY PETERSON

Acknowledgments

I WISH to express my gratitude and appreciation to all those who have helped and guided me in the preparation of this book. First and foremost to my artist and collaborator, Laura Louise Foster, whose accurate and detailed drawings are essential for this book based on pictured forms, and to her husband, H. Lincoln Foster, teacher and naturalist, for his continuous advice and help to us both; to Dr. Theodor Just, Chief Curator of Botany at the Chicago Natural History Museum, for his contribution to this book and for his generous interest, and to the Museum's staff for granting me permission to use the picture of the primitive coal forest; to Dr. Henry K. Svenson, Associate Curator of Botany and Forestry at The American Museum of Natural History, for the lengthy process of checking and correcting the manuscript and drawings; to Dr. Warren H. Wagner, Jr., for giving permission to quote from his article on the complexities of the Appalachian spleenworts; to Professor Irene Manton of Leeds and Dr. Standley Walker of Liverpool for giving me a glimpse at the mysteries of the cytology of ferns; to Mr. Francis Ballard and his assistants at the Herbarium at Kew for their help to me with the ferns of Great Britain; to Mrs. Helen Everitt, formerly of Houghton Mifflin Company, for fostering the initial idea that led to this Field Guide.

In addition I would like to thank the following for special help during the course of my work: Dr. Ralph C. Benedict, Professor G. Evelyn Hutchinson, Miss Elizabeth Ann Bartholomew, the late Dr. William T. Helmuth III, and those members of the staff of Houghton Mifflin who have helped us all to make the Field Guide Series a success.

Finally, to Roger Tory Peterson, whose attitude toward me and my work has confirmed the notion, as in all the other Field Guides, that the layman can enjoy and use the scientific approach.

BOUGHTON COBB

Cobb-Web
Falls Village, Conn.

Contents

Foreword

"If you have remarked errors in me, your superior wisdom must pardon them. Who errs not while perambulating the domain of nature? Who can observe everything with accuracy? Correct me as a friend, and I as a friend will requite with kindness."

LINNAEUS

To THOSE interested in nature and to those who perhaps want to specialize in one of the fields of the natural sciences, the ferns and their allies offer a good springboard for study. The ancient lineage of ferns, their interesting biology, the comparatively few numbers of orders, families, genera, and species (there are about 10,000 species of ferns and allies listed for the world; there are over 300,000 species of seed-bearing plants), and the presence of ferns in nearly all ecological systems make them objects of special interest to the scientist as well as to the layman.

Wherever we go, or wherever we are, in any part of the world except in the arid deserts or on the high seas, we are likely to find ferns. They are found sparingly in the Arctic and Antarctic Circles and in quantities in tropical jungles; on the tops of mountains and in low swamps; in dimly lit, moist, cave-like crevices and in sunny open fields; on high, dry, and wind-swept cliffs; in and on still waters of ponds or lakes; along highways, in towns and villages; and even in the cities, commonly displayed in florists' windows. Since some ferns are evergreen, these species can be observed in the wild in winter. Also, many ferns take kindly to pots and to terrariums, where they can be studied and appreciated indoors.

To the observer of nature the problems of identification and the questions of habits of the different species are two main interests. Ferns, so readily accessible wherever we are, constantly offer the observer material for these interests. The more easily identified are the more common ones. The number of species in our area is limited to about 100 or more. This relatively small number makes it possible to find them all. However, with the many hybrids, varieties, and forms the interest of the search does not end once all known species have been found. To date it remains the rare individual who has found and identified all the species of ferns and their allies which have been reported as indigenous to the area. Furthermore, there exists always the possibility of finding in the wild an escaped foreign species.

Unlike birds, ferns remain where we find them and consequently give unlimited opportunity for close-up observation. In addition, leaves can be taken home for more careful investigation, and plants or cuttings of the rootstocks of the more common ferns can be collected for transplanting. Spores of the more rare species may be propagated at home, though this is a delicate, precise, and often lengthy operation. (The lapsed time from the ripe spore to the first small new fern plant varies from a few weeks for the Osmundas to 15 or 20 years for some of the Lycopodiums.) If carefully and expertly done, however, enough specimens can be raised from spores for future study and appreciation without despoiling our rapidly vanishing wild flora.

The Field Guide

This *Field Guide* is of pocket size, and is brief and simple, with as few botanical terms or words as seemed possible. For further simplification, the keys for identification are based mainly on pictured forms and the key characteristics for the species are accentuated by diagnostic arrows. Important species have been accurately and faithfully portrayed from living specimens of mature growth and in fruiting state, with all parts of the plant illustrated, from the lowermost roots to the topmost leaves. All portraits are in the descriptive section on right-hand pages. The brief descriptive text for the species illustrated is always on the opposing left-hand page. No turning of pages is therefore necessary in the field. For more detailed descriptions, and especially for hybrids, varieties, and forms that may be local, endemic, or widespread I recommend the various fern books and pamphlets for specific states or localities listed in the Bibliography.

Area Covered

The area of northeastern and central United States and adjacent Canada covers that territory lying east of the 88th longitude, south of the 47th latitude, and north of the 36th latitude, and west of the Atlantic Ocean. In other words, the area is bounded by a line drawn southward from the top and middle of Wisconsin down to the southern border of Kentucky and eastward along its southern border and the southern border of Virginia to the coast, and from the top of middle Wisconsin *eastward* through southern adjacent Canada to the Atlantic Ocean.

Nomenclature

There is little agreement among botanists regarding either popular or scientific names. Though it is generally believed that genera and species are definable entities in nature, they have been set up by the mind of man, and minds (including scientific ones) are apt to vary. A plant that one person may consider to be a distinct species, another may hold to be only a variety of a species. In addition there is the great problem of just what genus a given species may belong to, especially the earliest name for that genus, and just what are the scientific limits of that genus. The reader must therefore be tolerant of the variations in names which he will find in different fern books. I have followed the nomenclature of Dr. Conrad V. Morton, who was in charge of the Pteridophyta in *The New Britton and Brown Illustrated Flora of the Northeastern United States and Adjacent Canada* (1952, 3 vols.), which is the most recently published authoritative work on the ferns and their allies of the regions covered by this *Field Guide*. Wherever mention is made in this guide of world-wide numbers of genera in a family, or numbers of species in a genus, I have followed the listings of Carl Christensen's *Index Filicum* (1906), and the Supplements of 1913, 1917, and 1934.

Fields for Exploration

From earliest times human activities have been filled with love and interest for plant and animal life, not only from the utilitarian view but also from the aesthetic. Man's attitude toward his natural environment has constantly advanced his observations of all things around him. This deep-seated sense of relation to his ecology is dramatically highlighted today by the large demand for guide books and other out-of-door literature. The annual attendance of the many thousands of persons at state and federal camping sites, even the sales of millions of hunting and fishing licenses, confirm a very high interest in nature and the outdoors. As a part of this general interest, there is a merging of the aesthetic and the intellectual in this inquiring attitude about nature, I believe — a sense of wonder often colored with religious and philosophical feeling. Our wider concept of time and space and our observation with instruments demand scientific explanations that nevertheless have aesthetic quality. The multiplication of problems offer increasing opportunities for observation and research by layman and trained scientist alike. The following points up some of the problems.

Many species of ferns may produce each season many millions of spores so tiny and light that they may be considered without exaggeration a normal ingredient of atmospheric dust. For most species the spores remain viable for many years and they seem to be impervious to extreme climatic conditions. The ferns, therefore, have greater mobility than the higher order of plants. Only a few years ago a station for *Asplenium adiantum-nigrum* was found near Boulder, Colorado. It is believed that there are no records, fossil or otherwise, which can show that this fern is or was indigenous to our continent. It is, however, common in Europe and Asia. It is supposed that the spores were carried from Asia to the Rocky Mountains by substratospheric air currents. With the more recent discovery of the jet stream in 1933 and its estimated speed of up to 400 miles per hour,* it seems probable that this jet stream quickly transported the spores from Asia to Colorado. Similarly, there are now first reports for *Asplenium septentrionale* in our western mountain area, as well as for *Ceterach officinarum* in our Southwest. Are the atomic test explosions in the Southwest sending us spores of our southwestern species and perhaps of these Asiatic immigrants?

Dr. Irene Manton (see Bibliography), in discussing the numbers of named types of species and hybrids of the *Dryopteris* in America, states that they do not exhaust the numbers of cytologically distinguishable entities which exist. She suggests that there is something else breeding with *Dryopteris spinulosa,* "typical" and possibly resembling it morphologically, that is of a different chromosome count, diploid not tetraploid.

The size and shape of ferns, I believe, are more dependent on their ecology than are these aspects of flowering plants. Variation in the morphology of a fern plant from the typical species, hybrid, or variety are termed "form" or *forma* (plural, *formae*). I have found that certain *formae* of some species revert to the typical when transplanted to another site. Explanations for this offer many opportunities for further investigation and research.

* "The Jet Stream," *The Aircraft Flash,* official Ground Observer Corps magazine, **3**: 5 (May, 1955).

A Field Guide to the Ferns

and Their Related Families
of Northeastern and Central North America

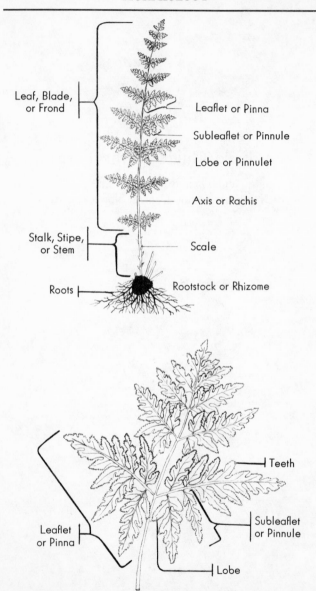

Leaf, Blade, or Frond

Leaflet or Pinna

Subleaflet or Pinnule

Lobe or Pinnulet

Axis or Rachis

Stalk, Stipe, or Stem

Scale

Roots

Rootstock or Rhizome

Teeth

Leaflet or Pinna

Subleaflet or Pinnule

Lobe

Morphology of a Fern

(Morphology — the study of form.)

Roots: Usual root forms are thin, wiry, black, forking, shallow-creeping, and grow from sides and undersides of rootstock.

Rootstock (Stock, Trunk, or Rhizome) supports roots below and stems and leaves above. Either short and thick, and almost completely buried, with only the growing parts of stems and leaves ascending in short trunks above ground, or (the more typical Rootstocks, better called Rhizomes) elongated, narrow, or thin, and growing horizontally below or on the surface of ground, with stems and leaves sprouting at intervals from upper surfaces. Rhizomes or Rootstocks perennial; stems and leaves evergreen or annual according to species and ecology. Rootstocks usually covered with scales or hairs.

Stalk (Stipe, or Stem) supports the leaf. Usually flat or concave in front, with rounded back, and covered with hairs or scales (particularly when young), of various shades of tans, browns, silvers, and black. Arrangements of Stalks growing from rootstock, whether in circles, pairs, individually, or in tufts, vary with genus or species.

Leaf (Frond, or Blade) is the flat, green, expanded part. Leaves vary in size and shape according to species. Some species have different sizes and shapes for fertile and sterile leaves. Fern Leaves not only perform function of photosynthesis, but fertile leaves bear, usually on undersides, the spores for reproduction, a function typical to ferns. Leaves vary by species from a simple undivided form to compound and decompound forms with laciness so characteristic of ferns in general.

Leaflets: When leaf is compound, divisions are known as Leaflets, or Pinnae, and leaf as whole is Once-cut, or Pinnate. When Leaflets are decompound, subdivisions are known as Subleaflets, or Pinnules, and leaf as whole is Twice-cut, or Bipinnate. When Subleaflets are divided again, divisions are known as Lobes, or Pinnulets, and over-all leaf is Thrice-cut, Lacy-cut, or Tripinnate.

Axis (or Rachis) is that part of stem carrying the leaflets. Similarly, where over-all leaf is simple that part of stem contained by leaf's surface is called the Midrib, the name also applied to central stems contained by leaflets, subleaflets, and lobes.

Stem supports leaf below axis, and similarly is the support for subleaflet or lobe.

Veins: Venation of fern leaves is an important distinguishing characteristic of the various species and genera. Position of spore case on underside of leaf and its relation to life-bearing Veins often identify the species.

How to Use the Keys in This Field Guide

A KEY, as used in reference to botany, is a table in which the chief characteristics of a group of plants are arranged to help in determining their names and species. It is an essential part of a field guide, and especially so if it is simple, easy to understand, and can be used rapidly. When we are in the field we want to recognize the commoner species as quickly as possible (to allow more time to identify the rare or unfamiliar).

Most botanical keys are based on matching verbal pictures to the ones made by the eye. Verbal distinctions of the genera are broken down into the verbal distinctions of the species and then into the variety, forma (special form with reference to shape), or hybrid. This for most of us is a tedious and often arduous process to follow and often impracticable in the field.

Since ferns present the human eye with singularly perfect examples of the architectonic design found in all plants, the keys in this book are based primarily on pictured forms. The leaves of young ferns are often nondescript and frequently very similar in form for several species, so the forms used here represent only those fern plants, or leaves, which are of average adult growth. Also, because the growth form of ferns is definitely affected by environment, the forms used are representative of those ferns as found in their most typical and most customary ecological systems, or environmental conditions.

I. The first and most simple pictorial key for recognition is a series of silhouettes of typical leaf forms for various ferns, grouped in accordance with their confusing similarity of form. Two diagnostic arrows for each fern are used to accentuate clearly and quickly their two most significant characteristics.

II. The second pictorial key is based on separating the ferns into four broad classifications of leaf form:

    a. Those with simple leaflets, i.e., those where the leaf, or frond, is cut into numbers of simple leaflets — Once-cut Ferns.

    b. Those with more complicated leaflets where the frond is not only cut into numbers of leaflets, but where these leaflets are cut again into subleaflets — Twice-cut Ferns.

    c. Those with lacy leaflets where the frond

is cut into leaflets, the leaflets into subleaflets, and the subleaflets cut again
into lobes — Thrice-cut Ferns.

d. Those with unique, distinctive, and non-
fernlike leaves.

The first three leaf forms, Once-cut, Twice-cut, and Thrice-cut,
are then separated into three types of over-all leaf shapes with
additional classifications as to approximate size. (The size includes
both the leaf and the stalk.)

a. Those which are broadest at the base.

b. Those which are semitapered to the
base, and

c. Those which are tapered to the base.

The shapes, structures, and characters of the leaves, leaflets,
subleaflets, lobes, and stalks are then simply classified and, finally,
the name of the fern is given with the numbers of the pages to turn
to for more detailed descriptions.

III. The third pictorial key shows the different typical spore
cases and the ways they are borne on the fertile leaflets of the
different genera and of those species that differ one from another
within the genus. (When ferns are in fruit, this key is a quick and
usually simple one to use, especially if one has a magnifying glass.)

Final, and usually positive, recognition of the fern under consideration is reached by turning to the two pages of full description.
The left-hand page not only describes the *style* (the quality of form)
and the *ecology* (the mutual relations of the fern with its sur-
roundings), but also the characters, structures, and types of the
leaves, axes, stalks, rootstocks, and roots, as well as the spores or
fruits, fruitcovers, and often the fiddleheads. The right-hand page,
facing the page of description, is a detailed drawing, or portrait,
of the complete fern in its full-blown fruiting state. Enlarged
drawings for better illustrating fruitdots and leaf forms, as well
as varieties and forms, are arranged as symphonic margins, or
marginalia, on the plates. In addition, diagnostic arrows are used
to emphasize the key characteristics of the species, with mention
made of those species of similar form which lack this combination
of characteristics. Each illustration has been drawn from a living
specimen, graphically emphasizing as nearly as possible the aesthetic qualities of its structure and form (style).

Pictorial keys are followed throughout the book, not only
for the True Ferns, but also for the Fern Allies.

Ferns of Unique or Unfernlike Forms

Diagnostic Arrows are for Key Characteristics

Hart's-tongue Fern 1. Leaf entire, acute wavy-edged. Blunt-tipped or forked. Very variable.
2. Short scaly stalk.

See page 160

Walking Fern 1. Leaf entire, long pointed tip. Base heart-shaped or with divergent wings.
2. Smooth slender stalk.

See page 108

Purple-stemmed Cliffbrake 1. Narrow, oblong entire upper leaflets.
2. Stalk and axis purplish brown.

See page 136

Filmy Fern 1. Leaves translucent.
2. Hardly any stalks; axis winged.

See page 166

Curly Grass Fern 1. Sterile leaves curly and hair-like.
2. Fertile leaves erect, topped by spore cases.

See page 164

Hartford Fern 1. Sterile leaves ivy-like.
2. Stalk vine-like.

See page 162

(These illustrations for all keys are not drawn to the same scale. They are merely to show differences in form.)

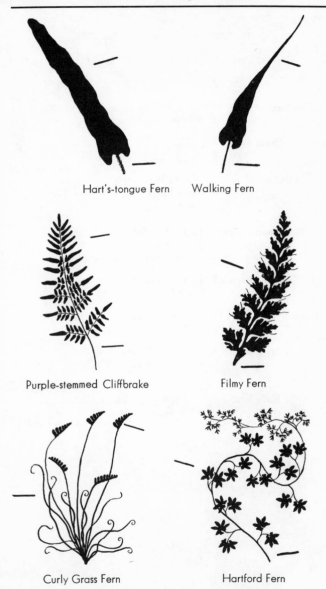

Hart's-tongue Fern

Walking Fern

Purple-stemmed Cliffbrake

Filmy Fern

Curly Grass Fern

Hartford Fern

Larger and Coarser Ferns

Crested Fern
1. Lowest pair of leaflets each an *equilateral* triangle.
2. Stalk rather tall and very chaffy.
See page 74

Interrupted Fern
1. Fertile leaf erect and interrupted.
2. Sterile leaf *shorter* and not as erect.
See page 170

Virginia Chain Fern
1. Leaflets ascending.
2. Tall purplish-brown stalk.
See page 124

Clinton's Fern
1. Leaf tall and erect.
2. Lowest pair of leaflets each a *broad-based triangle*.
See page 74

Cinnamon Fern
1. Fertile leaf pointed, clublike, cinnamon color.
2. Sterile leaf *taller* and *erect*.
See page 172

Goldie's Fern
1. Leaf broad ovate and slightly tilted.
2. Stalk longer than leaf.
See page 76

Evergreen Woodfern
1. Leaflets perpendicular to the axis.
2. Stalk *very* chaffy.
See page 68

Ostrich Fern
1. Sterile leaf plume-like.
2. Fertile leaf short, dark, and lyre-shaped.
See page 118

Male Fern
1. Leaf semi-tapering to bottom.
2. Stalk very chaffy.
See page 66

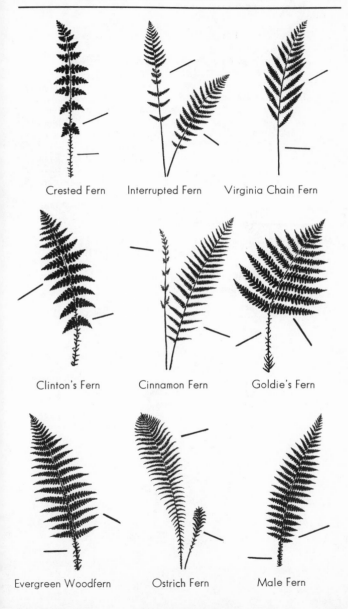

Crested Fern   Interrupted Fern   Virginia Chain Fern

Clinton's Fern   Cinnamon Fern   Goldie's Fern

Evergreen Woodfern   Ostrich Fern   Male Fern

Medium-sized Coarser Ferns

Christmas Fern 1. Leaflets eared at axis.
2. Stalk very chaffy.
See page 126

Braun's Holly Fern 1. Subleaflets spiny.
2. Stalk very stubby and chaffy.
See page 128

Sensitive Fern 1. Sterile leaves nearly opposite, *closely* spaced.
2. Fertile leaflets beadlike.
See page 120

Netted Chain Fern 1. Sterile leaflets *not* opposite, *widely* spaced.
2. Fertile leaflets narrow and constricted.
See page 122

Narrow-leaved Spleenwort 1. Leaflets narrow and pointed.
2. Slender, smooth stalk.
See page 114

Polypody
2 species
1. Leaflets alternate, winged at axis.
2. Smooth, shortish stalk.
See pages 130, 132

Christmas Fern

Braun's Holly Fern

Sensitive Fern

Netted Chain Fern

Narrow-leaved Spleenwort

Polypody

Medium-sized Delicate Ferns

Massachusetts Fern   1. Lower leaflets narrow at axis.
2. Pale and slender stalk.
See page 88

New York Fern   1. Lower pairs of leaflets diminish rapidly in size.
2. *Pale*, smooth, and slender stalk.
See page 86

Marsh Fern   1. Lower pairs of leaflets usually horizontal.
2. *Darkish*, smooth, and slender stalks.
See page   84

Lady Fern   1. Lower pairs of leaflets usually horizontal.
2. Scattered dark scales on stalk.
See page 110

Silvery Spleenwort   1. Lowest pairs of leaflets point downward.
2. Hairy stalks with scattered pale scales.
See page 112

Spinulose Woodfern   1. Finely cut, ascending leaflets.
2. Stalk coarse and very chaffy.
See page   68

Hayscented Fern   1. Long pointed finely cut leaf. Slightly hairy.
2. Stalk lustrous tan, hairy, brittle.
See page 116

Bulblet Fern   1. Leaf long and narrowly tapering to a point.
2. Stalk short, reddish, and smooth.
See page 156

Boott's Fern   1. Lacy-cut leaflets tilted like venetian blinds.
2. Stalk very chaffy.
See page 72

Massachusetts Fern   New York Fern   Marsh Fern

Lady Fern   Silvery Spleenwort   Spinulose Woodfern

Hayscented Fern   Bulblet Fern   Boott's Fern

KEY IE
Triangular-shaped Ferns and the Ferns with Other Distinctive Growth Forms

Broad Beech Fern 1. Broad triangular leaf.
2. *All leaflets* winged at axis.

See page 80

Long Beech Fern 1. Narrow triangular leaf.
2. Lowest pair of leaflets not winged at axis, and point downward.

See page 82

Bracken 1. Triangular leaf, branch-like form in 3 segments.
2. Subleaflets' tips distinct and pointed.

See page 134

Robert's Fern 1. Broad triangular leaf.
2. *Lowest and next lower pairs* of leaflets distinctly stemmed.

See page 49

Oak Fern 1. Broad triangular leaf.
2. *Only lowest pair* of leaflets distinctly stemmed.

See page 78

Royal Fern 1. Leaflets like locust tree leaves.
2. Feathery, cinnamon-colored fertile leaflets at top of leaf.

See page 168

Maidenhair Fern 1. *Whorled* growth form.
2. *Forked* purple-black stalk.

See page 140

Venus Maidenhair Fern 1. *Branching* growth form.
2. Purple-black stalk, *not forked*, upper stem zigzagged.

See page 142

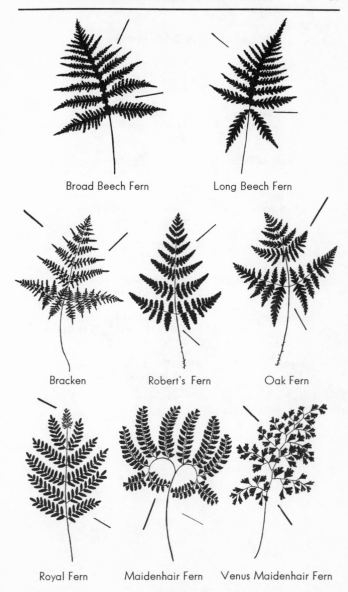

Broad Beech Fern   Long Beech Fern

Bracken   Robert's Fern   Oak Fern

Royal Fern   Maidenhair Fern   Venus Maidenhair Fern

Smaller, Rock-loving Ferns

Fragrant Cliff Fern
1. Leaf with *very* densely crowded leaflets and tapered to base.
2. Stalk *very short*.

See page 62

Lipferns
4 species
1. *Lower* leaflets widely spaced.
2. Stalk and axis dark, wiry, and brittle.

See pages 150, 152, 154

Fragile Fern
1. Leaf delicate and *smooth*.
2. Stalk slender, brittle, *brownish* at base.

See page 158

Blunt-lobed Woodsia
1. Rounded leaflets slightly *hairy*.
2. Stalk hairy, slender, *straw-colored*.

See page 144

Rusty Woodsia
1. Back of leaf *densely* hairy.
2. Scaly *dark brown* stalk.

See page 146

Smooth Woodsia
1. *Upper* leaflets crowded.
2. Tiny, delicate straw-colored stalk.

See page 148

Slender Cliffbrake
1. Sterile subleaflet fan-shaped.
2. Fertile subleaflets narrow and pointed.

See page 138

Alpine Woodsia
1. *All* leaflets widely spaced.
2. Entire stalk and most of axis chestnut brown.

See page 148

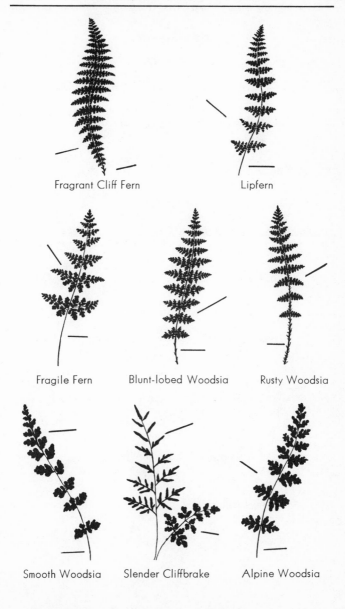

Fragrant Cliff Fern

Lipfern

Fragile Fern

Blunt-lobed Woodsia

Rusty Woodsia

Smooth Woodsia

Slender Cliffbrake

Alpine Woodsia

Spleenworts

Ebony Spleenwort 1. Leaflets eared, narrow, and
not opposite.
2. Stalk and axis dark and lustrous.

See page 90

Scott's Spleenwort 1. Long pointed tip to leaf,
leaflets irregular.
2. Stalk and axis brown.

See page 106

Black-stemmed Spleenwort 1. Leaflets eared, narrow, and
opposite.
2. Stalk and axis dark and lustrous.

See page 92

Maidenhair Spleenwort 1. Leaflets rounded, *not eared*.
2. Stalk and axis dark and lus-
trous.

See page 94

Lobed Spleenwort 1. Leaf long, pointed, with irregular lobed leaflets.
2. Stalk *brown at base*, green
above.

See page 104

Green Spleenwort 1. Oval leaflets tiny and opposite.
2. Stalk *brown at base*, green
above.

See page 98

Bradley's Spleenwort 1. Leaflets not opposite, *cut-
edged*, eared at base.
2. Stalk and *lower axis* dark and
lustrous.

See page 102

Wall Rue 1. Leaflets fan-shaped and *distinctly stemmed*.
2. Stalk slender and green.

See page 100

Mountain Spleenwort 1. Leaflets and subleaflets triangular with short stems.
2. Stalk dark below, green
above.

See page 96

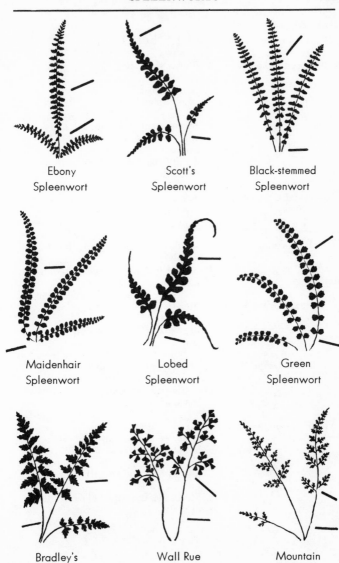

Ebony
Spleenwort

Scott's
Spleenwort

Black-stemmed
Spleenwort

Maidenhair
Spleenwort

Lobed
Spleenwort

Green
Spleenwort

Bradley's
Spleenwort

Wall Rue

Mountain
Spleenwort

KEY IH

Succulent Ferns

Cut-leaved Grape Fern   1. Sterile leaf broadly triangular, *acutely cut*.
   2. Sterile leaf branches near or below soil.

See page 186

Leathery Grape Fern   1. Sterile leaf broadly triangular with *blunted*, often overlapping leaves.
   2. Sterile leaf branches near or below soil.

See page 190

Daisyleaf Grape Fern   1. Sterile leaf *oval* and deeply cut.
   2. Sterile leaf branches *near top* of stalk.

See page 184

Rattlesnake Fern   1. Sterile leaf broadly triangular and deeply cut.
   2. Sterile leaf *not stemmed*, arising halfway up stalk.

See page 192

Triangle Grape Fern   1. Sterile leaf small, triangular, 3-*part*.
   2. Sterile leaf branches *near top* of stalk.

See page 184

Dwarf Grape Fern   1. Sterile leaf small, oval, *rounded outlines*, once-cut.
   2. Sterile leaf *near top*, often clasping spore case.

See page 184

Adder's-tongue Fern   1. Sterile leaf *entire*, oval.
   2. Leaf semi-clasping the stalk, about $\frac{1}{3}$ from top.

See page 182

Moonwort   1. Sterile leaf oblong with rounded *fan-shaped* leaflets.
   2. Sterile leaf branches below middle of stalk.

See page 188

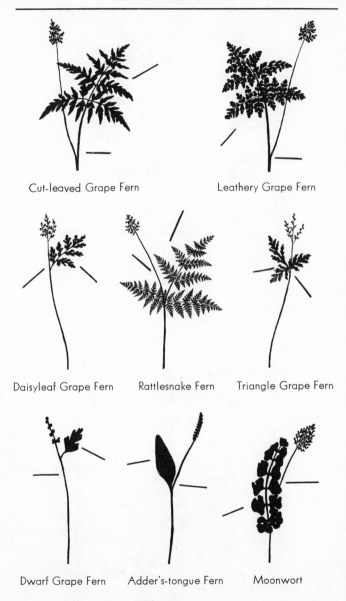

Cut-leaved Grape Fern   Leathery Grape Fern

Daisyleaf Grape Fern   Rattlesnake Fern   Triangle Grape Fern

Dwarf Grape Fern   Adder's-tongue Fern   Moonwort

KEY IIA
Once-cut Ferns

Total over-all height — 2 feet or more

a. LEAVES BROADEST AT BASE
   Stalks mostly smooth, stiff, and brittle
      Leaves broadly triangular; leaflets wavy-edged, or
      coarsely indented, upper leaflets winged at axis,
      two lowest leaflets sometimes pointing downward
      Sensitive Fern   p. 120

b. LEAVES SEMI–TAPERING TO BASE
   Stalks slender, smooth, green or light brown
      Leaves broadly oblong; leaflets broad-winged at
      axis throughout, edges finely toothed
      Netted Chain Fern   p. 122
   Leaves narrow lance-shaped; leaflets smooth-
   edged, narrow, pointed, not eared at base
   Narrow-leaved Spleenwort   p. 114
   Stalk short, stout, and very chaffy
      Leaves narrow lance-shaped, leathery; leaflets dis-
      tinctly toothed, eared at base   **Christmas Fern**   p. 126

Total over-all height — less than 2 feet

a. LEAVES BROADEST AT BASE
   Stalk and axis deep dark brown
      Leaves narrow with long pointed tips; leaflets
      mostly narrow, highly variable in size and shape
      Scott's Spleenwort   p. 106
   Stalks dark brown, axis green
      Leaves narrow with long pointed tips; leaflets
      mostly oval, fairly stable in size and shape
      Lobed Spleenwort   p. 104

b. LEAVES SEMI–TAPERING TO BASE
   Stalks green, smooth, and slender
      Leaves oblong, smooth, leathery, green on both
      sides; leaflets blunt-tipped, winged at axis
      Common Polypody   p. 130
   Stalks gray, scaly, and pock-marked, and slender
      Leaves oblong, leathery, green, and smooth above,
      scaly, pock-marked, and gray beneath; leaflets
      round-tipped, winged at axis   **Little Gray Polypody**   p. 132
   Stalks and lower axis dark lustrous brown, tufted
      Leaves delicate, ovate lance-shaped; leaflets ob-
      long, not opposite, eared at axes
      Bradley's Spleenwort   p. 102
   Stalks slender, brown at base, green above, tufted
      Leaves delicate, narrow lance-shaped; leaflets

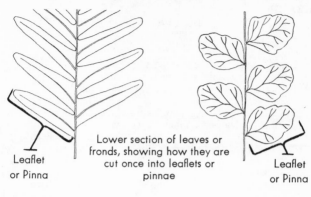

Lower section of leaves or fronds, showing how they are cut once into leaflets or pinnae

Leaflet or Pinna

Leaflet or Pinna

Leaf Shapes

Total length

Leaf, Blade, or Frond

Stalk, Stipe, or Stem

Leaf, Blade, or Frond

Stalk, Stipe, or Stem

Leaf, Blade, or Frond

Stalk, Stipe, or Stem

Broadest at base   Semi-tapered at base   Tapered to base

rounded, opposite, not eared at axes

Green Spleenwort   p. 98

c. LEAVES TAPERING TO BASE
   Stalks and axes dark and lustrous throughout
      Leaves narrow lance-shaped
         Leaflets narrow, blunt-tipped, eared at base, not
         opposite; lower leaflets hug axis

Ebony Spleenwort   p. 90

         Leaflets narrow, blunt-tipped, eared at base,
         often deflexed from axis, opposite

Black-stemmed Spleenwort   p. 92

         Leaflets rounded, not eared, opposite

Maidenhair Spleenwort   p. 94

KEY IIB

Twice-cut Ferns

Total over-all height — 2 feet or more

b. LEAVES SEMI–TAPERING TO BASE
    Stalks very scaly, particularly at base
        Leaves leathery, broad ovate, long stalk
                             Goldie's Fern   p. 76
        Leaves leathery, oblong ovate **Marginal Woodfern**   p. 64
        Leaves leathery, oblong lance-shaped
                            Clinton's Fern   p. 74
        Leaves leathery, narrow oblong lance-shaped
                            Crested Fern   p. 74
    Stalks smooth
        Leaves oblong lance-shaped; woolly tufts at base
        of leaflets   **Cinnamon Fern**   p. 172
        Leaves oblong lance-shaped; lacking woolly tufts
                       Interrupted Fern   p. 170
        Leaves oblong lance-shaped; long dark stalk
                  Virginia Chain Fern   p. 124
        Leaves ovate lance-shaped; subleaflets widely
        spaced   **Royal Fern**   p. 168
    Stalks pale, finely hairy
        Leaves oblong lance-shaped, finely hairy under-
        neath   **Silvery Spleenwort**   p. 112
c. LEAVES TAPERING TO BASE
    Stalks very scaly
        Leaves lance-shaped, prickly **Braun's Holly Fern**   p. 128
        Leaves lance-shaped; stalk chaffy   **Male Fern**   p. 66
    Stalks smooth
        Leaves broad lance-shaped   **Ostrich Fern**   p. 118

Total over-all height — between 1 and 2 feet

a. LEAVES BROADEST AT BASE
    Stalks hairy
        Lowest pairs of leaflets pointing downward
        Leaves as broad as long, axis winged
                       Broad Beech Fern   p. 80
        Leaves narrower than long; axis not winged at wide
        space between lowest pairs of leaflets
                       Long Beech Fern   p. 82
b. LEAVES SEMI–TAPERING TO BASE
    Stalks slender and smooth
        Leaves delicate, lance-shaped
            Veins of subleaflets forked   **Marsh Fern**   p. 84
           Veins of subleaflets not forked
                 Massachusetts Fern   p. 88

(*Continued on p. 24*)

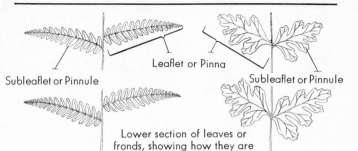

Subleaflet or Pinnule   Subleaflet or Pinnule

Leaflet or Pinna

Lower section of leaves or
fronds, showing how they are
cut once into leaflets or
pinnae, and then again into
subleaflets or pinnules

Leaf Shapes

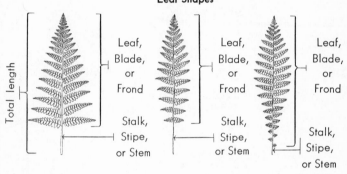

Total length

Leaf,
Blade,
or
Frond

Stalk,
Stipe,
or Stem

Leaf,
Blade,
or
Frond

Stalk,
Stipe,
or Stem

Leaf,
Blade,
or
Frond

Stalk,
Stipe,
or Stem

Broadest at base   Semi-tapered at base   Tapered to base

KEY IIB *continued*

c. Leaves tapering to base
  Stalks slender and smooth
    Leaves delicate, lance-shaped   **New York Fern**   p. 86

Total over-all height — less than 1 foot

a. Leaves broadest at base
  Stalks slender, green, and tufted
    Leaves ovate; subleaflets stemmed, fan-shaped
                                      Wall Rue   p. 100
  Stalks slender, dark brown at base, tufted
    Leaves oblong lance-shaped; subleaflets semi-
    stemmed, oblong   **Mountain Spleenwort**   p. 96
  Stalks slender, pale brown, slightly chaffy, not tufted
    Leaves ovate; fertile subleaflet narrow, pointed;
    sterile subleaflet fan-shaped   **Slender Cliffbrake**   p. 138
  Stems purplish brown, tufted
    Leaves lance-shaped; fertile subleaflets oblong;
    sterile subleaflets ovate
      Stems slightly chaffy
            Purple-stemmed Cliffbrake   p. 136
      Stems smooth   **Smooth Cliffbrake**   p. 57
b. Leaves semi–tapering to base
  Stalks brown at base, hairy, tufted, not jointed above
  rootstock
    Leaves oblong lance-shaped with white hairs
                       Mountain Woodsia   p. 58
  Stalks chestnut at base; smooth, tufted, jointed
  above rootstock
    Leaves narrow oblong lance-shaped, smooth
                           Alpine Woodsia   p. 148
  Stalks pale green at base; smooth, delicate, tufted,
  jointed above rootstock
    Leaves narrow oblong lance-shaped, delicate,
    smooth   **Smooth Woodsia**   p. 148
  Stalks black, wiry, smooth, with rusty brown hairs at
  base
    Leaves narrow oblong lance-shaped, smooth
                         Smooth Lipfern   p. 154
  Stalks dark brown, wiry, brittle, very hairy, tufted
    Leaves oblong lance-shaped, slightly hairy on top,
    densely hairy beneath; lower pairs of leaflets
    spaced widely apart   **Hairy Lipfern**   p. 152

KEY IIC

Thrice-cut or Lacy Ferns

Total over-all height — 18 inches or more

a. LEAVES BROADEST AT BASE
>Stalks tall, smooth, rigid, light brown, swollen at base
>>Leaves broadly triangular, usually divided into three parts, often parallel to the ground, coarse, leathery; subleaflets narrow oblong, often deeply lobed **Bracken** p. 134
>Stalks short, slender, smooth, pale red or straw color
>>Leaves triangular, narrow, long, tapering to the apex, lowly arching or pendent; subleaflets toothed or deeply lobed **Bulblet Fern** p. 156

b. LEAVES SEMI–TAPERING TO BASE
>Stalks light brown, coarse, and scaly
>>Leaves semi-delicate, very lacy, broad lance-shaped, subleaflets distinctly toothed
>>>**Spinulose Woodfern** p. 70
>>Leaves semi-delicate, lacy, narrow lance-shaped; subleaflets oblong, deeply cut, distinctly toothed, lowest pairs of leaflets triangular with very short stems, and tipped toward the horizontal
>>>**Boott's Fern** p. 72
>Stalks smooth, greenish or reddish, finely scaly at base
>>Leaves lance-shaped, delicate, subleaflets narrow oblong, blunt-tipped, finely toothed **Lady Fern** p. 110
>Stalks stoutish, brittle, shiny, chestnut-colored
>>Leaves ovate lance-shaped tapering to apex, slightly hairy underneath; subleaflets shallow-cut, blunt-toothed **Hayscented Fern** p. 116

Total over-all height — 18 inches or less

a. LEAVES BROADEST AT BASE
>Stalks very slender, round, slightly scaly at bases
>>Leaves delicate, broadly triangular, divided into three segments; subleaflets deeply cut, bluntly toothed **Oak Fern** p. 78

b. LEAVES SEMI–TAPERING TO BASE
>Stalks ascending from elongated rootstock, smooth, slender
>>Leaves membranous, ovate lance-shaped; subleaflets deeply cut, bluntly toothed, nearly winged to axes **Filmy Fern** p. 166
>Stalks slender, brittle, brown, and smooth
>>Leaves broad lance-shaped, delicate, smooth; leaf-
(*Continued on p. 26*)

KEY IIC *continued*

lets broadly spaced, deeply cut, variable in form
Fragile Fern p. 158
Stalks hairy, slender, straw-colored, semi-tufted
Leaves broad lance-shaped; leaflets mostly close together, semi-coarse, slightly hairy underneath; subleaflets deeply cut, blunt **Blunt-lobed Woodsia** p. 144
Stalks short, scaly, densely tufted
Leaves lance-shaped, smooth above, rusty scales underneath; leaflets crowded, deeply cut into rounded lobes **Rusty Woodsia** p. 146
Stalks short, stout, brown scales at bases
Leaves leathery, narrow lance-shaped; leaflets chaffy underneath, narrow lance-shaped, deeply cut into continuous blunt lobes; leaflets' stems at axes obscure **Fragrant Cliff Fern** p. 62
Stalks stout, covered with thick brown wool, tufted
Leaves oblong lance-shaped, upper surface slightly woolly, undersides thickly covered with whitish-brown wool; subleaflets oblong lance-shaped, deeply cut, terminal lobes prominently enlarged
Woolly Lipfern p. 150

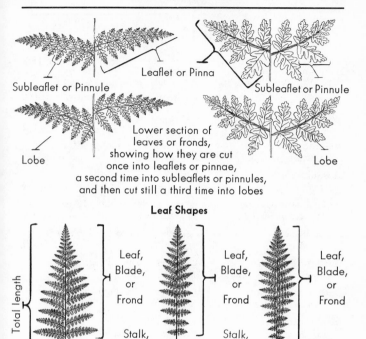

Subleaflet or Pinnule

Leaflet or Pinna

Subleaflet or Pinnule

Lobe

Lower section of
leaves or fronds,
showing how they are cut
once into leaflets or pinnae,
a second time into subleaflets or pinnules,
and then cut still a third time into lobes

Lobe

Leaf Shapes

Total length

Leaf,
Blade,
or
Frond

Stalk,
Stipe,
or Stem

Leaf,
Blade,
or
Frond

Stalk,
Stipe,
or Stem

Leaf,
Blade,
or
Frond

Stalk,
Stipe,
or Stem

Broadest at base   Semi-tapered at base   Tapered to base

Ferns of Unique Form

Hart's-tongue Fern
Phyllitis Scolopendrium
1 species. 12″± long by 1½″ wide. Often with forked or composite tip.   p. 160

Adder's-tongue Fern
Ophioglossum
2 species. 4″± high, 1″± wide.   p. 182

Walking Fern
Camptosorus rhizophyllus
1 species. 4″± long, 1″± wide at base.   p. 108

Mosquito Fern
Azolla caroliniana
1 species. ¼″ over-all.   p. 178

Water Shamrock
Marsilea quadrifolia
1 species. 8″ ± high, 1″ ± wide for leaf.   p. 178

Grape Fern
Botrychium
7 species. Up to 12″ high.   pp. 184 ff.

Hartford Fern
Lygodium palmatum
1 species. Vine-like growth up to 3′. Leaves 2½″±.   p. 162

Curly Grass Fern
Schizaea pusilla
1 species. 2″± high.   p. 164

Maidenhair Fern
Adiantum
2 species. 20″± high. Fragile, delicate leaflets in branching form.   pp. 140, 142

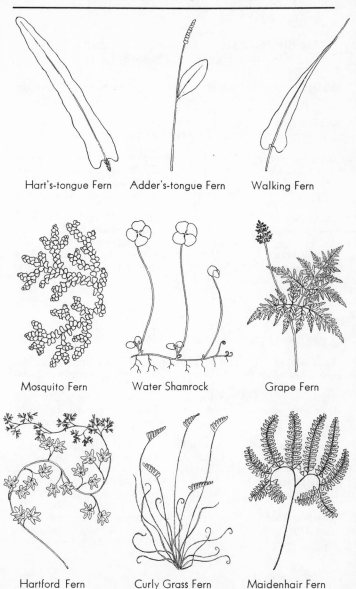

Hart's-tongue Fern   Adder's-tongue Fern   Walking Fern

Mosquito Fern   Water Shamrock   Grape Fern

Hartford Fern   Curly Grass Fern   Maidenhair Fern

KEY IIIA

Spore-bearing Leaves, Fruitdots, or Spore Cases of Genera Listed

Adder's-tongue Ferns or *Ophioglossum*	Spore cases in a spike, shaped like the rattles of a rattlesnake. On separate stem.
Grape Ferns or *Botrychium*	Globular spore cases in clusters like bunches of grapes. On separate stalks, or stems.
Osmunda Ferns or *Osmunda*	Globular spore cases in dense clusters on separate stalks, or leaf stalks.
Sensitive Fern or *Onoclea*	Spore cases enveloped by the fertile leaflets into rows of hard beads. On separate stalks.
Chain Ferns or *Woodwardia*	Fruitdots oblong halfway between midvein and margin. Indusium, or fruit-cover, opening toward midvein.
Ostrich Fern or *Matteuccia*	Fruitdots covered completely and tightly by overcurving margins of leaflets. Separate stalks.
Bracken Fern or *Pteridium*	Fruitdots in continuous lines around leaflets. Indusium formed by overlapping margins.
Cliffbrakes or *Pellaea*	Fruitdots in masses along margins of leaflets. Indusium formed by overlapping margins.
Rock Brakes or *Cryptogramma*	Fruitdots spreading to midrib. Indusium formed by overcurving margins. Separate stalks.
Lipferns or *Cheilanthes*	Fruitdots in bunches along but in from margins. Indusium formed by overcurving margins partially covering fruitdots.
Maidenhair Ferns or *Adiantum*	Fruitdots in from margins of lobes. Indusium formed by overcurving of margins.
Curly Grass Fern or *Schizaea*	Spore cases beadlike in two rows covering undersides of fingerlike leaflets. On triangular-headed separate stalks.
Climbing Fern or *Lygodium*	Fruitdots egg-shaped in double rows completely covering undersides of narrowed fertile leaflets. Scale-like indusium.

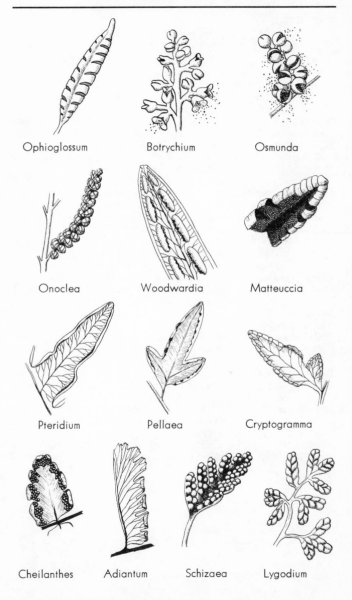

Ophioglossum   Botrychium   Osmunda

Onoclea   Woodwardia   Matteuccia

Pteridium   Pellaea   Cryptogramma

Cheilanthes   Adiantum   Schizaea   Lygodium

Fruitdots of Genera Listed

Woodferns
or *Dryopteris* — Fruitdots in scattered rows. Indusium, or fruitcover, rounded, kidney-shaped.

Marsh, Beech Ferns
or *Thelypteris* — Fruitdots usually in wide-apart rows near margins. Indusium narrow, kidney-shaped (lacking in Beech Ferns).

Woodsias
or *Woodsia* — Fruitdots scattered, clasped by star-shaped or fringed indusium from underside.

Holly Ferns
or *Polystichum* — Fruitdots in rows, usually close together and nearer midrib than margin. Indusium round with center stem.

Oak Ferns
or *Gymnocarpium* — Fruitdots small, few, scattered. Fruitdot rounded, kidney-shaped.

Bladder Ferns
or *Cystopteris* — Fruitdots scattered away from margins. Indusium hood-shaped, reaching up and partially over fruitdots.

Hayscented Fern
or *Dennstaedtia* — Fruitdots small on teeth of leaflets. Indusium nest-shaped holding spore cases like eggs.

Filmy Ferns
or *Trichomanes* — Fruitdots on marginal indentions of leaflets, inserted in funnel-shaped indusium with large bristle tip.

Polypodies
or *Polypodium* — Fruitdots round, prominent in two rows. Indusium lacking.

Walking Fern
or *Camptosorus* — Fruitdots scattered and irregular in size, shape, and placing. Indusium narrow, opening on one side.

Hart's-tongue Fern
or *Phyllitis* — Fruitdots long, narrow, prominent, at right angles to midvein. Indusium narrow, opening near one side.

Lady Ferns
or *Athyrium* — Fruitdots short, curved, oblique to midrib. Indusium narrow, curved, opening toward midrib.

Spleenworts
or *Asplenium* — Fruitdots short, straight, usually oblique to midrib. Indusium narrow opening toward midrib.

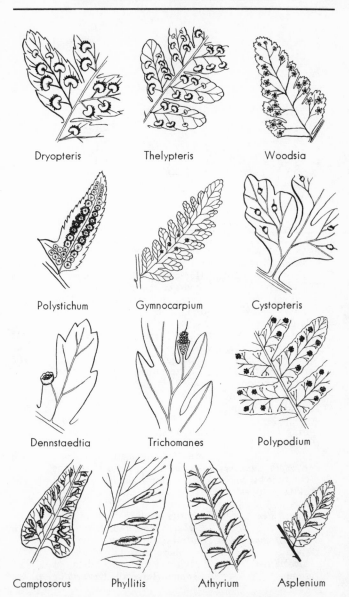

Dryopteris

Thelypteris

Woodsia

Polystichum

Gymnocarpium

Cystopteris

Dennstaedtia

Trichomanes

Polypodium

Camptosorus

Phyllitis

Athyrium

Asplenium

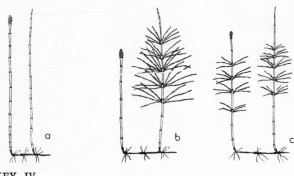

KEY IV

Horsetails

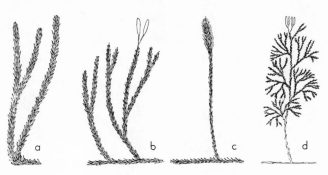

KEY V

Clubmosses

a. STEMS UPRIGHT WITHOUT CONES
  Closely formed tufts; leaves ascending
      Fir Clubmoss, *Lycopodium Selago*   p. 218
  Loosely formed tufts; leaves spreading
      Shining Clubmoss, *L. lucidulum*   p. 218
b. HORIZONTAL STEMS CREEPING; UPRIGHT STEMS WITH CONES
  Leaves ascending; one or more long-stemmed cones
      Staghorn Clubmoss, *L. clavatum*   p. 220
  Leaves spreading; single stemless cones
      Stiff Clubmoss, *L. annotinum*   p. 222
c. HORIZONTAL STEMS CREEPING; TOPS OF UPRIGHT STEMS LIKE BUSHY TAILS
  Lower part of upright stems with few and ascending leaves   **Bog Clubmoss,** *L. inundatum*   p. 224
  Lower parts of upright stems with many and spreading leaves   **Foxtail Clubmoss,** *L. alopecuroides*   p. 224
  Lower part of upright stems thin and almost leafless
      Carolina Clubmoss, *L. carolinianum*   p. 226
d. UPRIGHT TREE–LIKE GROWTH WITH CONES
  Horizontal stems deep in ground
    Single cones without stems
      Tree Clubmoss, *L. obscurum*   p. 228
    Three or four long-stemmed cones to the "candelabrum"   **Ground Cedar,** *L. tristachyum*   p. 230
  Horizontal stems subsurface-creeping
    One or two short-stemmed cones
      Savin-leaved Clubmoss, *L. sabinifolium*   p. 232
    Two or more long-stemmed cones to the "candelabrum"   **Running Pine,** *L. complanatum*   p. 232

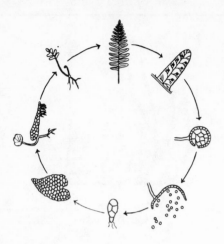

Life Cycle of a Fern

EACH OF the four classes of the Pteridophytes has its own characteristic behavior in producing, bearing, and propagating its spores. In turn the subdivisions, orders, families, genera, and species all have their own different distinctive behavioral patterns. It is by these differences that we commonly classify the various ferns and their allies.

The life cycle pattern within which ferns produce spores, spores develop into gametophytes, and the gametophytes produce the new fern plants is extremely interesting and little understood by many.

Even though the characteristic reproductive behavior of each family, genus, and species is given later in this handbook, an over-all understanding will be enhanced by a brief and simple description of the reproductive behavior of one of the more common ferns — *Dryopteris marginalis*, the Marginal Woodfern.

In summer, on the undersides of the subleaflets of the fertile leaves of this woodfern, there appear tiny greenish round specks. These specks mature rather rapidly and turn into dark brown spots.

They are called sori, from the Greek word meaning "heaps." These sori, or *fruitdots*, are tiny masses of spore cases, or sporangia, which contain the spores. In the case of the Marginal Woodfern, the sori are covered by a thin membrane, or a part of the skin of

the leaf. This protective membranous covering is called the indusium, or *fruitcover*. When the spore cases are ripe and fully developed, they push off this protective covering. The *spore case*, or sporangium, is a small round capsule made of a single layer of sterile skin mounted on a tiny stem.  The capsule is almost completely belted vertically by a jointed ring, called the *annulus*, which is unjoined at about "four o'clock." When the spores are ripe and the spore case is dry, the annulus breaks and bursts the spore case. The ring snaps backward rapidly to below a horizontal position and then snaps forward even more rapidly and catapults the spores some distance away. As the spore case and the annulus are most sensitive to moisture, breakage only occurs under dry conditions. The spores, therefore, are freed only when the air is dry, or when there is a dry wind which can better disperse them and give them more opportunity to land in suitable spots to develop first into their *prothalli* and later into their *gametophytes*. The spores of the Marginal Woodfern develop into gametophytes in about two weeks, and the gametophytes develop into the new young fern after about three and one half months. This varies, of course, in different ecological regions and with varying climatic conditions.

The Marginal Woodfern is not one of the largest ferns, nor has it many fertile, or spore-bearing, leaves. It produces, however, many hundreds of thousands of spores each season. Some of the larger ferns with many fertile leaves and more spore cases to their leaves produce millions of spores each season. (One botanist estimated 52 million spores on one *Dryopteris marginalis* plant.) This is hard to believe but can be readily appreciated when we take into consideration that each spore case contains, usually, 64 spores, and each fruitdot, or sorus, contains scores of spore cases with each tiny leaflet containing a dozen or more fruitdots. There are hundreds of leaflets on each fertile leaf and many leaves on a full-grown Marginal Woodfern plant.

When a spore finds itself in a suitable place in the form of a tiny bit of shady moisture at the proper temperature, it begins developing into a *prothallus*, or gametophyte. The prothallus starts as a one-celled body and promptly puts down a tiny rootlike hair to anchor it to the soil. Then by adding one cell to another, it enlarges into a small heart-shaped, green, membranous body about $\frac{1}{4}$ inch in size. The notched end is several times thicker than the apex, forming a kind of cushion. The sexual organs develop on the underside.

The male organs, or *antheridia*, are near the apex, and the female

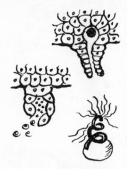

organs, or *archegonia*, are near the notch. Both male and female organs are microscopic in size. The female organ consists of a sterile neck, or chimney-like tube with its base imbedded in the cushion part of the gametophyte. The base holds one single egg. There are twenty or more female organs in one gametophyte. When the female organs are fully developed, they all bend toward the apex better to receive the sperms, or *antherozoids*. The male organs are more numerous than the female. They are short and bulbous, and each contains several sperms. The sperm is shaped like a corkscrew, with hairs, or *cilia*, at one end for propelling itself through moisture.

When the gametophyte is fully grown and the sex organs are fully developed, the thin skin of the male organ bursts if, and only when, there is contact with a tiny bit of moisture. At the same time the necks of the female organs open and exude a chemical that is attractive to the sperms and causes them to swim toward the open necks and enter and fertilize the egg. As soon as the one egg is fertilized the neck closes, as, it is believed, do all the other necks on that particular gametophyte. (Customarily only one plantlet develops from each gametophyte.) If, however, there is enough moisture present, sperms may swim to adjacent gametophytes and fertilize their eggs.

The time development of the gametophytes varies for different species. If the time development for two different species of the same family synchronizes exactly and their gametophytes are adjacent in the same tiny bit of moisture, one species can fertilize another species, and produce a hybrid. But even though it is common for several species of ferns to grow close together, hybrids are not as common as we imagine.

After fertilization, the egg develops. At first it is anchored to the base of the female organ in the cushion of the gametophyte.

Then it grows a root downward into the soil and a stem upward, which curves through the notch of the heart-shaped gametophyte. From the stem grows the first tiny leaf. Nutrition from the cushion lasts only long enough to have the root and the leaf develop sufficiently to become the independent plant again, with multiple roots, stems, and leaves, ready for the next cycle.

Such is the life cycle for the *True Ferns*.

The *Fern Allies* differ somewhat from this in general. Their spores are not born on the undersides of the leaves, but are usually in cone-like spikes — i.e., Horsetails and some Clubmosses;

or in special chambers between the leaves — i.e., some Spike-mosses and Quillworts; or in special individual cases, or *sporocarps* — i.e., Water Ferns. The spores of the Clubmosses, like those of the True Ferns, are all alike, at least in outward appearance, and their gametophytes have both male and female sex organs, whereas the Horsetails have spores of one kind but gametophytes of two kinds, male and female. The Water Ferns have two kinds of spores and two kinds of gametophytes. The Quillworts and Spike-mosses also have two kinds of spores and two kinds of gameto-phytes, which are small, or minute, and rudimentary; but the female gametophyte in the megaspore (large female spore) retains the fertilized egg and nourishes it until it has attained sufficient growth and strength for independence. Even though the alternation of generations exists here, it is of a highly modified form and close to that of the seed-bearing plants.

The Place of Ferns and Their Allies in the Plant Kingdom

A SIMPLE but widely used classification of the Plant Kingdom readily shows the place of ferns and their allies among other plants:

1. *Thallophyta*,* the thallophytes, comprise a large and varied group of about 125,000 species of aquatic and terrestrial plants, ranging in size from unicellular microscopic forms, such as bacteria, to large seaweeds or giant kelps attaining more than 100 feet in length. Customarily thallophytes are divided according to their mode of life: (a) algae — including green, red, and brown algae — are mainly aquatic, contain chlorophyll, and make their own food; (b) fungi — including bacteria, slimemolds, true fungi, and lichens — are mainly terrestrial, lack chlorophyll, and, with few exceptions, depend on other organisms for their food. Seaweeds and pondscums are algae; molds, yeasts, mushrooms, and toadstools are true fungi. Bark lichens and deermoss represent lichens, organisms formed by the union of a fungus with an alga.

2. *Bryophyta*,** the bryophytes, a group consisting of about 20,000 species, are represented by relatively small green land plants, the mosses, liverworts, and hornworts. Some lack true roots, stems, and leaves, and are always low-growing. In place of roots they possess hairlike filaments (*rhizoids*) with which they adhere to the ground. Like the thallophytes, they require water for sexual reproduction. Although some are aquatic, most species are terrestrial, occurring on the ground, on the bark of trees, and even on leaves of tropical trees.

3. *Pteridophyta*,† the pteridophytes, including ferns and their allies, represent the first true vascular plants with roots, stems, and leaves, but without flowers and seeds. Represented by only about 10,000 species, pteridophytes make up the smallest group of the plant kingdom. This group is usually divided into four classes: (a) the ferns proper (Filicinae); and fern allies, (b) horsetails (Equisetinae), (c) clubmosses and spikemosses (Lycopodiinae), (d) quillworts (Isoetinae). Grape ferns and adder's-tongue (order Ophioglossales), and water clovers and mosquito fern (order Hydropteridales) are here treated as succulent ferns and water ferns, respectively.

4. *Spermatophyta*,†† the spermatophytes, or seed plants, make up the largest and most important group of plants. They include

---

*From the Greek: *thallos* — young shoot; *phyton* — plant.
**From the Greek: *bryo* — tree-moss; *phyton* — plant.
†From the Greek: *pteris* — fern; *phyton* — plant.
††From the Greek: *sperma* — a seed; *phyton* — plant.

all evergreen and deciduous trees and shrubs, herbs, grasses, and other flowering plants. To date over 200,000 species have been described and classified, and many new ones are constantly being added to the list. Seed plants more than any other group determine the character and appearance of most plant communities and natural landscapes.

LIKE FLOWERING PLANTS, ferns and their allies are vascular plants, characterized by their internal vascular (conducting and mechanical) tissue that enables them to attain height, stature, and strength impossible without it. Lacking vascular tissue, algae, fungi, lichens, liverworts, and mosses are called non-vascular plants. Actually, most people think of plants only in terms of ferns and flowering plants, rarely of algae, fungi, lichens, mosses, liverworts.

Because of their complex internal structure, vascular plants can transfer water and nutrient materials obtained from the soil to their topmost leaves. This vascular tissue consists of two major regions, wood (*xylem*) and bast (*phloem*), variously grouped together as vascular bundles. The xylem region is the principal tissue through which water and the nutrient substances dissolved in it are conveyed from the soil to the tops of the tallest plants, whereas the phloem region functions as the downward pathway for the organic substances produced by the plant in the leaves. In addition to these most important functions, vascular tissues provide the mechanical support needed by land plants.

Ferns and their allies are also known as *vascular cryptogams*, in contrast to thallophytes and bryophytes, which make up the bulk of the cryptogams. In short, cryptogams are plants without flowers, whereas flowering plants are known as *phanerogams*. Thus the old terms cryptogams and phanerogams refer to modes of reproduction. These terms date from a period when reproduction in plants was poorly understood and are retained today solely for purposes of convenience.

All ferns and their allies produce spores, the typical and most common method of asexual reproduction. However, many ferns multiply vegetatively by creeping rootstocks, and one genus produces bulblets. Spores are contained in cases, known as sporangia. The seven orders of pteridophytes have distinct types of spore cases, which vary considerably from family to family and within families. In fact, fern families and their subdivisions down to genera and species are based primarily on the characters exhibited by their spore cases and the way these are carried.

When ripe, spores are ejected from spore cases and germinate under suitable conditions, i.e., when they come in contact with moisture. Then they produce a small, usually green, flat, thallus-like growth called the prothallus, or gametophyte (sexual phase). The sexual organs develop on the underside of the prothallus, and, after fertilization, give rise to new plants. Fern plants in turn

PLANT KINGDOM

THALLOPHYTA	BRYOPHYTA	*PTERIDOPHYTA*	SPERMATOPHYTA
ALGAE	MOSSES	*Ferns*	SEED PLANTS
FUNGI	LIVERWORTS	*Fern Allies*	
LICHENS			

RELATIONSHIPS OF THE FERNS AND THEIR ALLIES DESCRIBED IN THIS BOOK

PTERIDOPHYTES, Ferns and Their Allies

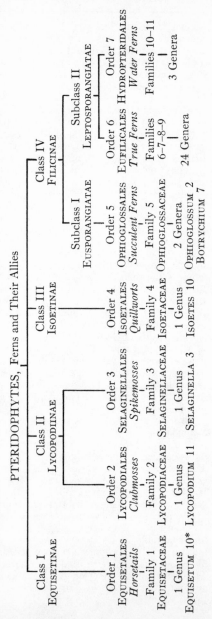

Class I
EQUISETINAE

Order 1
EQUISETALES
Horsetails
Family 1
EQUISETACEAE
1 Genus
EQUISETUM 10*

Class II
LYCOPODIINAE

Order 2
LYCOPODIALES
Clubmosses
Family 2
LYCOPODIACEAE
1 Genus
LYCOPODIUM 11

Order 3
SELAGINELLALES
Spikemosses
Family 3
SELAGINELLACEAE
1 Genus
SELAGINELLA 3

Class III
ISOETINAE

Order 4
ISOETALES
Quillworts
Family 4
ISOETACEAE
1 Genus
ISOETES 10

Class IV
FILICINAE

Subclass I
EUSPORANGIATAE

Order 5
OPHIOGLOSSALES
Succulent Ferns
Family 5
OPHIOGLOSSACEAE
2 Genera
OPHIOGLOSSUM 2
BOTRYCHIUM 7

Subclass II
LEPTOSPORANGIATAE

Order 6
EUFILICALES
True Ferns
Families
6-7-8-9
24 Genera

Order 7
HYDROPTERIDALES
Water Ferns
Families 10-11
3 Genera

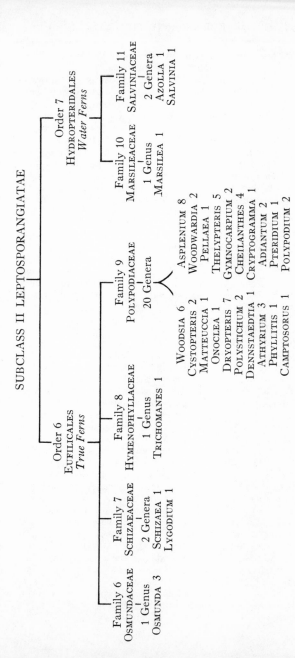

SUBCLASS II LEPTOSPORANGIATAE

Order 6
EUFILICALES
True Ferns

Order 7
HYDROPTERIDALES
Water Ferns

Family 6
OSMUNDACEAE
1 Genus
OSMUNDA 3

Family 7
SCHIZAEACEAE
2 Genera
SCHIZAEA 1
LYGODIUM 1

Family 8
HYMENOPHYLLACEAE
1 Genus
TRICHOMANES 1

Family 9
POLYPODIACEAE
20 Genera

WOODSIA 6
CYSTOPTERIS 2
MATTEUCCIA 1
ONOCLEA 1
DRYOPTERIS 7
POLYSTICHUM 2
DENNSTAEDTIA 1
ATHYRIUM 3
PHYLLITIS 1
CAMPTOSORUS 1

ASPLENIUM 8
WOODWARDIA 2
PELLAEA 1
THELYPTERIS 5
GYMNOCARPIUM 2
CHEILANTHES 4
CRYPTOGRAMMA 1
ADIANTUM 2
PTERIDIUM 1
POLYPODIUM 2

Family 10
MARSILEACEAE
1 Genus
MARSILEA 1

Family 11
SALVINIACEAE
2 Genera
AZOLLA 1
SALVINIA 1

*The number following the genus name refers to the number of species covered here.

produce spores, thus representing the asexual, spore-producing phase or generation (*sporophyte*). As the gametophyte is followed by a sporophyte, this sequence of stages known as alternation of generations is completed. In other words, each generation begins with a particular type of reproductive cells, grows, and ends with the production of a different type of reproductive cells. For instance, a spore gives rise to a prothallus, which produces sex organs (gametophyte stage of the prothallus). The fertilized egg gives rise to the fern proper, which in turn produces spores (sporophyte). As these generations alternate in regular sequence, they are both essential for completion of the life cycle. (See pages 36 ff.)

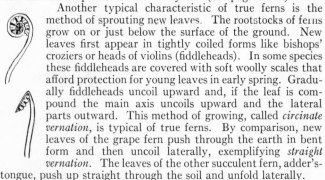

Another typical characteristic of true ferns is the method of sprouting new leaves. The rootstocks of ferns grow on or just below the surface of the ground. New leaves first appear in tightly coiled forms like bishops' croziers or heads of violins (fiddleheads). In some species these fiddleheads are covered with soft woolly scales that afford protection for young leaves in early spring. Gradually fiddleheads uncoil upward and, if the leaf is compound the main axis uncoils upward and the lateral parts outward. This method of growing, called *circinate vernation*, is typical of true ferns. By comparison, new leaves of the grape fern push through the earth in bent form and then uncoil laterally, exemplifying *straight vernation*. The leaves of the other succulent fern, adder's-tongue, push up straight through the soil and unfold laterally.

The system of veining (*venation*) in fern leaves provides another outstanding characteristic. Whereas the veins of most flowering plants branch irregularly, veins of fern leaves branch into two equal parts, so-called forked venation. In one case veins do not branch (Massachusetts fern); in a few cases branched veins form a net or chain (adder's-tongue, netted chain fern, and sensitive fern).

We think of all ferns as green. True, their leaves are completely green, but they are of various shades, ranging from the blue-green of cliffbrake to the dark, shining green of holly fern. Fern stems, however, are not always green. Some are black, others brown, tan, or even purple. Some species have woolly or hairy, tan or brown scales on the undersides of their leaves, and many have woolly or hairy stems. Not even the scales and wool are always of one color, as they may range from lustrous browns, through silvery tans to bright and dull ocherous yellows. Therefore, ferns are not entirely green and monochromatic. They are always colorful to the fern enthusiast who observes them first during their early growth and later in their particular ecological niches.

Practically all pteridophytes are perennial plants. Certainly all species dealt with in this handbook are perennial; one exception is the British annual gymnogram, *Anogramma leptophylla*, a delicate little fern found only in the Channel Islands.

The True Ferns

The Four Families and Twenty-four Genera Covered in This Book

I THE POLYPODIACEAE

THIS is the largest of the True Fern families, having listed for the world 171 genera with 7227 species. This family contains almost all of the species of the True Ferns. Because the differences between the genera and the species in this family are often so slight, many of the species have been moved within the family from one genus to another. Many changes have been made in the last few years, and probably many more changes will be made in the future. According to the classification of Morton in *The New Britton and Brown Illustrated Flora of the Northeastern United States and Adjacent Canada* by Henry A. Gleason (New York, 1952, 3 vols.), we have in the area covered in this book 20 genera with 54 species.

Typical for this family is the long-stalked spore case. The spore-case rings, or annuli, are vertical and interrupted by the stalk. The spore case breaks at about "4 o'clock," as described on page 37. The fruitdots, or sori, are borne on the undersides, or under margins, of the fertile leaves. Some species have fruit-covers, or indusia, some do not. The spores are without sex. The gametophyte, or prothallus, is heart-shaped, green, and terrestrial. The two sexual organs are borne on its underside. (See page 37.)

II THE HYMENOPHYLLACEAE

THIS family is usually known as the Filmy Fern family. It is of early origin, but not of great antiquity. It contains 4 genera with 651 species listed, which are widely distributed in warmer, moist or wet shaded areas, mainly in the tropics. In the area covered here we have only one genus with one species that is definitely rare and very local.

The Filmy Ferns have thin, delicate, and translucent leaves. They are small in size, even tiny. (A colony of one species can be covered by a twenty-five-cent piece.) For most species the leaves are made up of only one layer of cells with no stomata, or breathing pores. They require abundant moisture. Their rootstocks are slender and creeping, with a reduced root system that in some species is even absent and where the hairs of the rootstock act as rootlets. (Sometimes the hairs on the stalks or the hairs on the leaves act as rootlets.)

Typical for this family is the short-stalked, thin-walled spore case, which is round, or round disc shape, surrounded by an obliquely transverse, entire ring, or annulus, which splits obliquely. The fruitdots are borne at the ends of veins and on the margins of the fertile leaves. The indusium is sunk into the leaf tissue at the outer edges of the fertile leaves. For the genus *Trichomanes* it is shaped like a vase with two lips. The spore cases are piled up one on another from the bottom of the vase into a distinct and projecting stalk, which, after the spores are shed, persists as a long thin spike. The gametophyte, or prothallus, is thin, long, and profusely branched, not heart-shaped as in the Polypodiaceae family. The sexual organs are borne like stubby branches along its length.

III THE SCHIZAEACEAE

THIS family of 4 genera with 162 species listed for the world is found mainly in the tropics, but with some species in the northern temperate zones. The family contains genera and species which are widely different in size, shape, and form, and mostly of unfernlike appearances. The genus *Lygodium* is ivy-like in growth and form, and certain species attain a length of over 100 feet, while the genus *Schizaea* is grasslike in growth and form, and only a few inches tall. In our area we have two genera, each with only one species — one ivy-like and one grasslike. Both are rare; in fact, the Curly Grass is very rare, or found at present only in one locality.

Typical for this family are the egg-shaped, upright spore cases with short, thick stalks. They are solitary, not in groups, or sori. A number of each is borne on a contracted part of the fertile leaf. Near the narrower end of the spore case is a complete ring, or annulus, which, when breaking, splits the spore case horizontally. There are no true indusia, but the spore cases are covered by the margins of the fertile leaves. The gametophyte, or prothallus, is of a really primitive form, being thin, long, often branching, with the sex organs borne along its length like dwarf branches — similar to the gametophytes of the Filmy Ferns.

IV THE OSMUNDACEAE

(Named for Osmunder, the Saxon god of war.)

THE Osmundas, or Flowering Ferns, are one of the most primitive fern families. They are represented in our area by one genus with the three species: the Flowering Fern, *Osmunda regalis*; the Cinnamon Fern, *Osmunda cinnamomea*; and the Interrupted Fern, *Osmunda Claytoniana*. Thirteen species of the genus *Osmunda* are listed for the world — primarily in the temperate zones. The only other genus of the Osmunda family is *Todea*, which is solely indigenous to South Africa, New Zealand, and Australia.

The Osmundas are the largest and coarsest of our native ferns. They are well represented throughout the area and in some areas they are extremely common and widespread. Their rootstocks are massive, hard, often surface-creeping with their sprouting points ascending or erect. With older plants, the heavy coarse rootstocks arise a foot or more above the ground, like the trunks of tree ferns or small palm trees. The creeping rootstocks are increased each year by being constantly renewed at one end, while the oldest rootstocks at the other end die off. It is believed that they can live forever. Their roots are numerous, black, very wiry, and tightly matted together (each to each other, as well as to the rootstock). These matted masses of roots and rootstock are widely used in the culture of orchids.

The chief characteristics of the Osmunda family are their spores. They have no indusia (fruitcovers). They have no sori (fruitdots) or masses of spores like the true ferns. Their sporangia, or spore cases, are large and globular, thin-walled, with a short and stout stalk, and are formed from and on modified portions of the fertile leaves. The annulus, or spore-case ring, is developed from certain thickened cells of the spore case and is not a complete ring. It extends from one side to the opposite side, over the top of the spore case and down to the stalk of the spore case, and opens by a vertical slit. The spores are green and contain chlorophyll and must germinate promptly. The gametophytes are green and semi-heart-shaped, being longer and narrower than those of the true ferns.

THE GENERA

Family POLYPODIACEAE

Genus *Dryopteris*

(Greek: *drys* — oak, *pteris* — fern.
The majority of the species were usually found in oak woods.)

see pp. 62 ff.

IN THE world there are 1213 listed species, the largest number of species for any of the genera considered in this *Field Guide*. In our area there are listed 7 species, 1 fertile hybrid, and several varieties. The species of the genera *Gymnocarpium* and *Thelypteris* have at one time or another been included in the genus *Dryopteris*.

The species of this genus are generally woodland ferns, often evergreen, of medium size, with their sterile and fertile leaves substantially of the same shape and form. They are all definitely fernlike in appearance. Leaves are often leathery, much cut, dark green, frequently evergreen. Their leaflets and subleaflets are toothed or deeply cut. Their prominent indusia are kidney-shaped, and are attached to the underparts of the fertile leaflets or subleaflets by a marginal sinus (an indentation of a part of the edge of the indusium). The fruitdots, or sori, are round, numerous, and attached to the veins. The veins are free, forked, and end short of the margin of the leaflet or subleaflet. The rootstocks are coarse, scaly, and erect; short, creeping, or ascending at their tips. The stalks are stout and scaly and often grow in basket-like clusters, or tufts.

In the area included in this book these woodland ferns vary in their ecological preferences, from the low swampy areas to the high and dry rocky cliffs. The Crested and Clinton's Ferns like wet feet, while the rare, small Fragrant Cliff Fern is found only in crevices of the high and dry shaded rocky cliffs of northern regions. With the exception of the Fragrant Cliff Fern, it is not uncommon to find many of the *Dryopteris* species growing together, particularly in woodlands that have contiguous damp and dry areas. Such a region, which is usually a swampy spot in a sun-filtered wood, will have growing happily together the Crested Fern and the Clinton's Fern in the damp spots, the Boott's Fern with the former, and the Spinulose Woodfern (often with one or more of its varieties) and the Marginal Woodfern in the drier areas. Oftentimes the Goldie's Fern is added to this community, and in the most northerly regions, the Male Fern also.

Such a community of the different species of *Dryopteris* often produces many crossbreeds, or hybrids, and not only do we find

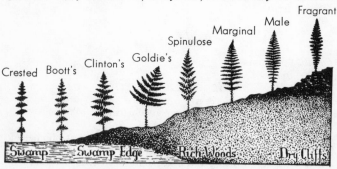

crossbreeds of the species, but crossings between the species and their hybrids, their varieties, their formae, and one with another, resulting in all kinds and sorts of forms varying more or less from the original parents. So common are these that it makes it almost impossible to list or describe them all. A dozen or more have been described in various books and pamphlets, and many dozens more merely given listings. There are, therefore, only described in this book the typical species of the genus *Dryopteris*, plus a few of the commoner varieties. One hybrid, Boott's Fern, is fully described in its most typical form, as it is often considered a species.

Genus *Gymnocarpium*

(Greek: *gymnos* — naked, *karpos* — fruit;
referring to their lack of indusia.)

see p. 78

THE two species of this genus found in our area are the Oak Fern, *Gymnocarpium Dryopteris* L., and Robert's Fern, *Gymnocarpium Robertianum* (Hoffm.) A. Br., also known as the Limestone Fern or Northern Oak Fern. (They were classified by Fernald in *Gray's Manual of Botany*, 8th ed., 1950, in the genus *Dryopteris*. Dr. Conrad Morton in *The New Britton and Brown*, 1952, has put them back into the genus *Gymnocarpium*.)

Oak Fern   Robert's Fern

They are both small, delicate, and triangular-leaved fragile ferns with similar fertile and sterile leaves. They are not evergreen. Their rootstocks are slender and wide-creeping. The stalks are fine, wiry brittle, and smooth, and longer than their leaves. Their leaves are of thin texture, with the lowest pairs of leaflets branching out from the main stem with prominent stems. Their fruitdots are round and have no indusia, or fruitcovers. The veins are simple or seldom forked and reach the margins of the subleaflets.

The Oak Fern is the more common of the two. Robert's Fern is rare in our area, found only in the cold and northerly regions on rocky ledges, usually limestone. Its leaf shape is more of an equal triangle. Its lowest pairs of leaflets moderately taper to their tips;

the lowest pair of leaflets of the Oak Fern taper abruptly, their lower subleaflets nearest the main stem being much longer than either their upper leaflets or their next adjoining subleaflets.

Genus *Thelypteris*
(Greek: *thelus* — female, *pteris* — fern)
see pp. 80 ff.

THELYPTERIS includes small to medium-sized ferns, mainly delicate and membranous. They are not evergreen. Their fertile and sterile leaves are mostly alike and cut into leaflets and subleaflets, which are not toothed. Their rootstocks are slender and creeping, stalks are straw-colored, slender, and slightly scaly — not chaffy. The fruitdots are round and attached to the veins on the undersides of the subleaflets about halfway between the midvein and the margin. Veins are usually free and forked and run to the margin of the subleaflet. (Veins of the New York Fern and the Massachusetts Fern are usually simple, *not forked*.)

The five species of this genus found in our area may be divided into two groups:

Group 1. The two Beech Ferns, which have triangular leaves, tilt about 45 degrees from vertical, and their fruitdots have *no indusia* (fruitcovers).

Long Beech Fern   Broad Beech Fern

Group 2. The Marsh Ferns, the Massachusetts Ferns, and the New York Fern have upright, narrow, oblong leaves, and their fruitdots are covered by pale, delicate, *kidney-shaped indusia*.

New York   Massachusetts   Marsh
Fern   Fern   Fern

These five species of the genus *Thelypteris* have been moved from one genus to another. In *Gray's Manual of Botany* (8th ed., 1950) and elsewhere they are classified in the genus *Dryopteris*, even though they have many characteristics differing from *Dryopteris*. Dr. Conrad Morton in *The New Britton and Brown* (1952) has now put them into the genus *Thelypteris* — a cosmopolitan genus of the temperate and subtropical areas.

Genus *Asplenium:* Spleenwort Ferns

(Greek: *a* — without, *splen* — spleen;
in reference to supposed medicinal properties.)

see pp. 90 ff.

THERE are listed 664 species of this genus, mostly tropical. Eight species occur in our area and as many or more hybrids, varieties, or forms.

The spleenworts are small evergreen ferns that grow from short, creeping, erect or ascending rootstocks, with fragile, slender, usually dark, wiry, and tough stalks. Their leaves usually grow in clustered forms with various degrees of cuttings, depending on the species. Their indusia, or fruitcovers, are narrow, usually straight, and attached at one side of a vein facing away from the midvein. Their veins are simple or forked and do not reach the margins.

One or more of the Aspleniums are to be found throughout our area. Many of the species crossbreed and produce hybrids or varieties, some of which have been given specific rank by certain authorities. In the Appalachians the Aspleniums form a complex group, ably described by Dr. Warren H. Wagner, Jr.* A small part of his description is quoted here.

Wherry (1925, 1936) pointed out that the Appalachian Aspleniums "form a series showing intermediates between certain long-recognized species." His basic end-point species were five in number: *Asplenium pinnatifidum* . . . *A. montanum* . . . *A. bradleyi* . . . *A. platyneuron* . . . and *A. rhizophyllum* (the walking-fern, usually treated as *Camptosorus rhizophyllus* but for the sake of simplicity retained as an *Asplenium* here). Detailed studies of the morphology of these five end-point species and comparisons of them with their various intermediates suggest that within the complex totalling 11 described entities, the real extremes are only three in number. These three species are *A. montanum*, *A. platyneuron*, and *A. rhizophyllum*. All the remaining taxa, commonly treated as species or hybrids — including the familiar *A. pinnatifidum* and *A. bradleyi* — lie somewhere between these three extremes in their morphology. . .

The Appalachian Aspleniums comprise 11 described taxa, of which 3 represent morphological extremes and the remainder intermediates. *A. ebenoides* is a usually sterile hybrid of *A. platyneuron* and *A. rhizophyllum* with 72 univalents at meiotic

*"Reticulate Evolution in the Appalachian Aspleniums," *Evolution*, 8: 103–18 (June, 1954).

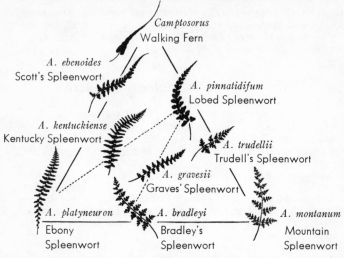

Camptosorus
Walking Fern

A. ebenoides
Scott's Spleenwort

A. pinnatidifum
Lobed Spleenwort

A. kentuckiense
Kentucky Spleenwort

A. trudellii
Trudell's Spleenwort

A. gravesii
'Graves' Spleenwort

A. platyneuron
Ebony
Spleenwort

A. bradleyi
Bradley's
Spleenwort

A. montanum
Mountain
Spleenwort

metaphase, although one population from Alabama is a fertile allopolyploid, forming 72 normal bivalents at meiosis. *A. bradleyi* is apparently the allopolyploid hybrid of *A. montanum* and *A. platyneuron*; it back-crosses with both parents. *A. pinnatifidum* likewise is evidently an allopolyploid hybrid, and its morphology, the irregularity of the leaves, and the pairing behavior of its putative backcross (*A. trudellii*) with one of the parents indicates that its parentage is *A. montanum* × *A. rhizophyllum*. *A. kentuckiense* and *A. gravesii* are both evidently trihybrids, the former 3n, the latter 4n, and *A. kentuckiense* morphologically represents the theoretical central point of the whole complex. A hypothesis of reticulate evolution is thus presented for the Appalachian Aspleniums which postulates that three original diploid species, *A. montanum*, *A. platyneuron*, and *A. rhizophyllum*, have given rise to 8 additional taxa through hybridization.

Genus *Camptosorus:* Walking Fern

(Greek: *kamptos* — bent, *soros* — a heap;
referring to the irregular arrangements of the fruitdots, or sori.)

see p. 108

FOR THIS genus, evidently derived from the genus *Asplenium*, there are only two species listed. One in northeastern Asia and the other in our area, *Camptosorus rhizophyllus* (L.) Link, the Walking Fern. The description given later for our species is adequate for that of the genus.

Genus *Athyrium*
(Greek: *a* — without, *thureos* — shield;
referring to lack of shieldlike appearance of indusium.)
see pp. 110 ff.

CARL CHRISTENSEN lists 68 species for the world, mostly tropical, although some species are common throughout the temperate zones. We have three species: the Lady Fern and Silvery Spleenwort, which are common, and the Narrow-leaved Spleenwort, which is uncommon though not rare. All are found throughout our area.

Many of the species of the genus *Athyrium* were originally grouped in the genus *Asplenium*, as the two genera have similar fruitdots and indusia. In fact, two of our species of *Athyrium* retain the common names of spleenworts.

The Athyriums differ from the Aspleniums in being large, *not* evergreen, terrestrial Woodferns with thick rootstocks, short and creeping, and with stalks that are stout, succulent, and of straw color; the Aspleniums are small, evergreen, rock-loving plants with small, semi-erect rootstocks and with thin, wiry, brittle, and dark stalks. The Athyriums, like the Aspleniums, have fruitdots that are narrow, arching, and attached at their sides to the forward parts of the veins.

The three species of the genus *Athyrium* in our area are quite different in leaf form. The Narrow-leaved Spleenwort has narrow pointed leaflets. The Silvery Spleenwort has narrow pointed leaflets with rounded semi-subleaflets, and the Lady Fern has lacy-cut subleaflets of varying degrees.

The Lady Fern, which is so common, has many variations. It is commonly separated into two varieties: Upland or Northern Lady Fern — var. *Michauxii* Mett., or var. *angustum* (Small) Rydb. — and Lowland or Southern Lady Fern. The leaf of the Upland Lady Fern is broadest near the middle, its spores pale brown, and its fruitdots larger and less hooked in shape than the Lowland Lady Fern (var. *asplenioides* [Michx.] Farw.), the leaf of which is broadest at the base and the spores dark brown. These differences seem to be not only due to geographic locations, but also to locations of high and low altitudes regardless of latitude. The inter-

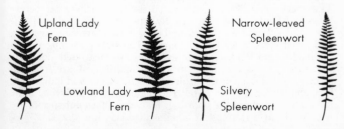

Upland Lady Fern

Lowland Lady Fern

Narrow-leaved Spleenwort

Silvery Spleenwort

grading of the varieties in the middle grounds make them almost impossible to classify properly as to the variety Northern or Southern. One variety, however, var. *rubellum*, is easy to distinguish, since its stalks are distinctly light wine color. It occurs in both the Upland and Lowland Lady Ferns and, I believe, in all their variations.

Genus *Dennstaedtia*
(Named for Augustus W. Dennstaedt, German botanist of early 19th century.)
see p. 116

THIS genus has listed 70 species, mostly in the tropical or semitropical areas of South America and Asia. In our area, there is only the one species: *Dennstaedtia punctilobula* (Michx.) Moore — the Hayscented or Boulder Fern.

Genus *Matteuccia*
(Named for Carlo Matteucci, an Italian physicist, 1800–68.)
see p. 118

FOUR species are listed for the world — three for Asia and one for North America and Europe. The species in our area is *Matteuccia Struthiopteris* (L.) Todaro, var. *pensylvanica* (Willd.) Morton — the Ostrich Fern. The description of the genus is the same as for the species.

Genus *Onoclea*
see p. 120

FOUND in eastern North America. Only one species found in North America and eastern Asia. Description of the genus is the same as for the species.

Genus *Woodwardia:* Chain Ferns
(Named for Thomas J. Woodward, an English botanist, 1745–1820.)
see pp. 122 ff.

TEN species of this genus are listed for the northern temperate zones and Central America, with two species in our area — *Woodwardia areolata* and *W. virginica*. The rootstocks are wide-creeping, dark, coarse, very scaly, and tough. The stalks are longer than the blades, and the leaves, not evergreen, are scattered along the rootstock. Veins are netted near the midrib, but are free and forked near margins of the leaflets. The fruitdots and indusia are long and narrow and are parallel to the midrib, or midveins. The indusia open toward the midrib or midvein. Both our species are ferns of the acid swamps, or other shaded acid wet places.

Genus *Polystichum*

(Greek: *polys* — many, *stichos* — rows; referring to many regular rows of fruitdots common in this genus. Christmas Fern often has so many fruitdots that they are confluent [massed together]. Braun's Holly Fern, however, has few, small, and well-spaced fruitdots. The description "many rows of fruitdots" applies primarily to our common Christmas Fern, *Polystichum acrostichoides*, and to the common Pacific Coast Sword Fern, *P. munitum*.)

see pp. 126 ff.

THE Polystichums are a large genus of 225 listed species found in both hemispheres, most abundant in the tropical mountains and in other cooler areas. They are coarse, rigid ferns quite tolerant of pH of the soil, and they are mostly evergreen. Their rootstocks are short, stout, either erect or horizontal, and very scaly. The leaves are narrow, wider in the middle, and taper up and down from the middle. They grow in bouquet-like clusters from a central rootstock. Their stalks are short, stout, and scaly. The leaflets and subleaflets are shiny, lustrous green, with bristly-toothed or holly-like edges.

Their fertile leaflets are usually narrower, especially when heavy with fruit, their veins forked and free. The indusium is round, with its center attached to the leaflet, leaving it open all around, like a shield. As the fruitdots grow, the indusium becomes funnel-shaped, then tubular, and finally, in certain species, the underside of the leaflet is completely covered by spores. Hence the name "acrostichoides" for our Christmas Fern — "like an *Acrostichum*." (*Acrostichum* is a genus of tropical fern that not only has masses of fruitdots covering the undersides of the fertile leaflets, but often on the top side as well.)

Two species, *P. acrostichoides* and *P. Braunii*, are described and illustrated as occurring in our area. *P. Lonchitis*, the Northern Holly Fern, found extremely locally in our most northerly and middle-western area, is not illustrated. This species is found locally only on the cliffs of our Canadian border. Its area east of the Rockies starts at the most northerly region of the Christmas Fern. However, on the Pacific Coast it is found in Southern California. It is quite like the Christmas Fern in form, except that its sterile and fertile leaves are similar, and its leaflets are close together, often overlapping.

P. acrostichoides, the Christmas Fern, common throughout our area, is widely variable in form, with all sorts of forkings, cuttings, and twistings of leaflets, which seem to persist in those forms, whereas *P. Braunii* (Braun's Holly Fern) is commonly stable in growth form.

Genus *Polypodium*

(Greek: *polys* — many, *pous* — foot; referring to the many "footprints"
left on rootstock where stalks have broken off.)

see pp. 130 ff.

THIS genus, with 1127 listed species, is widely distributed throughout the world, mostly in tropical and semitropical areas. There
are two species indigenous to the northeastern United States: the
Common Polypody, *Polypodium vulgare*, is widely and commonly
found in our northern area; and the Little Gray Polypody, *P.
polypodioides*, is widely and commonly found in our southern
area. Both, however, are uncommon in the sandy coastal
regions.

These two small ferns, with matlike growth form, are seldom
more than 10 inches high. They are evergreen. (Even though they
wither in a drought they promptly become green again after getting
moisture, and are therefore often referred to as Resurrection
Ferns.) Their leaves are oblong and leathery, and are once-cut
into narrow, oblong, blunt-tipped leaflets. The veins, which are
free and forked, do not reach the margins of the leaflets. There
is no difference between the fertile and sterile leaves. Their
fruitdots are round, naked, and prominent. Their stalks are
grooved on the upper sides and are jointed to the horizontally
creeping scaly rootstock.

The Common Polypody has 10 or more named forms, a fact that
recommends more than ordinary attention to this common and
widespread species.

Genus *Pteridium:* Bracken or Brake

(From Greek word for fern — *pteris*.)

see p. 134

THIS genus with only the one species — *Pteridium aquilinum* (L.)
Kuhn — is truly cosmopolitan and widely spread over the surface
of the world. There are, of course, many varieties that are more or
less geographically isolated. In our area the typical is var. *latius-
culum* (Desv.) Underw. — the eastern Bracken, which often has
variations in form as it approaches the boundaries of our area.

This rugged, prosperous genus has rootstocks that are widely
creeping over large areas, and their profuse leaves often exclude all
other plants. As their rootstocks and roots are often deep in the
ground, they are impervious to wet and cold or drought and heat.
They are generally considered the weed of the fern family. Their
proliferous and hardy reproduction by rootstock growth and
spreading has curtailed their reproduction by spores, which in
their genus is quite rare.

Genus *Pellaea:* Cliffbrakes
(Greek: *pellos* — dark; referring to dark stalks.)
see p. 136

IN OUR area we have only one species of 85 species listed for the genus *Pellaea* — *Pellaea atropurpurea,* Purple-stemmed Cliffbrake.

The Pellaeas are rigid ferns with stiff, brittle, powdery or slightly scaly purple or dark stalks. They are small rock-loving ferns with blue-green, simple, and entire leaflets and subleaflets. Their sterile and fertile leaflets and subleaflets are different in growth and form. They are often evergreen. Their rootstocks usually creep and entwine in the crevices of dry rocky ledges. The spores are borne at the edges of the veins a short way from the margins of the leaflets, which overlap them and make their characteristic false indusia. This overlapping of leaf margins makes the fertile leaflets into narrow, stiff, and constricted forms. The variety *Bushii,* the Smooth Cliffbrake, sometimes considered the species *Pellaea glabella,* is a more northerly, smaller fern, with more simply cut leaves and less powdery or scaly stalks.

Genus *Cryptogramma:* Cliffbrakes or Rock Brakes
(Greek: *kryptos* — hidden, *gramme* — line; referring to the lines of fruitdots hidden or covered by the overlapping of the margins of the fertile leaflets.)
see p. 138

THERE are listed 7 species of this genus in the world. In our area we have one indigenous species — *Cryptogramma Stelleri,* the Slender Cliffbrake — and an introduced species — *C. crispa,* the Parsley Fern.

These two ferns are small shade-loving, rock-loving plants with fragile, delicate, smooth, light-colored stalks, which are usually darker and slightly scaly at the base. Their sterile and fertile leaves are of different forms. The sterile weak and spreading, the fertile stiff and erect, with leaflets made narrow by the overlapping of their margins to cover the spore cases, making the false indusium. The veins are free, forked, not reaching margins; spore cases few at vein tips; and rootstocks slender, creeping, delicate.

The Slender Cliffbrake is distinctly rare and local, though found in many parts of our area — usually in the cooler sections in spite of its fragility. The Parsley Fern is a western species. (Where it has been introduced in our area it seems to thrive satisfactorily.) It differs from the Slender Cliffbrake in being more erect, more rugged, and more evergreen. Its sterile and fertile leaves are both erect and clustered, of thick texture. Its rootstock is coarse, erect. The Slender Cliffbrake is a fragile plant with a creeping, slender rootstock.

Genus *Adiantum:* Maidenhair Ferns

(Greek: *a* — without, *diainem* — to wet;
referring to way leaves shed water.)

see pp. 140 ff.

A LARGE and widely distributed genus found throughout the tropical and warm temperate zones, with 226 species listed. In our area, we have two species: *Adiantum pedatum* L., the Northern Maidenhair Fern, which occurs as far north as Alaska and northern Canada and as far south as Georgia and Louisiana; and *A. Capillus-Veneris* L , the Venus Maidenhair Fern, or Southern Maidenhair Fern, which extends from the southern parts of our area to tropical America.

Typical for this genus, and particularly for our two species, are the red-black or black thin, polished, smooth, brittle stalks that support drooping, delicate lacy leaves made up of fragile, fan-shaped, often overlapping leaflets. The fruitdots are borne on the outer edges, a little way in from the margins of the leaflets, which curl over the fruitdots and form false indusia. The veins are free and many times forked. The rootstocks are wide-creeping and spreading. Neither species is evergreen where frost occurs.

Genus *Woodsia*

(Named for the English botanist Joseph Woods, 1776–1864.)

see pp. 144 ff.

THIS genus has 37 species listed for the northern temperate, alpine, arctic, and antarctic zones of North and South America, Asia, and Africa. For our area, we list 6 species, 4 of which are illustrated in the descriptive section of this book. Two are fairly common throughout the area, two are fairly rare and confined to our most northerly area, and two are rare and local or found only in certain areas.

Typical for this genus is the inferior indusium, which is fixed to the underside of the leaflet. At first, with its lacerated segments it clasps the fruitdots like a fist, later opening and framing the fruitdots with a many-pointed star. The degree of lacerations of the indusium broadly differentiates the species. The fruitdots are round and often so numerous as to cover completely the backs of the leaflets. The similar fertile and sterile leaves, usually ever-green, grow in erect clusters from an erect and scaly rootstock. The stalks are short, stout, and, together with the leaves, leaflets, and axis, are covered with hairs, scales, or glands. (The stalks for some species are jointed above the rootstock.)

The two rare and local species — *W. scopulina* var. *appalachiana* (T. M. C. Taylor) Morton, and *W. oregana* var. *Cathcartiana* (B. L. Robinson) Morton — are really western species. *Scopulina*, or the Mountain Woodsia, has ragged-appearing blades, with distinctly toothed leaflets, and is distinguished by its many flat whitish hairs. It is reported from West Virginia and southwestern Virginia in our area. *Oregana*, or the Oregon Woodsia, is much like the Mountain Woodsia and the Blunt-lobed Woodsia, but without the flat white hairs, and its indusium breaks into many fine threadlike segments.

Genus *Cheilanthes:* Lipferns

(Greek: *cheilos* — lip or margin, *anthos* — flower; referring to way edges of leaves curl over submarginal lines of spore cases.)

see pp. 150 ff.

APPROXIMATELY 100 species of Lipfern are listed for the world, primarily in the tropical or subtropical zones. Of the 4 species recorded for our area, two — the Smooth and the Woolly — are found in our most southerly regions. The Hairy (most common) is not recorded for the northeastern area, and the Slender is rare and local in the Middle West, except in Wisconsin, where it is reported to be common.

The Lipferns are lovers of dry and rocky places. During droughts they curl up and look dead but quickly recover after rain. Like the Rusty Woodsia and the Little Gray Polypody, they are often referred to as Resurrection Ferns.

The Lipferns are small, evergreen or semi-evergreen, sturdy ferns, usually hairy or woolly. They grow in small tufts from short and compact rootstocks covered with rusty brown scales. The firm green leaves, which are intermingled with the dead stalks, are twice- or thrice-cut into divisions which are often beadlike in appearance. There is little difference between the sterile and fertile leaves. Their veins are free and forked and do not run to the edges of the leaves. The rounded spore cases are in lines at the ends of the veins, well within the margins of the leaves, and the edges of the leaves curl over these linear submarginal spore cases and form a more or less continuous false indusium — typical of the Lipferns. The stalk is usually shorter than the blade, and the axis is distinctly dark throughout and quite brittle.

Our 4 Lipferns are uncommon, different, and interesting little ferns. They are most easily distinguished from other small ferns by their round-tipped leaflets and their purplish dark brown stalk and axis. Their common names of Slender, Smooth, Hairy, and Woolly are truly descriptive for each species. *Cheilanthes Feei* is slender, *C. alabamensis* smooth, *C. lanosa* very hairy, and *C. tomentosa* very woolly.

The Slender Lipfern, *Cheilanthes Feei*, is so local in the western part of our area that a full description is not given in this *Field Guide*. In brief, it looks like a small and slender Hairy Lipfern, with a quite smooth stalk about the same length as its blade. Its leaflets are more rounded and beadlike, similar to those of the

Woolly Lipfern, and its rootstock is more compact and shorter than that of the Hairy, and more like the chunky erect rootstock of the Woolly. The very short, creeping rootstock gives it a tufted growth form more like the Woolly with its erect rootstock.

Genus *Cystopteris:* Bladder Ferns
(Greek: *kustis* — bladder, and *pteris* — fern;
referring to the inflated indusium.)
see pp. 156 ff.

THIS genus contains 18 species. One or more species is reported throughout the temperate and tropical zones. They are delicate ferns of the rocky woodlands, with creeping scaly rootstocks, with smooth, often polished, light-colored stalks, and much cut, not evergreen, leaves that grow usually in tufts. The veins are free, simple or forked, and reach the margins of the leaflets. Typical for the genus is the roundish, thin, hoodlike, or deeply convex, indusium that faces outward. The younger Bladder Ferns are easily confused with the young Woodsias. There are two species in our area.

Genus *Phyllitis*
(Greek: *phyllon* — a leaf.)
see p. 160

THERE are listed 8 species of this genus in the world, mostly occurring in the temperate zones and Central and South America. In our area we have only one rare species — *Phyllitis Scolopendrium* (L.) Newm. var. *americana* Fern. (D.).

Typical of the genus are the tongue-shaped, leathery, glossy, evergreen simple leaves with their long, narrow, and prominent fruitdots, which are borne in pairs alternately on the upper and lower parts of the veins, their indusia opening toward each other. The rootstocks are short, scaly, and erect. The leaves, which grow in spreading irregular clusters, have short, stout, and very scaly stalks.

Family SCHIZAEACEAE

Genus *Lygodium*
(Greek: *lugodes* — flexible.)
see p. 162

THERE are listed 39 species for this genus, mostly tropical and subtropical. In our area there is only one species, *Lygodium palmatum*. However, south of our area, *Lygodium japonicum* (Thunb.) Sw. escaped from cultivation many years ago and has spread to South Carolina and westward to Texas.

Genus *Schizaea*
(Greek: *schizein* — to split.)

see p. 164

THIS genus contains 29 species, usually tropical or subtropical. One species, however, is found in our area in southern New Jersey — also outside our area in Nova Scotia and Newfoundland.

Family HYMENOPHYLLACEAE

Genus *Trichomanes:* Filmy Ferns
(Greek: *trichomanes* — soft hair; referring to projecting hair of fruitdots.)

see p. 166

THIS genus contains 330 species, mostly tropical. One is found in our area.

Family OSMUNDACEAE

Genus *Osmunda*
see pp. 168 ff.

THREE species are represented in our area. See pages 46–47 for family characteristics.

FRAGRANT CLIFF FERN
Species: *Dryopteris fragrans* (L.) Schott

Style: When luxuriant, forms large bouquet-like bunches of dead brown leaves with green living leaves occupying the center. Usually seen as small isolated plants with only a few dead and a few living leaves.

Ecology: Dry cliffs, rocky banks, and talus slopes, usually limy and with a northern exposure. Rare, local; northern areas only.

Leaves: 12″± tall; 2½″± wide; evergreen, beset with glands that give off a fragrance; submembranous in our variety (the typical arctic plants have smaller leathery leaves and closer leaflets), lanceolate, narrowed at both base and apex, and twice-cut.

Leaflets: Up to 1″± long; 15 to 40 pairs; often inrolled and usually covered by fruitdots on the lower surface.

Axis: Chaffy, with wide-spreading, broad, thin brown scales.

Stalk: Up to nearly 5″± long; covered with shining brown to reddish scales.

Rootstock: Short and thick, nearly vertical; covered with brown scales and by the curled and withered leaves of previous years.

Roots: Black, rather sparse.

Fruitdots: Very large, soon becoming confluent and imparting a chocolate-brown color to the lower surface of the leaflets. Indusium kidney-shaped.

Marginalia: a. Sterile leaflet. b. Underside of fertile leaflet.
Diagnostic Arrows: 1. Double-tapered leaves. 2. Withered leaves of previous year.

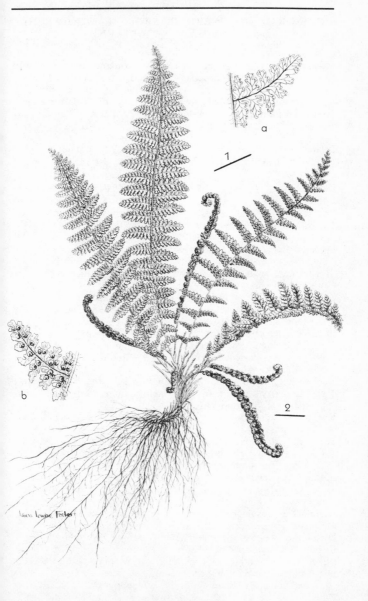

MARGINAL WOODFERN (EVERGREEN WOODFERN; LEATHERLEAF WOODFERN)
Species: *Dryopteris marginalis* (L.) Gray

Style: Leathery, evergreen, dark green woodland fern growing in scattered individual graceful clumps among roots and rocks. Six or more ascending leaves form a bouquet from an exposed and prominent rootstock, which simulates trunk of a small tree fern, or small palm tree. Together with the Christmas Fern is conspicuously green among dry leaves and snowpatches in winter woods.

Ecology: Hardy, evergreen, and abundant throughout wooded areas in all altitudes, from high ledges to wooded rocky lowlands; along banks; in ravines; and on rocky slopes, wherever there are semi-shaded pockets of light rich soil, either acid, alkaline, or neutral.

Leaves: 18"± high; 6"± wide; oblong ovate; ascending and arching; leathery; blue-green above, light green beneath; evergreen.

Leaflets: Lance-shaped and rapidly tapering to a point; deeply cut into 20± pairs of subleaflets, not opposite; quite widely spaced near axis; wide-spreading with tips arching upward; short-stemmed.

Subleaflets: Blunt-tipped; edges serrated or lobed; coarse texture; slightly chaffy beneath. Veins forked, or free and curving.

Axis: Pale, slightly scaly, grooved in front.

Stalk: Swollen at base; stout, brittle, grooved in front; covered with bright golden-brown scales, particularly at base; brownish green above, dark red-brown at base; stalk about $\frac{1}{4}$ to $\frac{1}{3}$ length of leaf.

Rootstock: Stout; ascending; shaggy with large golden-brown slightly hairy scales; many prominent withered stalks and leaves persisting throughout year.

Roots: Many; shallow-spreading from rootstock or base of stalks; often exposed.

Fruitdots: Marginal; large; prominent; single or in well-spaced rows; develop early; gray at first, dark brown when ripe in July or Aug. Indusium kidney-shaped and prominent.

Fiddleheads: Densely covered with golden-brown "fur."

Marginalia: a. Fruiting subleaflet. b. Fruiting leaflet. c. Fruiting subleaflet, forma *elegans*. d. Leaflet, forma *elegans*.

Diagnostic Arrows: 1. Marginal fruitdots. 2. Exposed rootstock. 3. Blunt Subleaflets. 4. Leaflet rapidly tapering to point. 5. Chaffy stalks. 6. Withered leaves and stalks. Combination of these characteristics lacking in similar species: Male Fern, Crested Fern, Goldie's Fern, and Spinulose Woodfern or other Woodferns.

Lunna Louise Foster

MALE FERN
Species: *Dryopteris Filix-mas* (L.) Schott

Style: Rare fern in our area, but common fern in Europe. Looks like the Marginal Woodfern, but is true green, not blue-green; stalk is shorter and stouter, and fruitdots are nearer midvein than margin.

Ecology: Found in rocky wooded areas of most northerly areas of Maine, Vt., Mich., and N.Y.

Leaves: 18″± tall; 8″± wide semi-tapering to base, widest ⅔ from tip. Yellow-green, semi-evergreen, leathery. Cut into 20± pairs of narrow long-pointed leaflets.

Leaflets: Long, oblong, narrow; cut almost to midvein into 24± pairs of short forward-pointing, or rounded subleaflets or lobes with slightly toothed margins. Veins simple and forked.

Axis: Green, flat-faced, prominent, scaly beneath.

Stalk: 4″± long; short, stout; flat-faced, green, densely scaly with brown scales.

Rootstock: Thick, short, erect, very scaly.

Roots: Black, wiry, thickish, quite numerous.

Fruitdots: Large, prominent, nearer midvein than margin. Indusium kidney-shaped, often with hairy edges.

Marginalia: a. Leaflet. b. Fertile subleaflet. c. Sterile subleaflet.
Diagnostic Arrows: 1. Short stout stalk. 2. Toothed subleaflets. 3. Fruitdots near midvein. Similar to Marginal Woodfern, which has a larger stalk, rounded subleaflets, and fruitdots along the margins of the lobes.

Laura Louise Foster

SPINULOSE WOODFERN AND ITS VARIETIES
Species: *Dryopteris spinulosa* (O. F. Müll.) Watt

Evergreen Woodfern — var. *intermedia* (Muhl.) Underw.
Fruitful Woodfern — var. *fructuosa* (Gilbert) Trudell
Mountain Woodfern — var. *americana* (Fisch.) Fern. or
Dryopteris austriaca (Jacq.) Woynar

Style: Spinulose Woodferns, and their varieties, are the lacy-cut, usually evergreen, larger plants of woodland which truly typify the ferns. Delicate, green, lance-shaped, much cut leaves rise in circular clusters from central, coarse, and scaly rootstocks, in isolated bouquets or in close-together colonies. They are the "greenery" so commonly used by florists and called "fancy ferns."

Ecology: In rich moist woods throughout our area. Mountain Woodfern in the cooler, higher, and more acid regions; Spinulose Woodfern in the wet sub-acid and woodland swamps; and the Evergreen and Fruitful Woodferns in the drier regions where there is limy or neutral soil.

Leaves, Leaflets, & Subleaflets: See page 70 and illustration.
Stalk: 12″± tall; stout, shorter than blade, densely scaly.
Rootstock: Thick, coarse, scaly, variable. Spinulose, creeping; Evergreen and Fruitful, semi-erect; Mountain, creeping or semi-erect.
Roots: Black, wiry, widely spreading, variable.
Fruitdots: See page 70 and illustration.

Marginalia: a. Lowest leaflet, Spinulose Woodfern. b. Fruiting sub-leaflet, Spinulose Woodfern. (This specimen had a semi-erect or almost erect rootstock, more typical for the Evergreen Woodfern.)
Diagnostic Arrows: 1. Semi-erect coarse rootstock with leaves growing in bouquet-like clusters. 2. Lacy-cut, lance-shaped leaves. 3. Very scaly stout stalks. Similar species: Lady Fern, with slim and smooth stalks; Marginal Woodfern does not have lacy-cut leaves.

SPINULOSE WOODFERN AND ITS VARIETIES

THE Spinulose Woodfern and its varieties are so closely alike in almost every way that it is most difficult to separate them. Even though they may be separately classified, as is endeavored here, they crossbreed so readily that there are often many varieties of varieties, or forms of varieties of the species. Their preferences as to habitat are not always lived up to, and the supposedly distinguishing characteristics of the size, shape, and color of scales, of the size and placing of fruitdots, and the shapes and cuttings of the leaves, leaflets, and subleaflets are all extremely variable from plant to plant, even with plants found within the same station.

a. Leaf of **Spinulose Woodfern.** 30″ ± tall. Ascending leaflets. Scales on stalk pale brown.

b. Leaf of **Evergreen Woodfern.** 30″ ± tall. Leaflets perpendicular to axis. Scales on stalk brown.

c. Leaf of **Mountain Woodfern.** 36″± tall. Leaf broadly triangular. Leaflets perpendicular to axis. Scales on stalk have dark brown centers.

d. Bottom leaflet of **Spinulose Woodfern.** Rapidly tapering outline. Upper and lower subleaflets nearest axis nearly opposite. First lower subleaflets prominently longer than the second.

e. Bottom leaflet of **Fruitful Woodfern.** Gradually tapering outline. Subleaflets nearly opposite, but first lower subleaflet approximately same length as second.

f. Bottom leaflet of **Evergreen Woodfern.** Outline tapers to a long slender tip. Subleaflets nearly opposite, but the first lower subleaflet is shorter than the second.

g. Bottom leaflet of **Mountain Woodfern.** Outline broadly tapering. Lower subleaflet nearest axis *very much longer* than second and more nearly opposite second upper subleaflet and almost as wide as the two short upper subleaflets together.

h. Subleaflet of **Spinulose Woodfern.** Lobing not prominent, slightly toothed, teeth sloping toward tip. Fruitdots small, and near tips of veins. Indusia smooth.

i. Subleaflet of **Fruitful Woodfern.** Lobing more prominent, slightly toothed, teeth not sloping toward tip. Fruitdots numerous, very large, partway down from tips of veins. Indusia glandular.

j. Subleaflet of **Evergreen Woodfern.** Lobing prominent, distinct, with divergent teeth. Fruitdots small, partway down from tips of veins. Indusia glandular.

k. Subleaflet of **Mountain Woodfern.** Lobing prominent, distinct, divergent, with prominent teeth. Fruitdots few, near tips of veins. Indusia slightly glandular.

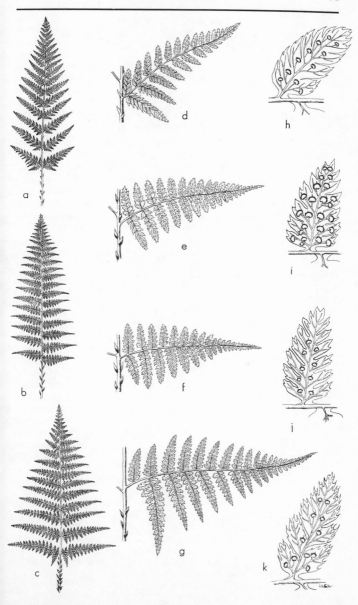

BOOTT'S FERN

Species: *Dryopteris* × *Boottii*. (Tuckerm.) Underw.
(A hybrid between *D. spinulosa* var. *intermedia* and *D. cristata*.)

Style: Fairly common, supposedly fertile hybrid Woodfern which has the lacy-cut leaves of the Evergreen Woodfern and the narrow shape of the Crested Fern. Variable in form between the two.

Ecology: In low weed thickets on damp slopes, in moist wet woods, sub-acid soil. Found throughout our area.

Leaves: 30″± tall; 6″± wide, widest near middle; tips pointed, semi-tapering to base. Fertile leaves taller, more erect, not evergreen. Sterile leaves are evergreen. Widest below middle. Cut into 12± pairs of lacy-cut leaflets with pointed ends.

Leaflets: 3″± long. Lower leaflets short-stemmed, broader and shorter, slightly tilting forward and upward, and often widely spaced. Cut into 8± subleaflets winged to midrib, margins with distinct and forward-pointing teeth. Veins once-forked.

Axis: Green, smooth, lower parts slightly scaly.

Stalk: 8″± long; stout, straw color above, dark brown below, many pale brown scales. Fertile stalks taller and more erect.

Rootstock: Dark brown, scaly, stout, ascending.

Roots: Black, wiry, wide-spreading, quite deep-rooted.

Fruitdots: Small, *near midvein*, usually only on upper leaflets. Indusium kidney-shaped, glandular.

Marginalia: a. Triangular basal leaflet. b. Fertile subleaflets, showing fruitdots near midvein.

Diagnostic Arrows: 1. Erect fertile leaf with lower leaflets widely spaced and tilting up to the horizontal. 2. Fruitdots small and near midvein. 3. Shorter, less erect sterile leaves with leaflets closer together. 4. Lacy-cut distinctly toothed leaflet. Similar species: Spinulose Woodferns' leaflets are not widely spaced and tilting; Crested Fern does not have lacy-cut leaflets.

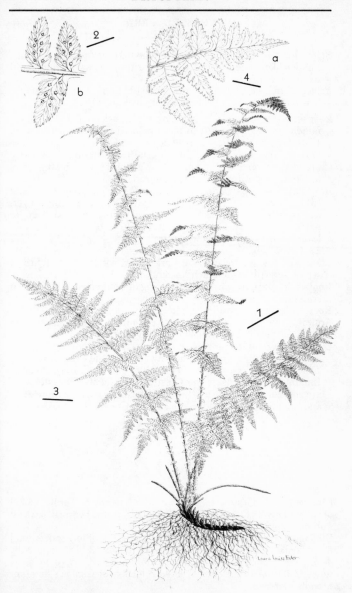

Laura Louise Foster

CRESTED FERN
Species: *Dryopteris cristata* (L.) Gray

Style: Firm-textured, bluish-green Woodfern of the damp woods. Ladder-like, wide-spaced leaflets tilting toward horizontal readily identify it.

Ecology: In wet, swampy woods in shade or sun; marshes where it is not too exposed. Throughout our area. Quite common.

Leaves: 30″± tall; 5″± wide; narrow lance-shaped, widest above middle, tapering upward to blunt-pointed tip and downward to 1″± lowest leaflets. Fertile leaves taller, very erect, more narrow, not evergreen. Sterile shorter, semi-erect, slightly broader, evergreen. Smooth yellow-green. Cut into 20± pairs of almost opposite short-stemmed leaflets.

Leaflets: Lowest pair broad triangular 1″± long, distinctly tilting to the horizontal. Lower leaflets widely spaced, getting longer, less triangular, and less widely spaced as they approach upper parts. Veins twice-forked. Cut into 6± blunt-pointed sub-leaflets with slightly toothed margins.

Axis: Green, slightly scaly on lower parts.

Stalk: 10″± long; green above, dark below, with many dull brown scales. Fertile stalk much longer, almost ⅓ length of blade.

Rootstock: Dark brown, stout, creeping or semi-erect, many brown scales.

Roots: Black, wiry, wide-spreading, numerous.

Fruitdots: Prominent, halfway between midvein and margin. On upper leaflets only. Indusium kidney-shaped, not glandular.

Clinton's Fern is considered a true species by some — *D. Clintoniana* Dowell — and by others a variety of the Crested Fern — *D. cristata* (L.) Gray, var. *Clintoniana* (D. C. Eaton) Underw. Inhabits same areas as the Crested, most of its characteristics are the same except it is larger, and fertile leaves are more alike and are not narrow ladder-like as with Crested Fern.

Marginalia: a. Growth form of var. *Clintoniana*. b. Fertile leaflet of Crested Fern. c. Lower sterile leaflet of Crested Fern. d. Lowest sterile leaflet of Clinton's Fern.

Diagnostic Arrows: 1. Narrow upright leaf with widely spaced and tilting leaflets. 2. Small triangular lowest leaflet. 3. Tall scaly stalk. 4. Clinton's Fern, showing broader, taller leaves with more uniformly spaced, not tilting leaflets. 5. Lowest leaflets of Clinton's Fern not broadly triangular.

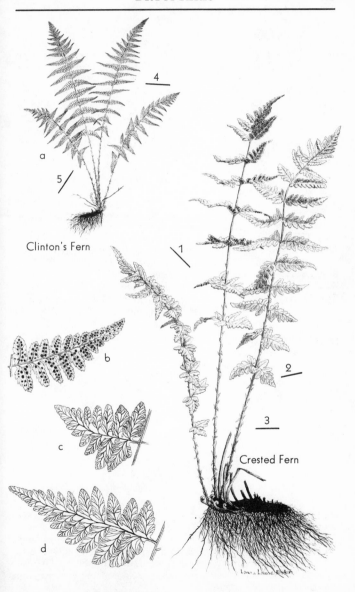

4

a

5

Clinton's Fern

1

b

c

2

3

d

Crested Fern

GOLDIE'S FERN
Species: *Dryopteris Goldiana* (Hook.) Gray

Style: The giant of our Woodferns. Its golden-green color, large coarse size, and backward-tilting blades are its characters of identification.

Ecology: In moist and rich soils of cool woods throughout our area. In shade or partial shade of well-drained and rocky slopes of higher regions.

Leaves: 4'± tall; 12" wide; abruptly pointed at tip, slightly narrowed at base. Leathery texture, green-bronze tint; evergreen. Cut into 12± not opposite pairs of leaflets.

Leaflets: Double-tapered with short stems — abruptly pointed tip semi-tapering to axis. Bottom leaflets 8"±, often tilting downward and outward. Cut almost to midveins into 18± subleaflets or lobes mostly opposite, rounded or forward-pointed tips, margins slightly toothed at ends of veins. Veins simple and forked and twice forked; prominent.

Axis: Green, distinct, with pale scales.

Stalk: 16"± long; thick, straw-colored, very scaly at base, scaly throughout. Scales pale tan with dark centers.

Rootstock: Short, stout, semi-erect, very scaly.

Roots: Black, coarse, widely spread, numerous.

Fruitdots: Quite small, widely spaced, nearer midvein than margin. Indusium kidney-shaped, persistent, smooth.

Marginalia: a. Double-tapered leaflet. b. Fertile subleaflet showing veins and fruitdots.

Diagnostic Arrows: 1. Blades tipping backward from stalk. 2. Long and scaly stalks. 3. Downward- and outward-pointing lowest pair of leaflets. 4. Fruitdots nearer midveins. The double-tapered leaflet, location of spores near midveins, and golden-green color distinguish it from Marginal Woodfern.

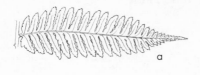

Laura Louise Foster-

OAK FERN
Species: *Gymnocarpium Dryopteris* (L.) Newm.

Style: Like a tiny, delicate, bright yellow-green Bracken. Its triangular leaves are divided into three distinct parts, which from short slender stalks they tilt almost to the horizontal, often forming a wavy carpet over woodland floor.

Ecology: In moist, sub-acid, shaded, rocky soil. Along the slippery edges of trout streams. Found throughout our area in those higher wooded regions which are cool, damp, and shaded.

Leaves: 5″± tall; 5″± wide, broadly triangular. Divided into 3 triangular leaflets with distinct stems; the two lower leaflets are opposite each other and about $\frac{3}{4}$ as long, or longer than the remainder of the entire leaf, frond, or blade. Stem of upper or middle leaflet $\frac{3}{4}$″± long, usually more than twice the length of the stems of the two lower leaflets.

Subleaflets: 8″ ±; lance-shaped, blunt-pointed, in opposite pairs, deeply cut into blunt lobes.

Axis: Green and delicate.

Stalk: 5″± long, longer than blade; few scales; yellow-green, slender, brittle, dark at base.

Rootstock: Slender, black, scaly, long-creeping. Produces leaves all summer.

Roots: Black, tiny, wiry, sparse.

Fruitdots: Small, round, few, near margin — naked. No indusium.

Fiddleheads: Small, green, delicate, developing into threes — one for each of the 3 divisions of blade. Produced all summer like little green fists among the leaves.

Marginalia: a. Underside of fertile subleaflet.
Diagnostic Arrows: 1. Horizontal growth. 2. Triangular 3-part leaf. 3. 3 fiddleheads of developing 3-part leaf. 4. Shallow-creeping slender rootstock. Its delicate and small size and slender, shallow-creeping rootstock distinguish it from similar fern, the Bracken.

a

Laura Louise Foster.

BROAD BEECH FERN
Species: *Thelypteris hexagonoptera* (Michx.) Weatherby

Style: Larger and more erect of two Beech Ferns. Found in sunny open spots in the woods, in dry or semi-moist areas. Unlike the Long Beech Fern, it cares not for rocks or running water.

Ecology: In rich woods throughout our area, but more abundant in southern regions. Prefers the moist or dry rich woodland soils where the New York Fern abounds.

Leaves: 24″± tall; broad, triangular, 16″± wide at base. Tilts backward from upright stalk; slightly hairy, dull green; not evergreen. Cut into 12± almost opposite pairs of leaflets, *all of which are winged* at axis. Two lowest pairs quite widely spaced with the *axis between broadly winged*.

Leaflets: Long, double-tapered, widest at about middle. Lowest pair often point downward and are the largest and broadest and most distinctly winged at axis. Cut almost to midvein into 20± blunt-pointed subleaflets with somewhat distinctly lobed, often toothed margins. Veins forked, unforked, and several times forked.

Axis: Stout, green, winged throughout — with whitish scales.

Stalk: 16″± long; longer than blade. Quite slender, straw-colored, smooth above, darker and slightly scaly and hairy at base.

Rootstock: Slender, very scaly, black, widely creeping and branching.

Roots: Black, scaly, numerous, creeping, and branching.

Fruitdots: Small, round, scattered near margins, naked. *No indusium.*

Marginalia: a. Upper side of lowest leaflet, showing double-tapering and winged axis. b. Fertile subleaflet and scattered fruitdots.
Diagnostic Arrows: 1. Tilting leaf growth. 2. Lowest leaflet winged at axis also. 3. Winged axis. 4. Subleaflets, distinctly lobed margins.
Similar species: Long Beech Fern axis not winged between the two lowest pairs of leaflets, and subleaflets not indented.

Laura Louise Foster.

LONG BEECH FERN (NARROW BEECH FERN; NORTHERN BEECH FERN)
Species: *Thelypteris Phegopteris* (L.) Slosson

Style: A small light green fern of narrow triangular shape. Favorite habitat is a wet pocket near cool and running water; often lives under small waterfalls. Where it grows on dripping cliffs leaves grow drippingly downward.

Ecology: On cliffs, in ravines, on shaded banks along streams and brooks. In colonies in the semi-shade of rich and moist woodlands. Seldom far from rocks. Found throughout our area; common in northern or higher regions.

Leaves: 12″ ± tall. Backward-tilting blade. Narrow, triangular, with rapidly tapering tips; lowest pair of leaflets *characteristically drooping downward and outward* and distinctly spaced from next upper pair. Often hairy above and beneath. Yellow-green; not evergreen. Cut into 12 ± pairs of nearly opposite stemless leaflets.

Leaflets: Long, quite narrow, with long pointed tips. All but bottom pair semi-tapered to and semi-winged at axis. Bottom pair *distinctly* tapered to axis and *not winged*. Cut almost to midvein into 18 ± rounded lobes with hairy margins. Midvein and veins scaly and hairy. Veins forked.

Axis: Green, quite stout, scaly and hairy above and beneath.

Stalk: Medium-slender, scaly and hairy, variable in length.

Rootstock: Slender, black, scaly, branching and creeping. Produces leaves all summer.

Roots: Black, wiry, branching, quite numerous, often deep in soil.

Fruitdots: Small, near margins. Usually on lower leaflets. Rarely on points — naked. *No indusium.*

Marginalia: a. Double-tapering basal leaflet. b. Fertile subleaflet with fruitdots.
Diagnostic Arrows: 1. Rapidly tapered pointed tips. 2. Downward-pointing lowest leaflets. 3. Free space on axis between lowest leaflets and next upper leaflets.

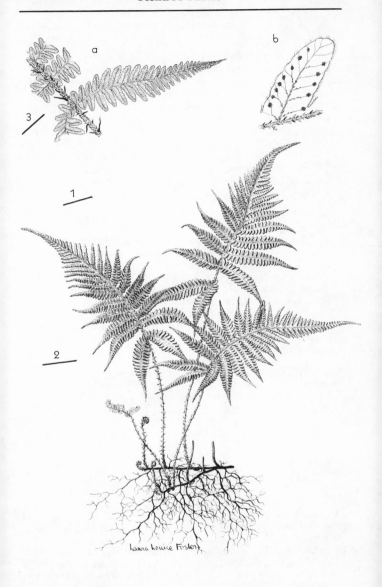

Laura Louise Foster

MARSH FERN
Species: *Thelypteris palustris* Schott

Style: One of our most common ferns. In sunny moist meadows almost as common as the grasses. This thin, green, and delicate medium-sized fern produces leaves throughout summer. Uncoiling fronds mingle with those fully developed, which turn and twist with the sun and wave with the breeze, often forming a dancing mass of fernery.

Ecology: In moist open sun and partial shade. In rich, sweet, muddy soil, but seldom in standing water. Open woodlands, wet meadows, and along ditches and streams. Common throughout our area.

Leaves: 18″ ± tall; 6″ ± wide; lance-shaped with pointed tips and widest almost at base. Thin, delicate, scattered, green or yellow-green; not evergreen. Fertile leaves more erect and with relatively longer stalks. Cut into 12 ± pairs of nearly opposite stemless leaflets.

Leaflets: Lance-shaped, cut nearly to midvein into 12 ± rounded or blunt-tipped lobes, margins not toothed. *Lowest pair* and other leaflets *perpendicular to axis.* Fertile leaflets *narrow* and constricted by margins curving over fruitdots. Veins forked. (Some fertile leaflets' veins not forked.)

Axis: Green, slender, and smooth.

Stalk: 9″ ± long; longer than blade; smooth, slender, pale green above, black at *base.* Stalks of fertile leaves much longer than those of sterile.

Rootstock: Slender, black, few scales, widely creeping and branching.

Roots: Black, wiry, shallow, creeping, not numerous.

Fruitdots: Numerous, mostly on upper leaflets in close rows near midvein. Indusium pale, narrow kidney-shaped, slightly hairy.

Marginalia: a. Sterile subleaflets showing forked veins. b. Basal leaflet not tapered to axis. c. Fertile subleaflets and partially covered fruitdots.

Diagnostic Arrows: 1. Twisting growth form. 2. Tall, slender, smooth stalk. 3. Fertile subleaflets curving over fruitdots. These characteristics not found in similar species: Massachusetts and New York Ferns and Silvery Spleenwort.

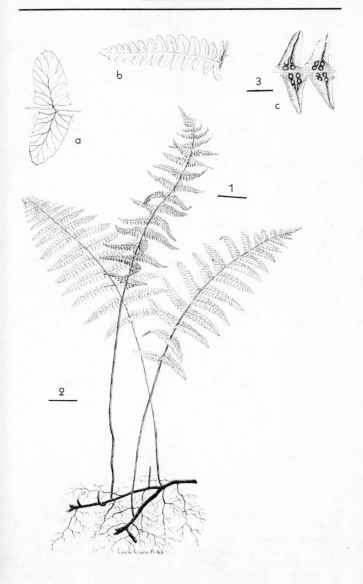

NEW YORK FERN
Species: *Thelypteris noveboracensis* (L.) Nieuwl.

Style: Common yellow-green, delicate, medium-sized fern growing in colonies of three or more leaves to a tuft and spreading through those areas in our woodlands where sunlit areas occur.

Ecology: Common throughout our area in sunny spots of mixed woodlands and drier edges of swamps. Most abundant in semi-moist regions, in opposition to the Marsh Fern, which prefers the wet. The two species seldom found close together.

Leaves: 18″ ± tall; 6″ ± wide, tapering from middle up to pointed tip and down to near rootstock. Delicate, thin, yellow-green; not evergreen. Grows in tufts along rootstock. Finely hairy underneath. Fertile leaves larger, narrower and more upright. Cut into 20± pairs of *never opposite* stemless leaflets.

Leaflets: Long, pointed, narrow lance-shaped cut nearly to midvein into narrow round tufted lobes or subleaflets. Lowest leaflets often minute in size. Veins *rarely forked*.

Axis: Green, pale, smooth or slightly hairy.

Stalk: 8″ ± long; light green, smooth or slightly hairy above, brown and slightly scaly at base.

Rootstock: Dark brown, slender, slightly scaly, widely creeping and branching, but producing leaves in semi-tufts.

Roots: Black, wiry, shallow, creeping and branching, sparse.

Fruitdots: Few, small, near margins. Indusium kidney-shaped; pale, quite persistent, slightly hairy.

Marginalia: a. Long tapering leaflet. b. Sterile lobe, or subleaflet, showing simple veins. c. Fertile subleaflets and fruitdots.

Diagnostic Arrows: 1. Double-tapering leaf. 2. Tiny bottom leaflets close to rootstock. 3. Leaf growing in semi-tufts of 3 leaves from branching rootstock. Combination of these characteristics not found in similar species: Marsh and Massachusetts Ferns and Silvery Spleenwort.

MASSACHUSETTS FERN
Species: *Thelypteris simulata* (Davenp.) Nieuwl.

Style: This species, a newcomer, was described in 1894. Evidently had been overlooked on account of its similarity to Marsh and New York Ferns and Silvery Spleenwort.

Ecology: In cedar, spruce, larch, and sphagnum swamps. In moist, acid, shady woods. Local, though found throughout our area. Quite rare in northern regions. Its ecology is halfway between open and wet of Marsh Fern and shade and dry of New York Fern.

Leaves: 24″ ± tall; 6″ ± wide; erect; lance-shaped with pointed tip and slightly narrowed at base, widest near middle. Thin, yellow-green; not evergreen. Fertile leaves more erect, with relatively longer stalks. Cut into 18 nearly opposite stemless leaflets.

Leaflets: Oblong, *narrowed* near axis (particularly the lower ones), cut almost to midvein into 15± pairs of blunt lobes, margins not toothed. Lowest pair tip downward, rarely upward, veins *not forked.*

Axis: Green, slightly hairy above, smooth beneath.

Stalk: 8″± long; shorter than blade; slender, yellow-green and a little hairy above, light brown and few scales at base.

Rootstock: Slender, black, few scales, rapidly wide-creeping and branching.

Roots: Small, black, wiry, sparse. Younger roots with many hairlike rootlets.

Fruitdots: Small, distinct. Indusium pale, narrow kidney-shaped.

Marginalia: a. Sterile lower leaflet showing taper to axis. b. Section of fertile leaflet and fruitdots. c. Section of fertile leaflets showing veins not forked.

Diagnostic Arrows: 1. Downward-tipping and tapering lowest pair of leaflets. 2. Hairy new roots. 3. Slender, slightly scaly stalks. 4. Simple, not forked veins. Similar species: Silvery Spleenwort has coarse hairy stalks, coarse rootstock with many roots, and long narrow fruitdots; veins simple. Marsh Fern has smooth stalk, veins mostly forked, leaflets not tapering to axis. New York Fern, veins simple, leaflets rapidly diminishing in size almost to rootstock.

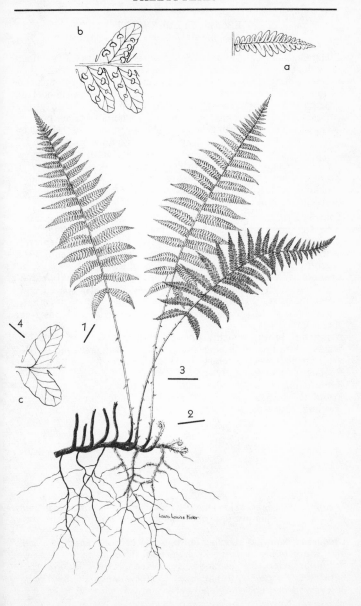

EBONY SPLEENWORT
Species: *Asplenium platyneuron* (L.) Oakes

Style: One of most widespread Spleenworts in our area. In summer its foot-high (or more) ladder-like fertile leaves, with their shining dark stems and axis, stand out prominently through the undergrowth in fields or woods, and especially as silhouettes against roots and rocks, alongside which they like to grow. Usually found as one, two, or three plants — sometimes in colonies. In the South grow to height of 18″ or more. (Leaflets of sterile leaves vary considerably and afford many known varieties and forms. Var. *proliferum,* not uncommon, has a proliferous growth on stem, which often sprouts into a new leaf.)

Ecology: Found throughout the area in shaded woods, fields, and along banks, walls or fences in all kinds of well-drained rocky soils, even in full sun, if reasonably moist though not wet.

Leaves: Fertile leaves 15″ ± over-all; erect, tall, narrow, tapering to top and bottom. Sterile leaves shorter, spreading, and pendent; often flat on ground. Fertile leaves dark green and semi-evergreen; sterile more numerous, lighter green, and evergreen. Both cut into 18 or more pairs of leaflets.

Leaflets: Fertile leaflets narrow oblong, pointed, distinctly eared at base, with toothed or serrated edges, distinctly spaced and not opposite. Sterile leaflets more rounded, closer together, and only slightly eared, with less toothed edges. Veins free and forked.

Axis: Dark brown, smooth, shining throughout.

Stalks: Dark brown, shining, smooth; short, stiff, erect and brittle for fertile leaves; extremely short and pendent for sterile leaves.

Rootstock: Thick, usually erect; few scales.

Roots: Numerous, wiry, dark, widely spreading.

Fruitdots: Short, straight, often confluent. Indusium silvery when young, soon withering.

Marginalia: a. Sterile leaflet. b. Fertile leaflet. c. Leaflet of var. *incisum.* d. Proliferous leaf and stalk growing from old stalk, var. *proliferum.*

Diagnostic Arrows: 1. Leaflets not opposite and are eared. 2. Tall and erect fertile leaves. 3. Short and pendent sterile leaves. 4. Sterile leaflets more rounded and crowded together. The Kentucky Spleenwort, page 52, is supposedly halfway between the Ebony Spleenwort and Lobed Spleenwort in growth and form.

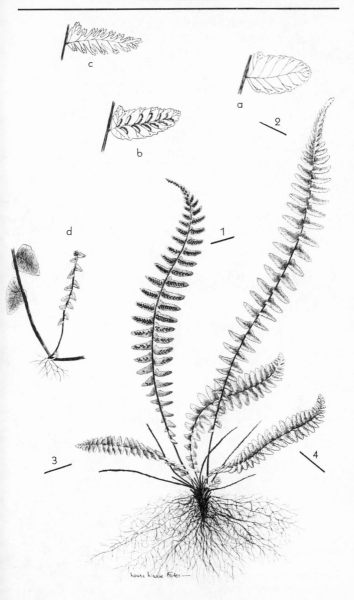

BLACK-STEMMED SPLEENWORT
Species: *Asplenium resiliens* Kunze

Style: Southern counterpart of the Ebony Spleenwort, but with leaflets more rounded and more opposite, like leaflets of Maidenhair Spleenwort, although more widely spaced. Grows in evergreen, erect tufts with fertile and sterile leaves approximately the same in form, size, and erectness.

Ecology: Grows in locations similar to that of and with Ebony Spleenwort — at bases of rocks and stones in semi-shaded areas of fields, woods, and cliffs. The Ebony is found with it in southern areas, but it is not found with the Ebony in our northern areas.

Leaves: 8″ ± over-all; all stiffly erect, narrow, tapering to top and bottom; dark green; evergreen; tufted. Cut into 20 ± distinctly spaced leaflets.

Leaflets: Mostly opposite; blunt-tipped, toothed edges, halberd-shaped or slightly eared at bases; imperceptibly stemmed; lower leaflets reflexed and wide apart.

Axis: Distinctly dark brown, almost black; smooth, shining.

Stalk: Short, stiff, brittle; dark brown or black; shining, erect.

Rootstock: Short, creeping or half erect, with black stiff scales.

Roots: Quite numerous, fine, dark, and widely spreading.

Fruitdots: Oblong, nearer margin than midrib, prominent, often confluent.

Marginalia: a. Underpart of fertile leaflet.
Diagnostic Arrows: 1. Leaflets opposite, semi-eared, and oblong. 2. Black-stemmed throughout. 3. Lower leaflets usually wide-spaced. Ebony Spleenwort's leaflets are not opposite and lower leaflets are usually crowded together.

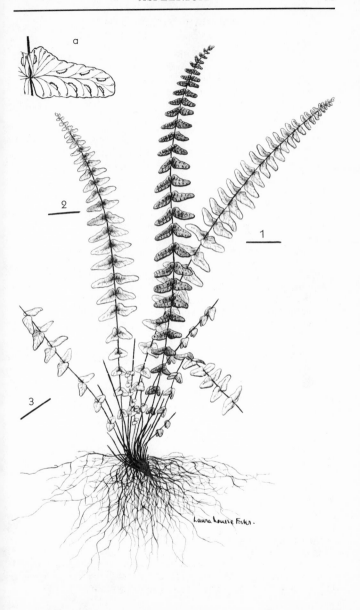

a

2

1

3

Laura Louise Foster.

MAIDENHAIR SPLEENWORT
Species: *Asplenium Trichomanes* L.

Style: Daintiest and one of prettiest ferns. Its spreading and tumbling leaves form dense rosettes on moist and shaded moss-covered surface of cliffs and boulders. Sterile leaves lie on surface the year round, while the late-sprouting fertile leaves are erect, fresh, bright green, spritely, and wither when winter arrives.

Ecology: A rock-loving, lime-loving tiny fern found throughout the area (except along the coast), wherever there are moist shaded crevices in moss-covered limestone outcroppings.

Leaves: 5″± over-all; fertile leaves upright, sterile leaves usually flat to surface of rocks, long and narrow and tapering from middle to top and bottom. Evergreen and dark green. Cut into 20± pairs of leaflets.

Leaflets: Tiny, $\frac{1}{4}$″± long; rounded or semi-oblong, with slightly toothed margins; imperceptibly stemmed and opposite. Upper leaves crowded, often overlapping; lower leaflets wider spaced but close together. Veins free and forked.

Axis: Dark, purplish-brown throughout.

Stalk: Very short, dark purplish brown; brittle, wiry.

Rootstock: Short, erect or ascending, with dark brown scales.

Roots: Short, compact, numerous, dark, and wiry.

Fruitdots: Few, short, often confluent. Indusium present though fragile.

Marginalia: a. Underside of fertile leaflet.
Diagnostic Arrows: 1. Opposite and rounded leaflets. 2. Short stalks. 3. Spreading rosette-like growth form. Similar species: Black-stemmed Spleenwort has opposite oblong and semi-eared leaflets; Ebony Spleenwort has eared leaflets which are not opposite.

MOUNTAIN SPLEENWORT
Species: *Asplenium montanum* Willd.

Style: A small, delicate, bluish-green, uniformly shaped delicate fern, which grows in drooping tufts, usually down and out of the crevices of overhanging rocks. It looks like a cross between a Wall Rue and a young Fragile Fern.

Ecology: In shaded and sheltered crevices of sandstone, gneiss, and shale, where there are tiny pockets of acid soil. Quite widely distributed in acid soil south of New England.

Leaves: 4″ ± over-all; oblong, slightly leathery, broadest at base and cut into 6 or more pairs of leaflets, which are cut again; more drooping than erect; growing in tufts; evergreen. Sterile and fertile leaves the same.

Leaflets: Ovate oblong; distinctly stemmed; coarsely, irregularly indented edges. Veins few, free, forked, or simple.

Axis: Broad, flat, and green.

Stalk: ⅓ length of leaf; slender, fragile. Brown at base, green above. Smooth.

Rootstock: Short, usually creeping; dark chaff at apex.

Roots: Short, sparse, wiry, close-creeping.

Fruitdots: Few, mostly elliptical, often confluent. Indusium thin and fragile.

Marginalia: a. Underside of fertile leaflet. b. Underside of fertile subleaflet.

Diagnostic Arrows: 1. Distinctly stemmed widely spaced leaflets. 2. Long stalks — dark at base, green above. 3. Subleaflets indented not lacy-cut. Similar species: Wall Rue has stemmed and widely spaced palm-shaped leaflets; Bradley's Spleenwort has stalks dark throughout and lacy-cut leaflets; Trudell's Spleenwort, page 52, is supposedly halfway between the Mountain Spleenwort and the Lobed Spleenwort in growth and form.

GREEN SPLEENWORT
Species: *Asplenium viride* Huds.

Style: A rare, delicate, tiny fern that grows in little green tufts and
  gives the appearance of a small, fragile, light green, green-
  stemmed Maidenhair Spleenwort, with which it often grows.

Ecology: Found only in our most northerly regions. At one time
  reported as only in Vt. In cool, moist, and shaded crevices of
  limestone.

Leaves: 3″± over-all; delicate, linear oblong, semi-erect, evergreen. Fertile and sterile leaves the same. Cut into 12± pairs
  of leaflets; lower and middle leaflets widely spaced.

Leaflets: Rounded, wedge-shaped, not eared but often with slightly
  indented or toothed edges; lower leaflets with short stems; opposite or sub-opposite. Veins free and forked below; upper veins
  not forked.

Axis: Green and delicate.

Stalk: Thin, delicate, and flexible; much shorter than leaf; brown
  and scaly at base, green and smooth above.

Rootstock: Short; more erect than short-creeping.

Roots: Small, sparse, delicate, slightly spreading.

Fruitdots: Two or three to leaflet, seldom more. Indusium thin
  and fragile.

Marginalia: a. Underside of fertile leaflet.

Diagnostic Arrows: 1. Semi-erect form. 2. Widely spaced leaflets,
lower and middle. 3. Short stems. Key characteristics: delicate and
green axis and upper stalks. Stalk shorter than leaf but longer
than Maidenhair Spleenwort and Ebony Spleenwort, with which it
might be confused.

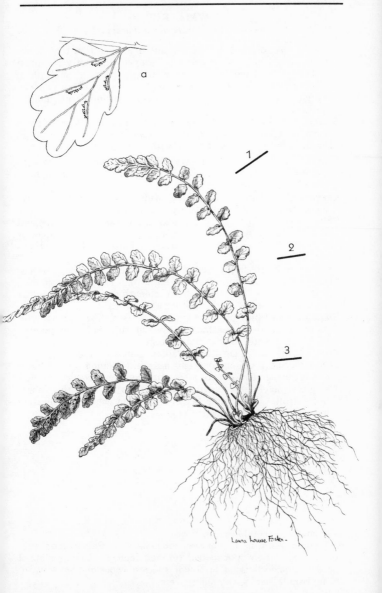

Laura Louise Foster.

WALL RUE
Species: *Asplenium Ruta-muraria* L.

Style: A tiny, delicate, semi-green and evergreen fern that grows in branched clusters of small fan-shaped, distinctly stemmed leaflets with prominently stemmed and palmate subleaflets; often growing flat on mossy surfaces in crevices of rocky cliffs. Fragile, not common, and unfernlike in its miniature fanlike growth.

Ecology: On sheltered cliffs, in smallest seams and crevices of limestone outcroppings, in shade or semi-shade. Withering in drought but quickly recovering with moisture.

Leaves: 3″ ± high; bluish- or olive-green; slightly leathery; smooth; evergreen; ovate-shaped. Cut into leaflets and subleaflets, both of which have prominent stems.

Leaflets: Broad ovate; branching, widely spaced, not opposite; distinctly stemmed; cut into 3 to 7 subleaflets.

Subleaflets: Predominantly fan-shaped, but variable in shape and size; distinctly stemmed to midrib; edges toothed, indented, or fringed. Veins free or many-forked or fan-shaped. Sometimes netted.

Axis: Smooth, green, grooved in front; delicate.

Stalk: Up to 2″ ± long; usually longer than leaf. Very slender, somewhat rigid, grooved in front; smooth and green, except at very base, where stalk is dark brown and scaly.

Rootstock: Creeping or, more commonly, ascending. Short, with many old dead stalks attached; covered with many tiny pointed dark brown scales hidden among roots.

Roots: Many, fine, blackish; spreading from each stalk.

Fruitdots: Short, oblong, on veins near and opening toward outer of outside segments of subleaflet; often confluent, covering underside completely. Frequently every subleaflet, even the tiniest bears fruit. Ripe June–Sept. Indusium whitish, delicately membranous, with hairy cut edges.

Marginalia: a. Fertile leaflet.
Diagnostic Arrows: 1. Stemmed subleaflet. 2. Palm-shaped subleaflet. 3. Widely spaced and stemmed leaflets. Combination of these characters lacking in similar species: Mountain Spleenwort, young Fragile Fern, young Bulblet Fern.

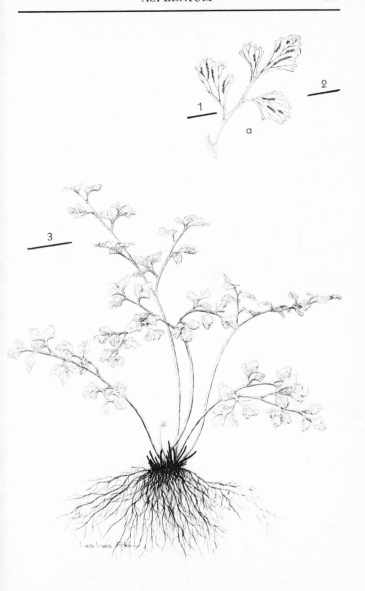

1

2

a

3

BRADLEY'S SPLEENWORT
Species: *Asplenium Bradleyi* D. C. Eaton

Style: A small, lustrous, brown-stemmed, evergreen, rock-loving fern that grows erect in tufts, with leaves cut once into triangular leaflets having prominently toothed edges and slightly eared at bases.

Ecology: A rock-loving fern found from N.Y. west; often on high and dry bare cliffs, in very acid soils. Rare and local; not abundant.

Leaves: 6″± over-all; linear, oblong; broadest at base and narrowly tapering to tip; once-cut into 10 or more pairs of leaflets. Very variable.

Leaflets: Ovate oblong or triangular; eared at base; edges deeply toothed. Lower leaflets distinctly stemmed, upper leaflets stemless.

Axis: Lower half shining dark green, upper half lighter green.

Stalk: ½ length of leaf; dark and lustrous brown. Long, erect, wiry.

Rootstock: Short, creeping, nearly erect; numerous black scales.

Roots: Small, dark, wiry, slightly spreading from rootstock.

Fruitdots: Short, numerous, dark brown; midway between margin and midvein; seldom confluent. Indusium ample and membranous.

Marginalia: a. Underside of fertile leaflet.

Diagnostic Arrows: 1. Leaflets eared and lacy-cut. 2. Leaflets with very short stems. 3. Dark stalk throughout. Similar species: Mountain Spleenwort has deeply indented leaflets not lacy-cut; stalk is dark at base and green above, and leaflets have prominent stems. Graves' Spleenwort, page 52, is supposedly halfway between Bradley's Spleenwort and Lobed Spleenwort in growth and form.

LOBED SPLEENWORT
Species: *Asplenium pinnatifidum* Nutt.

Style: Like a long-stemmed, more upright and deeply lobed Walking Fern, with the same long, tapering, and pointed leaves, but greener and more crinkled.

Ecology: In rocky, usually inaccessible crevices of acid soil from N.J. south and west. Common in a few high and dry restricted areas.

Leaves: 6″ ± over-all; broadest at base, tapering to a point; thick, semi-erect lower half, distinctly and deeply lobed, getting less and less tapering to a long and pointed tip. Sterile and fertile leaves the same; evergreen.

Leaflets: Merely lobings of leaf; considerable differences in sizes, shapes, and numbers. Veins much forked, fan-shaped, mostly free.

Axis: Green and smooth.

Stalk: ⅓ over-all size; green except for dark brown at base.

Rootstock: Short and erect.

Roots: Small, wiry, dark, creeping into pockets of crevices.

Fruitdots: Variable in shape, from the typical *Asplenium* linear shape to a semi-rounded form. Often varying on single leaf; often confluent. Indusium distinct and long-lasting.

Marginalia: a. Underside of fertile leaflet.
Diagnostic Arrows: 1. Rather uniformly lobed leaflets. 2. Long pointed tips usually curling downward. Similar species: Scott's Spleenwort has irregular leaflets in shape and size; long pointed tips usually point upward. Walking Fern sometimes has indented leaves that resemble Lobed Spleenwort's.

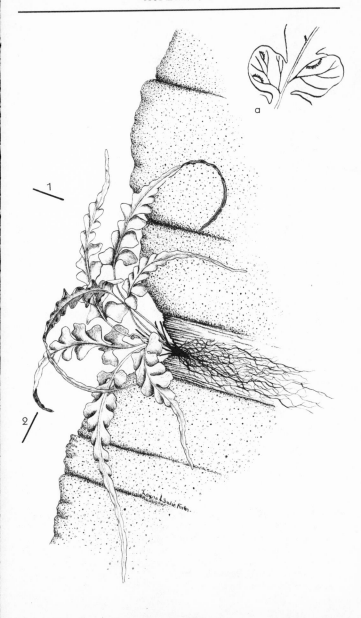

SCOTT'S SPLEENWORT
Species: *Asplenosorus ebenoides* (R. R. Scott) Wherry
or *Asplenium ebenoides* Gray, B. & B.
A hybrid between *Aspl. platyneuron* × *Campt. rhizophyllus* —
Ebony Spleenwort and Walking Fern

Style: Interesting, very variable, and rare. Supposedly earliest
established hybrid of the ferns, and occasionally fertile. A
favorite of the author's, since many isolated stations of one or
two plants are within walking distance of his home.

Ecology: Widely distributed from Vt. to Mo. and Ala. Reported
in our area from Vt., N.Y., Mass., Conn., Pa., N.J., Md., Ill.,
Va., and Ind. Limestone outcroppings and cliffs. Found often
near or with Walking Fern. Usually as isolated plants.

Leaves: 12″ ± long (usually 5″ to 6″, seldom up to 18″); wider at
base, long-tapering to point. Exceedingly variable. Lower ⅓
cut partway or entirely to axis into leaflets of variable shape and
form. Upper ⅓ usually uncut but with wavy, indented, or
straight margins all the way to point. Evergreen. Grows in
tufts; smaller leaves flat to ground, longer leaves usually pointing
upward. Sometimes leaf tip sprouts new plant. See Walking Fern.

Leaflets: Variable in size, shape, and form even on same leaf.
Veins free and forked, rarely netted.

Axis: Lower ⅓ brown, upper ⅔ green.

Stalk: Short, brittle, shining purplish brown.

Rootstock: Vertical, short, dark, stubby.

Roots: Black, wiry, sparse, shallow-creeping.

Fruitdots: Linear, nearer midvein than margin. Indusium silvery,
at an angle to and on one side or both sides of midvein or axis;
dull brown when mature.

Marginalia: a & b. Enlargements of underside of fertile leaf showing
variations in form of leaflets, veinings, and fruitdots.
Diagnostic Arrows: 1. Short stubby rootstock with sparse roots.
2. Arching though up-pointing leaf. 3. Variable forms and cuttings
of leaflets on one leaf. 4. Less cut and less variable leaf of same
plant. Combination of these characteristics not typical for similar
species: Walking Fern and Lobed Spleenwort.

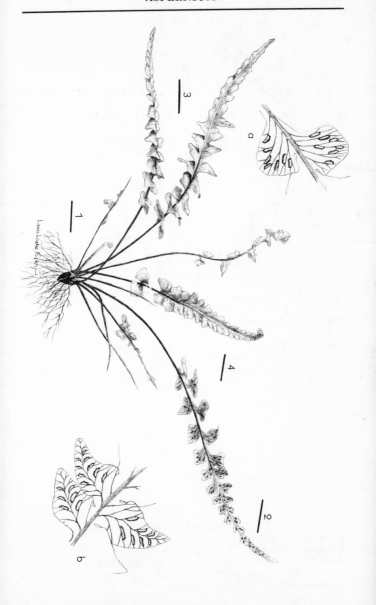

WALKING FERN
Species: *Camptosorus rhizophyllus* (L.) Link

Style: An interesting little evergreen fern that walks. Long, narrow, fine-pointed, arching leaves radiate from their rootstock. Those tips touching ground customarily sprout new plants. Often old plants surrounded by family of attached plantlets, so it walks and spreads.

Ecology: On shaded, moss-grown faces of limestone cliffs, rocks, and boulders, or on edges or in cracks and crevices of moist limestone outcroppings, usually northerly exposure. Sometimes on ground. Quite rare and local, reported from all states in our area where limy soil exists.

Leaves: 6″± long; 1″± at base. Evergreen, slightly leathery, shining green above, paler below; smooth, usually heart-shaped at base, elongated; triangular, tapering to long, fine, thin point. Leaves grow in star-shaped tufts, young plants flat to ground; older plants have semi-erect and/or arching leaves whose tips, when touching ground, sprout new plants. Forma *auriculatus* often sprouts new plants from pointed basal tips. Leaves variable in form with margins wavy or indented, but always narrow, long, and pointed when mature. Veins freely areolate, or in netted form.

Stalk: Short, flattened, and grooved face; dark brown and scaly at base, green and smooth above.

Rootstock: Short, slender, erect, with lustrous brown, well-spaced scales.

Roots: Short, compact, sparse, shallow-creeping.

Fruitdots: Scattered over undersurface of leaf from base to tip; brown. Some parallel to midrib, some oblique, some in pairs, some joined and some scattered — because of following netted veins. Indusium inconspicuous.

Marginalia: a. Base of fertile leaf and fruitdots. b. Forma *auriculatus*. c. Forma *Boycei*.

Diagnostic Arrows: 1. Plantlet growing from tip. 2. Leaf with heart-shaped base and long narrow tip. 3. Jumbled and scattered fruitdots. Combination of these characteristics lacking in similar species: Scott's Spleenwort and Hart's-tongue Fern.

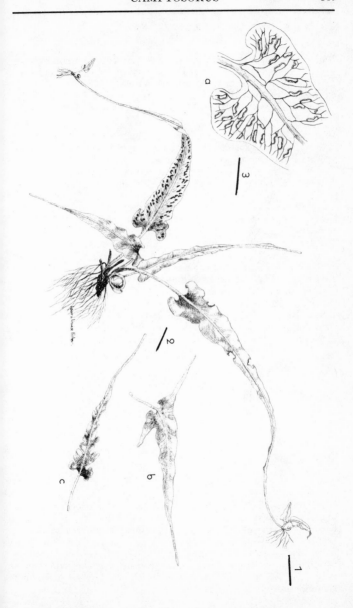

LADY FERN
Species: *Athyrium Filix-femina* (L.) Roth

Style: A rather large, showy, vigorous, lacy-cut, common fernlike fern. Variable in shape of blade, cuttings of leaflets and subleaflets, and color of stalks and fiddleheads.

Ecology: Common throughout our area, usually in fairly moist semi-shade. Meadows, fields, woods, ravines, along stone walls, and under trees.

Leaves: 30″ ± tall; 10″ ± wide; broad lance-shaped with pointed and lax tips, smooth throughout, slightly reduced at base. Variable in form. Grows in circular clusters. Not evergreen. Cut into 24± pairs of not opposite upward-pointing leaflets.

Leaflets: 8″ ± long; $1\frac{1}{2}$″ ± wide; narrow pointed tips; lower leaflets short-stemmed. Cut again into 12± pairs of subleaflets.

Subleaflets: Deeply cut and toothed; variable; thin-pointed or blunt-tipped. Veins once- or twice-forked.

Axis: Pale, slightly grooved or flat in front; smooth.

Stalk: Usually shorter than blade, fairly short, flat or grooved in front. Smooth or with few pale scales, particularly at base. It is green, but in forma *rubellum* pale wine color.

Rootstock: $\frac{3}{8}$″± thick; 4″± long; very scaly, shallow-creeping, often branching and sometimes semi-erect. Customarily with many old dead stalks attached. Often exposed like Osmundas.

Roots: Black, wiry, widespread, abundant.

Fruitdots: Short, curved, or even horseshoe-shaped, often crossing veins — dark brown. Indusium hairy, arching, prominent.

Marginalia: a. Sterile subleaflet. b. Section of fertile leaflet. c. Leaf of Upland Lady Fern. d. Leaf of Lowland Lady Fern.

Diagnostic Arrows: 1. Lax tips. 2. Growth form in circular clusters from horizontally creeping rootstock. 3. Cut and toothed subleaflets. 4. Smooth stalks with few pale scales. Often confused with: Spinulose Woodferns, which have scaly stalks; the Marsh Ferns, which don't have toothed subleaflets; and Hayscented Fern, which has hairy stalks and does not grow in circular clusters.

Laura Louise Foster

SILVERY SPLEENWORT
Species: *Athyrium thelypteroides* (Michx.) Desv.

Style: Soft dull green, rather tall fern named for the many prominent silvery fruitdots, which together with yellowish hairs give
pale sheen to leaves when waving in wind.

Ecology: In rich, moist, well-drained woods, or other semi-shaded
moist areas. Found throughout our area. Fairly common.

Leaves: 36″ ± tall; 8″ ± wide; lance-shaped, pointed at tip, tapering to base. Yellowish green and hairy, particularly when first
full-blown. Not evergreen. Cut into 18 ± pairs of not opposite
leaflets.

Leaflets: 6″ ± long; $\frac{3}{8}$″ ± wide; narrow, pointed, no stems, with
fuzzy yellow-green hairs beneath. Deeply cut into rounded
semi-subleaflets with wavy margins. Lowest pair of leaflets
usually pointing downward. Veins mostly not forked.

Axis: Pale green; slightly scaly, very hairy.

Stalk: Stout, green, hairy, slightly scaly and dark at base. Usually
much shorter than blade.

Rootstock: $\frac{1}{4}$″ ± thick; 5″ ± long; black, creeping, seldom branching, sometimes semi-erect; light brown scales.

Roots: Wiry, black, abundant.

Fruitdots: Narrow, long, usually straight, silvery at first, later
light brown. Indusium arching, silvery then light brown.

Marginalia: a. Section of underside of fertile leaflet, showing shape
and location of fruitdots, and rounded semi-subleaflets. b. Type of
leaflet with rounded subleaflets. c. Type of leaflet with blunt subleaflets.

Diagnostic Arrows: 1. Lowest pair of leaflets pointing downward.
2. Narrow double-tapering blade. 3. Short, stubby, hairy stalks.
4. Rounded, not toothed, subleaflets. Often confused with: Lady
Fern, which has cut subleaflets; Cinnamon and Interrupted Ferns, which
have coarser and smooth stalks.

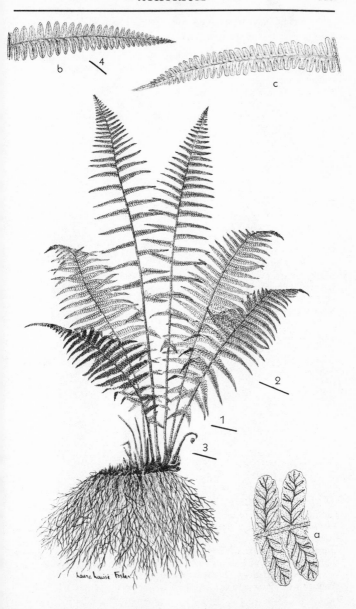

Laura Louise Foster

NARROW-LEAVED SPLEENWORT
Species: *Athyrium pycnocarpon* (Spreng.) Tidest.

Style: Rather tall, slender, pale green, narrow-leaved, once-cut fern that grows in almost circular clusters of 5 or 6 leaves from each rootstock.

Ecology: In open sunny spots in moist woodlands, or glades, in swamps, meadows, or ravines, in non-acid soil with plenty of moisture. Not common, but found throughout our area, usually in isolated colonies.

Leaves: 36″± tall; 6″± wide; narrow lance-shaped with sharp-pointed tip and slightly reduced at the base. Fertile leaves narrower, more erect and with longer stalks than arching and flexible sterile leaves. Not evergreen. Leaves cut into 20± pairs of not opposite leaflets.

Leaflets: 3″± long; ¼″± wide; narrow, long, with sharp-pointed tips. Base rounded or heart-shaped. Lowest leaflets with tiny stems. Margins slightly wavy, not toothed or cut. Sterile leaflets lax and often slightly twisting; fertile stiff, straight, and very narrow. Smooth throughout. Veins once- or twice-forked.

Axis: Pale green; slightly hairy beneath.

Stalk: Shorter than blade; stout; green above, slightly scaly and dark at base. Stalks of fertile leaves appreciably longer, stiffer, and more erect than sterile.

Rootstock: ¼″± thick; creeping, seldom branching; short, scaly, dark brown.

Roots: Wiry, black, abundant, often in masses.

Fruitdots: Long, slightly curved, run from midvein almost to margin; one-sided, attached to forward edges of veins, dark brown when ripe. Indusium long, narrow, arching, conspicuous.

Marginalia: a. Underside of sterile leaflet. b. Underside of fertile leaflet. c. Section of fertile leaflet showing shape and location of fruitdots.

Diagnostic Arrows: 1. Growth form of fertile and sterile leaves. 2. Narrow pointed leaflets. Margin wavy, not toothed. 3. Rounded or heart-shaped base of lower leaflet and tiny stem. Only remotely similar to young sterile leaves of Christmas Fern.

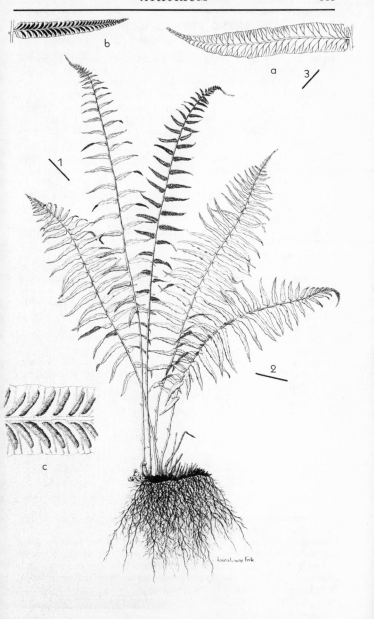

HAYSCENTED FERN (BOULDER FERN)
Species: *Dennstaedtia punctilobula* (Michx.) Moore

Style: Brittle yellowish-green fern, tending to become ragged in late summer. Sterile and fertile fronds similar, erect or somewhat arching; usually occur in large patches.

Ecology: Dry, partially shaded woodlands and open pastures; often covering large areas of hillside pastures to exclusion of everything else. Rapidly spreads by rootstocks, and difficult to eradicate. Southward often confined to moist sandstone ravines.

Leaves: 16″± tall; yellowish-green and not evergreen. Arise singly or in small groups. Glandular. Usually lance-shaped and widest near the bottom. Cut into 20± pairs of leaflets.

Leaflets: Close together and not exactly opposite, oblong or lanceolate with acute tips; prominently bristly, hairy on the lower surface. Not stalked.

Subleaflets: Numerous, opposite, oblong; bearing the small fruitdots on indentations of margin.

Axis: Slender; light brown to straw-colored; hairy.

Stalk: 7″± tall. Dark brown or almost black at the base, becoming light or reddish brown above. Smooth or with a few scattered hairs.

Rootstock: Horizontal and slender, rapidly growing; the older parts dark brown and nearly smooth, the younger parts clothed with numerous reddish-brown hairs.

Roots: Rather short, brownish; more abundant toward the young growth.

Fruitdots: Very small, placed at margins of leaflets. Surrounded by cup-shaped indusium. Spores mature in late summer and autumn.

Marginalia: a. Upper side of leaflet. b. Underside of fertile subleaflet. c. Cup-shaped indusium.

Diagnostic Arrows: 1. Narrow lance-shaped blades with narrowly pointed and relaxed tips. 2. Smooth or slightly hairy stalks. 3. Leaves growing singly along creeping rootstock. Distinguished from Lady Fern by its widely spreading growth in single leaves and from Woodferns by smooth, slender, brittle stalks.

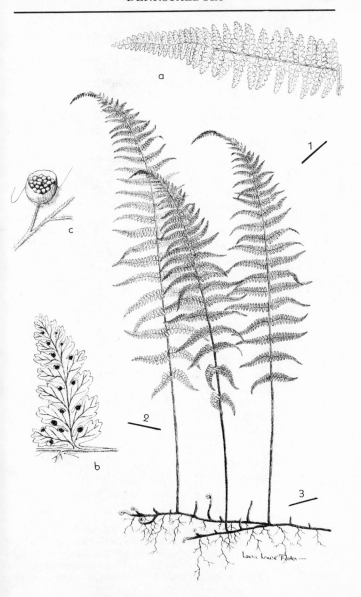

a

1

c

2

b

3

Laura Louise Foster

OSTRICH FERN
Species: *Matteuccia Struthiopteris* (L.) Todaro

Style: One of our largest ferns. A tall, erect, and gracefully arching plant growing in basket-like tufts of ostrich-plume-shaped leaves of dark rich green. Early withering with first frost, but throughout winter leaving its dark brown, stiff, erect, lyre-shaped compact fertile fronds.

Ecology: Along streams and riverbeds, in swamps, on slopes and flats with plenty of wet and some sunshine. In low, wet, open woodlands. Throughout our area. More common in East.

Sterile leaves: 60″± tall; 14″± wide; oblong lance-shaped. Widest near top, with rapidly pointed tip, base gradually tapering down to 1″± bottom leaflets. Not evergreen. Cut into 40± pairs of alternate long narrow-pointed ascending pairs of leaflets.

Sterile leaflets: Deeply cut into 30± pairs of not opposite sub-leaflets, or lobes, rounded oblong and forward-pointing. Veins not forked. Lower leaflets winged at axis or clasping axis.

Fertile leaves: 24″± tall; lyre-shaped; stiff, hard, green at first, dark brown later. Cut to midrib into leaflets that are contracted and clasp fruitdots, forming hard "pods" 2″± long, $\frac{1}{3}$″± thick.

Axis: Green, stout, slightly covered with whitish hairs.

Stalks: Sterile stalk 12″± tall; much shorter than blade; rigid, stout, dark brown and deeply grooved in front, green and flat-faced above; rounded back. Fertile stalk dark, stiff, erect, about same length as blade.

Rootstock: Stout, with dark brown scales. Erect, projecting symmetrical crowns. Spreads by numerous underground runners producing next year's plants.

Roots: Black, wiry, numerous, quite deep in ground.

Marginalia: a. Leaflet of sterile leaf. b. Sterile subleaflets, or lobes. c. Podlike fertile leaflets. d. Detail of fertile leaflet tip.

Diagnostic Arrows: 1. Arching basket-like growth form. 2. Stout, erect rootstock. 3. Runners. 4. Lyre-like dark fertile fronds enlarged. New York Fern has same general double-tapering shape; young Ostrich Fern may be confused with it.

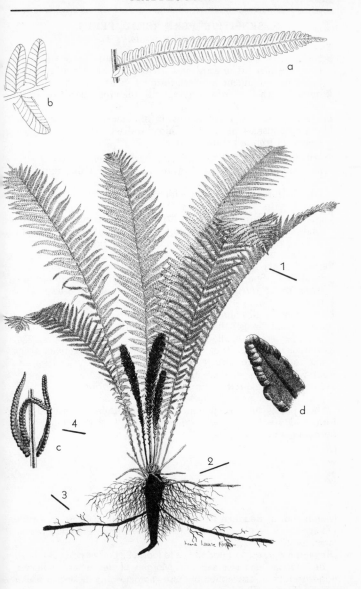

SENSITIVE FERN (BEAD FERN)
Species: *Onoclea sensibilis* L.

Style: Sturdy, coarse, unfernlike fern, with broad, almost triangular leaves, which tilt upward and backward. Most readily recognized by prominent network-forming veins. Common. Dies quickly with first frost, leaving only the erect, beadlike, fertile spikes.

Ecology: In damp or wet places; in full sun or shade, on banks, along woodsides, in meadows, along walls, or at edges of woods. Reported from all states in area.

Sterile leaves: 2′ ± tall; leathery, light grass-green, scattered white hairs on undersurfaces. Cut into 12 ± nearly opposite pairs of leaflets.

Sterile leaflets: Lower pairs widespaced with lowest or next to lowest pairs the longest and tapering at both ends. Upper leaflets winged at axis, with little or no tapering toward axis. Margins wavy. Larger plants with strong, often deep indentations. Edges smooth. Veins depressed, prominent, and in conspicuous net form.

Fertile leaves: 12″ ± tall; upright, compact, with numerous short branches. Spore cases contained in small hardened beadlike divisions of fertile leaflets, which become dark brown when mature.

Axis: Smooth, glistening; pale tan or yellow.

Stalk: Usually longer than leaf; yellow, with brown and thickened base; few scales; shallow furrow on face.

Rootstock: Brown, stout, usually smooth; extensively creeping and forking, near surface.

Roots: Numerous, matted, fibrous.

Fiddleheads: Pale red, in prominent mass in spring.

(When plants have been mowed over or otherwise injured, the forma *obtusilobata* occurs, where fertile leaves resemble the normally sterile leaves.)

Marginalia: a. Beadlike fertile leaflet. b. Netted veins. c. Fertile subleaflet. d. Fertile subleaflet, forma *obtusilobata*. e. Fertile leaflet, forma *obtusilobata*.

Diagnostic Arrows: 1. Beaded fertile leaf. 2. Lower pairs of leaflets widely spaced and stemmed. 3. Margins of sterile leaf indented, edges smooth. Combination of these characteristics lacking in similar species, Netted Chain Fern.

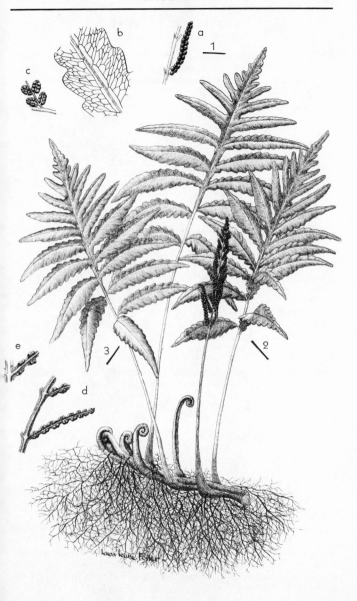

NETTED CHAIN FERN
Species: *Woodwardia areolata* (L.) Moore

Style: Like a small Sensitive Fern and consequently often overlooked. However, more glossy green, less coarse, being almost
translucent. Margins of leaflets are wavy and fine-toothed, not
deeply lobed or indented as so common for Sensitive Fern.

Ecology: In shade and swamps and wet woods. Most common
along coastal areas, sometimes in semi-brackish waters. Reported from all states.

Sterile leaves: 2′± tall; 6″± wide; oval, acutely pointed tips;
glossy green, somewhat membranous. Cut into 10± pairs of
nearly opposite leaflets.

Sterile leaflets: Sharp-pointed, narrow; wavy margins; fine-toothed
edges winged at axis, except lower pairs, which have slight stems.
Third lowest pair usually longest. Veins raised, prominent, and
in conspicuous net form (areolated).

Fertile leaves: Contracted when mature. Wider-spaced, more
narrow than sterile, with linear lobes frequently recurved over
the sausage-shaped rows of chainlike fruitdots, which usually
occupy the entire width of the leaflet.

Axis: Prominent, olive-colored, slightly scaly on underside.

Stalk: Usually longer than leaf; stout; yellow-green above, shining
chestnut-brown at base. Flattened and slightly grooved face.
Few scattered brown scales.

Rootstock: Rather slender, deep brown; clothed at apex and occasionally along length with glistening pale brown scales. Extensively creeping and forking.

Roots: Rather sparse, brown, and slender.

Fruitdots: Oblong, halfway between midvein and margin. Indusium wrapped over fruitdots; slightly leathery.

Marginalia: a. Section of leaflet showing netted veins. b. Fertile
leaflet in contracted mature form.

Diagnostic Arrows: 1. Lowest pair of leaflets not winged at axis.
2. Fertile leaf with long, thin, and contracted leaflets. 3. Wavy
margin to leaflet with finely toothed edges. Combination of these
characteristics lacking in similar species, Sensitive Fern.

VIRGINIA CHAIN FERN
Species: *Woodwardia virginica* (L.) Smith

Style: Tall, upright fern with very long, dark purple-brown stalk and axis. Leaves in close masses, growing from creeping root-stock. Often mistaken for Cinnamon Fern, which grows in clusters from individual crowns.

Ecology: In sphagnum bogs, swamps, muddy watery spots in woods. Rooted mostly in water, often a foot or more deep. Acid and shady locations. Reported from all our states, especially near the coast.

Leaves: 4′± tall; 10″± wide; broadest in middle; leathery in texture. Cut into 15±, almost opposite, fairly close-spaced leaflets. Sterile and fertile the same.

Leaflets: Narrow, oblong, pointing upward, tapering to both ends. No stems. Cut ¾ way to midrib into subleaflets with a narrow wing remaining along axis of leaflet.

Subleaflets: Round or seldom pointed at apex, slightly pointing toward tip. Inner veins netted, chainlike; outer veins free and forked between fruitdots and margin.

Axis: Lower portion dark purple-brown, upper portion dull green; smooth and shiny face with several grooves; slight ridges at bases of leaflets.

Stalk: Very long, twice or more the length of the blade; distinctly dark, shining purple-brown. Face grooved with two lateral lines running to base. Lower stalk swollen, almost tuberous at rootstock; of spongy tissue, slightly scaly and deeply grooved.

Rootstock: ½″± thick; coarse; widely creeping in mud and ooze. Growing tip covered with glistening brown scales, which are also scattered along rootstock.

Roots: Few, scattered, elongate, of slender fibers.

Fruitdots: Chainlike, elongate, in double rows along midvein of subleaflets, along wings parallel to axis, also in two rows at leaf's apex. Often occupying nearly all lower surface of leaf. Indusium leathery, inconspicuous, same dark brown color as fruitdots.

Marginalia: a. Subleaflets. b. Leaflet. c. Fertile subleaflets.
Diagnostic Arrows: 1. Swollen bases of stalks. 2. Tall black stalk. 3. Upward-pointing leaflets. 4. Chainlike rows of fruitdots. Combination of these characteristics lacking in similar species: Cinnamon Fern and Interrupted Fern.

CHRISTMAS FERN
Species: *Polystichum acrostichoides* (Michx.) Schott

Style: Green at Christmas. Lustrous rich-green tapering leaves grow in bouquet-like clusters cascading from a central rootstock. Spiny-toothed, holly-like leaflets and evergreen leaves make it a popular Yuletide decoration.

Ecology: Hardy, evergreen, and abundant in most areas. Prefers but does not demand rich limy soil. Grows in colonies, but more often singly or in twos and threes. Common on rocky shaded slopes; along wooded streambanks; in ravines; beside stone walls; in shaded or semi-open spaces; sometimes in swamps. Rocky or sandy soil.

Leaves: 3′ ± high; 4″ ± wide; leathery, lance-shaped, taper rapidly upward from about middle. Grow in circular, arching clumps from central rootstock. Fertile leaves taller, more rigid, more erect. In winter fertile leaves wither, sterile stay evergreen, though often prostrated by frost. Often second growth in late summer. Very variable.

Leaflets: Lance-shaped, prominently eared; short-stemmed; bristle-tipped, incurving teeth. Two lowest leaflets almost opposite and deflexed; lower and middle leaflets alternate and horizontal; upper leaflets scythe-shaped pointing upward, especially when in fruit. Lowest fruited leaflets ⅔ size of next lower unfruited leaflets. 20 to 40 pairs. Veins forked and free, with sterile leaflets many times forked and fertile leaflets' veins often meshed.

Axis: Very scaly, grooved in front; green.

Stalk: Shorter than leaf; brown at base, green above; very scaly; lower stalk flattened in front, ridged slightly at sides; swollen at base; upper stalk slightly grooved in front.

Rootstock: Short; horizontal or erect; very scaly; with many withered stalks and leaves. Pale brown.

Roots: Medium short; numerous; growing from rootstock or from extreme base of stalks.

Fruitdots: Numerous, round, at end of veins; in two or more rows near midrib; confluent, often covering back of leaflet completely; red-brown; ripe June–Oct. Spores bean-shaped. Indusium circular, entire, rough-edged; fixed at center.

Fiddleheads: Scaly and stout, silvery gray-haired. Prominent in early spring.

Marginalia: a. Typical sterile leaflet. b. Typical fertile leaflet. c. Forma *cristatum*, forked-tip leaflet. d. Forma *crispum*, leaflet wavy. e. Forma *incisum*, leaflet sharply cut and toothed. (This forma also bears additional fruitdots on tip ends of middle and lower middle leaflets of fertile leaf.) f. Forma *Gravesii*, sterile leaflet blunt with midrib projecting.

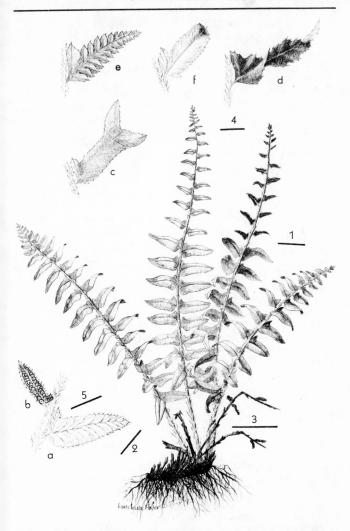

Diagnostic Arrows: 1. Sharp reduction in size between fruited and next-lower unfruited leaflet. 2. Down-pointed two lowest leaflets. 3. Scaly stalk. 4. Rapidly tapering top part of fertile leaf. 5. Eared leaflet. Combination of these characteristics lacking in similar ferns: Braun's Holly Fern, Narrow-leaved Spleenwort, and the Polypodies.

BRAUN'S HOLLY FERN
Species: *Polystichum Braunii* (Spenner) Fée

Style: Shiny, spiny, scaly, holly-like fern. Lustrous dark green leaves, up to 3′ long, arch upward and outward from circumference of a central, individual, stout, and very scaly rootstock.

Ecology: Found in cool deep woods of our northern sections, particularly in rocky, moist, shaded spots; along running brooks, on rocky slopes, or in cool ravines. Most luxuriant and deep green plants found where moisture and coolness are combined with deep shade and filtered sunlight of our northern woods and forests. Circumneutral soil.

Leaves: 24″± long. Thick, rigid, often arching, elliptical leaves taper from about center downward to base and upward to tip. Over-all length about three times the extreme width. Partially evergreen.

Leaflets: Lower middle, middle, and upper leaflets lance-shaped and pointed; lowest leaflets oblong and blunt. In 20 to 40 pairs, spaced fairly close together but not overlapping.

Subleaflets: Oblong or ovate; slightly eared at top near leaflet's axis; shiny, of slightly leathery texture with bristly, forward-pointing teeth. Subleaflets nearest main axis hug closely to it; together with their scales and scales of axis, this makes main axis appear very thick. In 6 to 18 pairs, spaced very close together, often overlapping.

Axis: Grooved in front, flat sides, back very scaly; pale brown.

Stalk: Very short; flat in front; thickly covered with medium-brown large scales and pale hairs. Stalk often scarred where scales have been worn off.

Rootstock: Very scaly; stout; medium brown. Circular arrangement of from 5 to 8 light brown knuckles the year round. Five to 8 leaves rise from the circumference. Usually withered leaves attached to rootstock.

Roots: Clump of numerous small, wiry, black rootlets reach down and outward a foot or more, depending on soil.

Fruitdots: Small, round; in two rows nearer midvein than margin; ripen Aug. or Sept. Indusium entire, circular, shieldlike, with a ragged edge; fixed at center.

Fiddleheads: Very woolly; cinnamon-brown.

Marginalia: a. Underside sterile leaflet.   b. Sterile subleaflet. c. Fertile subleaflet, showing spore cases after indusium has withered. d. Underside fertile leaflet.

Diagnostic Arrows: 1. Short, very scaly stalk. 2. Small fruitdots in two rows near center vein. 3. Subleaflets close to axis. 4. Prickly, sharp, forward-pointing teeth. Combination of these characteristics lacking in similar ferns: Christmas Fern, the Polypodies.

COMMON POLYPODY
Species: *Polypodium vulgare* L.

Style: Thoreau refers to the "fresh and cheerful communities" of the Polypody in early spring. French Canada names it *tripe de roche*, referring to its rich, lustrous, velvety, mantle-like growth over rocky surfaces. This small, evergreen, vigorous, and common fern, growing in matlike form, smooths and makes green and fresh the rugged contours of rocky woods.

Ecology: Abundant throughout the area at all altitudes where rocks and cliffs provide surfaces affording rich, woody, often very shallow, sub-acid soil. Shade or semi-shade. Most luxuriant in cool damp shade along watercourses. On stumps or old logs, or from tiny cracks in limestone cliffs. Rare in sandy, rockless coastal areas.

Leaves: 12″ ± long; oblong lance-shaped, or triangular; variable in form; leathery; deep green on both sides, often lustrous golden color above; wavy. Taller leaves erect and spreading, lower leaves spreading, small young leaves often prostrate. Leaf cut almost to axis into 10 to 20 pairs of leaflets.

Leaflets: Smooth above and beneath; entire or toothed; wavy. Lowest pair nearly opposite and almost same size as lower and middle leaflets. Upper leaflets more blunt and diminish evenly and rapidly in size to a prominent blunt or pointed tip. Veins obscure, free, 1 to 3 times forked, sometimes netted.

Axis: Smooth, green, slender. Appears sunken below flat plane of leaf's upper surface and slightly raised on undersurface.

Stalk: Up to ⅓ length of leaf. Slender, round, smooth, light dull green. Knobbed at base where attached to rootstock.

Rootstock: Horizontal, widely spreading and creeping; producing rows of leaves. Slender, ¼″ ± thick; densely covered with cinnamon-colored scales. Profusely scarred from broken-off, knob-jointed withered stems. Often exposed.

Roots: Short, dark, fine; spreading or matted; shallow-rooted.

Fruitdots: Large and round; red-brown; in two rows or scattered; more numerous on upper leaflets; often confluent. Lower leaflets rarely fruit-bearing. Fruitdots at ends of free veins, halfway to midrib, appear marginal on account of size. Ripe in summer, often borne all year. No indusium.

Marginalia: a. Undersurface of leaflet. b. Segment of leaf showing a variable cut-leaf form.

Diagnostic Arrows: 1. Slender, smooth green stalk. 2. Blunt-tipped, leathery leaflets; green and smooth on both sides. 3. Leaflets winged at axis. Combination of these key characteristics lacking in similar ferns: Little Gray Polypody, young Christmas Fern, and Narrow-leaved Spleenwort.

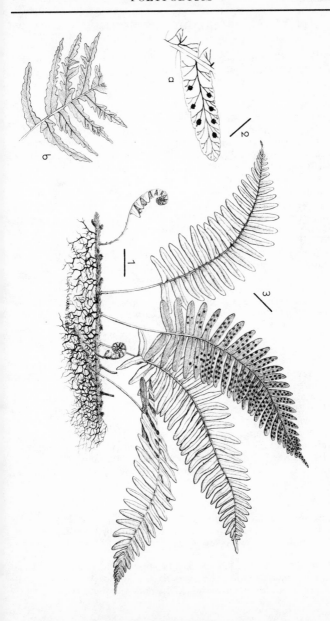

LITTLE GRAY POLYPODY (RESURRECTION FERN)
Species: *Polypodium polypodioides* (L.) Watt

Style: Small, evergreen fern of southern areas, usually growing like ivy on trunk of trees, along tops of old branches, stumps, logs, or rocks; in shade and semi-shade. In dry weather curls up and appears dead. However, with return of moisture, promptly uncurls and becomes green again. Consequently, one of its names is Resurrection Fern.

Ecology: Abundant in warmer southern areas. Prefers epiphytic life on stumps, logs, old wooden buildings, and, most commonly, on lower horizontal branches of ancient live oak trees, together with Spanish moss. In its more northern area found on rocks, stumps, or logs in acid or subacid soil pockets.

Leaves: 8″± tall; oblong ovate; leathery; blunt-tipped. Taller leaves erect or spreading. Smaller leaves often prostrate. Deep green and smooth above, light gray-green and densely scaly beneath. Cut to, or almost to, axis into 6 to 12 pairs of leaflets.

Leaflets: Narrow, rounded tips, often with wavy edges. Not opposite. Lowest and lower leaflets about same size. Under-surfaces pale grayish-green, prominently pock-marked with pointed gray scales, which have dark reddish-brown centers. Veins obscure, 1- to 3-forked, free; sometimes netted. Midrib sunken on upper surface of leaflet, also with prominently raised pale dots from the stems of the fruitdots on the undersurface.

Axis: Upper surface smooth and green. Undersurface pale grayish-green, densely scaly and pock-marked.

Stalk: ⅓± length of leaf. Slender, round; densely chaffy and pock-marked, with dark-centered gray pointed scales. Knobbed base jointed to rootstock.

Rootstock: Woody, slender, horizontally creeping; cordlike. Finely covered with sharp-pointed small pale scales with brown centers.

Roots: Short; many; fine, dark, creeping; often matted.

Fruitdots: Round, rather small but prominent. Reddish-brown. In two rows or scattered; near margin. More numerous on top leaflets, but often all leaflets of a fertile leaf bear fruitdots. Naked, no indusium. Fruitdots often obscured by scales.

Marginalia: a. Leaf curled under dry conditions. b. Underside of leaflet. c. Enlarged section of underside of leaflet. d. Upper side of leaflet, showing sunken midrib and raised dots from stems of fruitdots on undersurface.

Diagnostic Arrows: 1. Pock-marked leaflets. 2. Chaffy stalks. 3. Dark-centered, pointed scales on undersurface of leaflets. 4. Sunken midrib on upper surface of leaflet. Combination of these characteristics

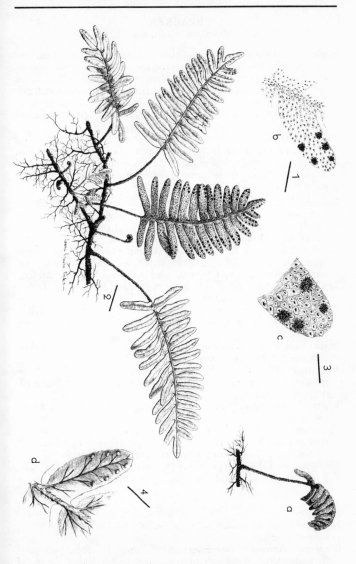

lacking in similar ferns: Common Polypody, young Christmas Fern, and
Narrow-leaved Spleenwort.

BRACKEN
Species: *Pteridium aquilinum* (L.) Kuhn

Style: Commonest of our ferns; strong and coarse. One of earliest to appear and continues to produce new leaves all season. Often grows in large colonies of over knee-high, wavy, dark green, almost horizontal leaves, particularly in neglected lands where only rankest weeds will grow. Killed by first frost, it wilts fast, often producing sizable areas of crisp brown erect growth.

Ecology: Widespread throughout the area. At home in many places; usually indicates poor and barren soil. In full sun, woods, old pastures, burned-over areas; sandy semi-shaded areas, and thickets. Rarely in rich, moist, and limy areas so typical for most ferns.

Leaves: 3′ ± long; 3′ ± wide; triangular or ovate; reflexed almost horizontal to ground; coarse texture; usually divided into 3 nearly equal parts: two lower parts almost opposite, distinctly stemmed, and cut into leaflets and subleaflets; upper part ovate, cut into leaflets, lower of which are cut again in lessening degrees approaching pointed tip, where uppermost leaflets are simple, narrow, oblong, blunt-tipped, and not even cut to midrib.

Leaflets: Oblong, with distinctly narrowed and blunt tips. Lower leaflets cut into subleaflets.

Subleaflets: Narrow, close together, variable in cutting and shape; usually with characteristic narrowed blunt tips; slightly hairy tips and midveins.

Stalk: Tall, about same length as leaf; smooth, rigid; green, then turning dark brown, semi-grooved in front.

Rootstock: ½″ ± thick; dark; scaleless; sometimes hairy; deep-growing and far-creeping, 15′ or more long, and sometimes 10′ deep in ground.

Roots: Stout, black, wide-spreading, sparsely scattered along rootstock.

Fruitdots: In narrow lines near margins of leaflets, covered or partially covered by their reflexed edges; silvery at first, dark brown later. Indusium formed by overlapping margin.

Fiddleheads: Like an eagle's claw, covered with silvery gray hair; 3 sections of leaf uncoil like opening of a claw.

Marginalia: a. Subleaflets of basal leaflet. b. Underside of fertile subleaflet or lobe.

Diagnostic Arrows: 1. Narrowed tip to leaflet. 2. Leaflet with variable subleaflets. 3. Smooth and grooved stalk. Other thrice-cut triangular ferns in our area — Oak Ferns, Beech Ferns, and Rattlesnake Fern — do not have combination of these 3 characteristics.

PURPLE-STEMMED CLIFFBRAKE
Species: *Pellaea atropurpurea* (L.) Link

Style: Stiff, wiry fern with brittle, lustrous, purple stems and widely spread, narrow, pointed bluish gray-green leaflets. Grows from crevices in exposed and weather-beaten limestone cliffs, where there seems little or no earth for nourishment. Evergreen; rare, local, and choosy of habitat.

Ecology: On dry and exposed limestone cliffs; in holes in masonry; at bases of limestone boulders and wherever there are limy, dry cracks or crevices, with medium exposure, throughout our area.

Leaves: 12″± tall; clustered and branching; leathery, dull blue-green; evergreen; variable.

Leaflets: Lance-shaped to linear, simple to compound, sometimes triangular or halberd-shaped at base, or even heart-shaped; margin inrolled; veins free and forked; leaflets often covered with powder.

Subleaflets: Usually similar to leaflets in shape.

Axis: Dark brown, smooth, or very frequently covered with slender brown hairs.

Stalk: About as long as leaf. Dull to glistening dark purplish-brown, usually with appressed, light brownish hairs; wiry and powdery.

Rootstock: Very short, erect or ascending, densely covered by lustrous brown pointed scales.

Roots: Very copious; deep brown or nearly black; thin and fibrous.

Fruitdots: Borne beneath margins of fertile leaflets or subleaflets; pale brown. No indusium. Spores mature in middle of summer.

Marginalia: a. Fertile leaflet showing rolled-in edges covering spore cases.

Diagnostic Arrows: 1. Stiff erect purple stems. 2. Halberd-shaped leaflets.

SLENDER CLIFFBRAKE
Species: *Cryptogramma Stelleri* (S. G. Gmel.) Prantl

Style: Fragile, tiny, almost translucent fern. Rare; hides in deep
   moist shade and its few small delicate-green sterile leaves wither
   and disappear in early summer. Fragile, slender, upright fertile
   leaves, which resemble the Cliffbrakes, disappear few weeks
   later. Sparse low-creeping growth together with small size and
   fragility and short season make it one of our rarest ferns.

Ecology: Found in our northern area and then only in moist, very
   limy soil; in cool and deeply shaded spots; in or on elevated,
   dimly lit dripping ledges; or in tiny, wet, dark pockets in limestone cliffs.

Leaves: 3″± high; smooth, frail, scattered, membranous; sterile
   and fertile leaves different in growth and form. Fertile erect
   and taller, lance-shaped; sterile smaller, decumbent, frail, ovate.

Leaflets: 6 or more pairs. Fertile leaflets narrow lance-shaped and
   spreading. Sterile leaflets ovate with broadly rounded outlines
   and with a crinkly appearance.

Subleaflets: Fertile: narrow, pointed lance-shaped, distinctly
   stemmed. Sterile: rounded fan-shaped; toothed edges, short
   stems, often overlapping or crowded; very delicate and almost
   translucent. Veins free and forked.

Axis: Green; smooth.

Stalk: Longer than leaf; delicate, smooth, weak; pale green above,
   pinkish-brown at base.

Rootstock: Slender, creeping, with pale brown scales and a few
   hairs.

Roots: Fine, sparse, shallow-spreading.

Fruitdots: Along ends of veins at edges of fertile subleaflets.
   Edges of subleaflets curve over and make a false indusium, often
   covering the whole back of the subleaflet.

Marginalia: a. Sterile leaflet. b. Fertile subleaflet.
Diagnostic Arrows: 1. Tall fertile stalk. 2. Lance-shaped fertile subleaflet. 3. Crinkly, rounded sterile subleaflet.

MAIDENHAIR FERN (NORTHERN MAIDENHAIR)
Species: *Adiantum pedatum* L.

Style: Circular or horseshoe-like flat fronds borne on slender erect stalks. Each stalk divides into two recurving parts that bear leaflets on outer rim, the larger leaflets being in middle.

Ecology: In rich shaded soil, often in ravines or beneath moist rocky banks; most abundant in limestone areas.

Leaves: Variable in size according to richness of soil, but flat fronds reach a size of 16″± by 10″± under most favorable conditions.

Leaflets: Bluish green, usually 5 or 6 on each branch of stalk. Elongate; longest ones closest to branching of stalk.

Subleaflets: Extremely variable in shape, with practically no stalks. Vary from fan-shaped to oblong, alternately arranged, entire on lower edge but with upper edge more or less incised.

Axis: Recurved, slender, black to chestnut-brown like stalk; not scaly.

Stalk: 20″± long; shining black or dark brown, and smooth except for scales at very base. Stalks often conspicuous on ground after leaves have died down.

Rootstock: Extensively creeping, grayish brown, frequently with remains of old broken stalks, and with light brown scales near the growing end.

Roots: Slender, grayish, mostly near growing end of rootstock.

Fruitdots: 1 to 5; on upper margins of leaflets. Indusium white to yellowish green, very thin, rounded to linear in shape.

Marginalia: a. Underside of fertile subleaflet.
Diagnostic Arrows: 1. Whorled growth form of leaves almost parallel with ground. 2. Shining dark slender stalks. 3. Fiddleheads multiple in form, wine-red in color.

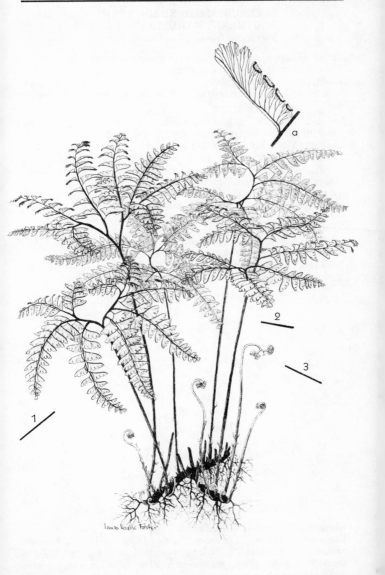

Laura Louise Foster

VENUS MAIDENHAIR FERN
(SOUTHERN MAIDENHAIR FERN)
Species: *Adiantum Capillus-Veneris* L.

Style: Hanging vertically on wet limestone rocks, usually in spray of waterfalls, often evergreen.

Ecology: Not common, because of lack of suitable environments, such as shaded waterfalls of limy water, wet walls of limestone sinks, etc.

Leaves: Up to 20″ ± long; lanceolate to ovate oblong; usually partly covered by trickling water; mostly twice compound.

Leaflets: Very thin; lanceolate to ovate; mostly compound near leaf base but becoming single toward apex of leaf; individual segments with a wedge-shaped base and variously lobed apex, segments up to $\frac{3}{8}$″ in length.

Axis: Brownish, zigzag, very slender and brittle.

Stalk: About $\frac{1}{3}$ length of leaf; shiny, black or dark chestnut. Very slender, scaly at base, but otherwise shining and smooth.

Rootstock: Horizontally creeping, slender, giving off several leaves in a tuft. Covered with shining brown scales.

Roots: Slender, rather numerous, brownish.

Fruitdots: Thin and papery, half-moon-shaped, at upper margins of leaf segments. Indusium white to yellowish green; thin, rounded.

Marginalia: a. Fertile subleaflet.
Diagnostic Arrows: 1. Slender, brittle, black stalks. 2. Pendent growth form of leaves. 3. Stalk between subleaflets zigzag. 4. Palm-shaped subleaflet. Northern Maidenhair Fern grows in whorled form; its leaflets long, narrow, and one-sided.

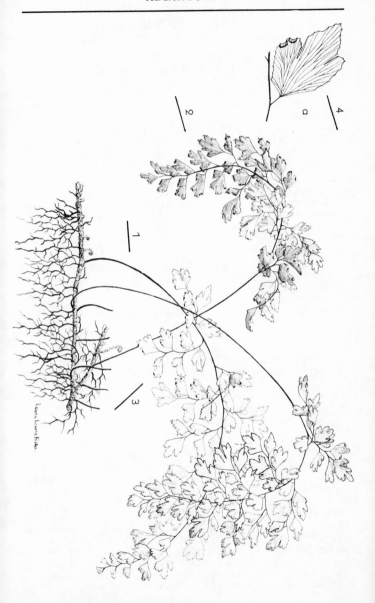

BLUNT-LOBED WOODSIA
Species: *Woodsia obtusa* (Spreng.) Torr.

Style: Our commonest and largest Woodsia. Evergreen in our northern areas. Produces new leaves throughout its season. Distinguished by downy stalks and undersides of leaves and by blunt-lobed lower leaflets. Full green and more delicate and larger in shade; pale green, smaller and coarser when exposed to sunlight.

Ecology: Rare in northern area, common in limestone areas. Shaded rocky banks and cliffs, dry rocky woods in neutral moist but not acid soil. Found in all states in our area. Seldom in exposed locations.

Leaves: 14″± tall; 3″± wide; 2 pairs of lower leaflets much shorter at base. Cut into 15± pairs of widely spaced, almost opposite, short-stemmed leaflets at right angle to axis and stalk.

Leaflets: Hairy underneath, particularly when young; upper leaflets pointed, lower leaflets blunt or rounded. Fertile leaflets often very narrow and pointed when exposed to full sun.

Subleaflets: 8± stemless, sub-opposite, rounded, oblong pairs are deeply cut into lobes rather than distinct subleaflets. Finely and irregularly toothed.

Axis: Grooved in front; hairy; pale yellow to shining brown; slightly scaly.

Stalk: Dark orange at base, yellow above; prominent scales, brittle, readily breaking off at base, not jointed above base; many and conspicuous downy white hairs when young. Stalk nearly hidden by broken-off short stalks.

Rootstock: Short, stout, nearly erect; scaly, dark.

Roots: Rather sparse, black, fibrous, with many dense and quite long rootlets.

Fruitdots: Pale brown, usually in rows, often close together when mature. Indusium small disc under and over fruitdot, which splits into 5 or 6 irregular segments, making a starlike frame for fruitdot.

Marginalia: a. Section of fertile leaflet. b. Underside of fertile leaflet, with edges turned under. c. Upper side of fertile leaflet, with edges turned under. d. Sterile leaflet. e & f. Indusium expanded and indusium half open.

Diagnostic Arrows: 1. Hairy stalk and axis. 2. Blunt-tipped lower leaflets. 3. Widely spaced leaflets. 4. Star-shaped opened indusium. Combination of these lacking in other Woodsias and the Lip-ferns, and Fragile Fern. Most closely resembles the Fragile Fern and grows in the same location and is of the same size, but is downy or hairy, more robust and more blunt-leaved, and has yellow stalk. When young, very difficult to distinguish.

Laura Louise Foster

RUSTY WOODSIA
Species: *Woodsia ilvensis* (L.) R. Br.

Style: Small, coarse, light green fern with silvery white undersides that turn to rusty brown in fall and during dry seasons, but become green again after moisture. Sometimes called a Resurrection Fern. Grows in tufts in dense mats. More pointed leaves, more compact growth, more rusty and woolly and coarser than the more common Blunt-lobed Woodsia. Its old stalks, broken off at the joints, form rough and typical stubble.

Ecology: On high rocky ledges and crests of precipices in acid soil. Full sun with dry mosses, or moist soil well drained in rocky crevices. Reported as found in northerly and higher and exposed regions.

Leaves: 6″± tall; 1″± wide; stiff, erect, pointed tips, slightly reduced at base; undersides covered with dense white wool, which turns later to rusty brown. Cut into 12± pairs of nearly opposite stemless leaflets. (Second and third lowest leaflets often stemmed.) Thick, membranous, dark brown above; smoothish.

Leaflets: Oval and slightly pointed; usually cut into 7 variable and rounded lobes, or stemless subleaflets.

Axis: Hairy, scaly; flattened and grooved in part; green.

Stalk: Brown below, shading to green above; stout, brittle, shining, hairy and scaly, jointed about 1″ above rootstock, forming a bristly stubble after stalks have broken off at the joints. Flattened and grooved in front to below joint.

Rootstock: Short, stout, dark brown, erect, with abundant and toothed and pointed brown scales.

Roots: Fine, lacy, with many tiny rootlets.

Fruitdots: Small, near margin, usually hidden by wool. Indusium a tiny disc on the undersurface of the fruitdot. Its outer edges are fringed around with many long hairlike appendages that radiate and often overlap the fruitdot.

Fiddleheads: Silvery white; prominent in the green and brown tufts. Present spring through fall.

Marginalia: a. Underside of fertile leaflet. b. Upper side of sterile leaflet. c. Underside of fertile stemmed leaflet, showing lobed or stemless subleaflets. d. Fruitdots and veins.

Diagnostic Arrows: 1. Stubble-like broken-off stalks. 2. Erect, pointed narrow leaf. 3. Fruitdot with long radiating hairs. Combination of characteristics lacking in similar species: Blunt-lobed Woodsia, Smooth Woodsia, and Lipferns.

ALPINE WOODSIA
Species: *Woodsia alpina* (Bolton) S. F. Gray

Style: Very small, very rare, evergreen fern growing in semi-rigid, erect, dense tufts. Slightly scaly and hairy. Dark stalks distinguish it from Green Spleenwort and Smooth Woodsia, with which it often grows.

Ecology: In high altitudes in cool crevices of limestone. Moist northerly areas; reported from Maine, N.H., Vt., N.Y.

Leaves: 4″± tall; ½″± wide; slightly narrow at base, usually blunt-tipped, delicate; slightly hairy undersides. Cut into 14± pairs of stemless, not opposite leaflets.

Leaflets: Deeply cut, usually into 5 lobes. Veins free or forked.

Axis: Slightly scaly and hairy; green; grooved face.

Stalk: Short; dark brown at base, shading up to yellowish green; shiny, slightly scaly, jointed above base.

Rootstock: Fairly stout, upright, with toothed brown scales.

Roots: Fine, hairlike, numerous.

Fruitdots: Small, distinct, very near margin. Indusium a tiny disc with many long hairlike appendages radiating outward and surrounding fruitdot from underside.

SMOOTH WOODSIA
Species: *Woodsia glabella* R. Br.

Style: A tiny rare northern evergreen fern growing in erect densely clustered tufts from small erect rootstocks. Pale green and smooth throughout. Its leaves are narrow, its leaflets almost fan-shaped. Easily mistaken for the Alpine Woodsia, Rusty Woodsia, or Green Spleenwort.

Ecology: In high altitudes, on shaded, moist, limestone crevices. Northern area reported from N.Y. west and north.

Leaves: 3″± tall; ⅓″± wide; narrow, oblong, pointed tips; pale, green, delicate; fertile and sterile same. Once-cut into 10± pairs of leaflets.

Leaflets: Oval shape; cut usually into 3 pear-shaped lobes. Lower pairs widely spaced, opposite, almost stemless, deeply cut, and reduced in size. Veins free-forked, not to margin.

Axis: Smooth, green.

Stalk: Shorter than blade; straw color; delicate; face grooved, smooth above, jointed above base, scaly below joint.

Rootstock: Tiny, slender, upright, with brown scales.

Roots: Fine, hairlike, sparse.

Fruitdots: Small, distinct, near margin. Indusium a tiny disc on underside of fruitdot, with few, short, hairlike appendages surrounding the fruitdot.

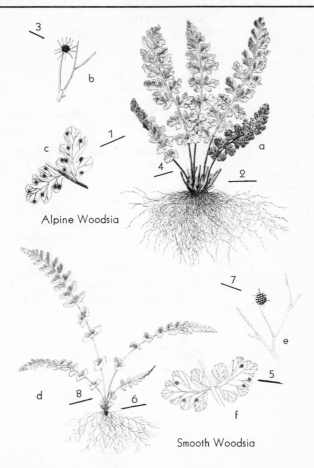

Alpine Woodsia

Smooth Woodsia

Marginalia: Alpine Woodsia: a. Growth form. b. Fruitdot. c. Underside of fertile leaflet. Smooth Woodsia: d. Growth form. e. Fruitdot. f. Underside of fertile leaflet.

Diagnostic Arrows: Alpine Woodsia: 1. Deeply cut leaflets. 2. Stout rootstock with numerous roots. 3. Fruitdot with long radiating hairs. 4. Stalk dark at base. Smooth Woodsia: 5. Fan-shaped leaflets. 6. Tiny rootstock with few roots. 7. Fruitdot with short radiating hairs. 8. Stalk pale color throughout. Both these species easily confused with Green Spleenwort and the smooth phase of the Rusty Woodsia.

WOOLLY LIPFERN
Species: *Cheilanthes tomentosa* Link

Style: Brown, woolly, shriveled, curled mass in dry weather; furry tannish-green, tufted little fern plant when enjoying moist conditions; a typical "Resurrection plant."

Ecology: Southern area. Dry rock ledges; crevice-loving; satisfied with various rocky locations where it is high and dry.

Leaves: 8″± over-all; oblong lanceolate, clustered; thrice-cut; evergreen; densely woolly, or tomentose, especially on undersides, with brownish-white articulated hairs.

Leaflets: 20± pairs, widely spaced and almost opposite below; close together at upper parts; ovate oblong in shape, with rounded tips; slightly hairy above, densely woolly beneath.

Subleaflets: Deeply cut; very rounded; veins free.

Axis: Whitish scales and hairs.

Stalk: Stout, short, erect, with whitish scales hidden under dense dark tan wool; tufted growth.

Rootstock: Stout, short, densely chaffed with brown dark-banded scales; erect.

Roots: Short, small, black; shallow-creeping.

Fruitdots: Marginal, firm, covered by continuous overlapping and overcurving of subleaflets' edges. No indusium.

Fiddleheads: Continuous throughout season; more folded than coiled or circinate.

Marginalia: a. Upper side of sterile leaflet. b. Underside of sterile subleaflet. c. Upper side of fertile leaflet. d. Underside of fertile subleaflet.

Diagnostic Arrows: 1. Coarse and woolly stalks. 2. Crowded and woolly leaflets on woolly axis. 3. Tufted growth, coarse erect rootstock. Hairy Lipfern is hairy, not woolly; its stalks are hairy and slender; its leaflets, especially lower ones, are widely spaced.

HAIRY LIPFERN
Species: *Cheilanthes lanosa* (Michx.) D. C. Eaton

Style: Bluish-green when fresh; a rusty, dead-looking little cliff-loving fern when dry. Dead look quickly disappears after rain or heavy moisture.

Ecology: Dry rocky ledges in middle and southern areas. Not in lowlands, nor high altitudes. Rare, but found in certain areas quite often.

Leaves: 8″± over-all; narrow. oblong lanceolate; evergreen, slender; hairy throughout, with tan-gray hairs; blades 3 times± length of stems; broadest near base.

Leaflets: 12± pairs; lanceolate; mostly opposite and ascending; slightly hairy above; densely hairy beneath; crowded at tops; wide-spaced below.

Subleaflets: Veins free; rounded throughout, both fertile and sterile.

Axis: No scales but often white hairs turning to tan-gray when mature.

Stalk: Short, wiry, slender, brittle; black-brown or dark purple; hairy; no scales.

Rootstock: Short; creeping; covered with pale brown scales; slender, often contorted; produces short rows of leaves in semi-tufts.

Roots: Short, small, black, shallow-creeping; not matted; few.

Fruitdots: Prominent dark brown; partially covered by interrupted incurving of subleaflet's edges. No indusium.

Marginalia: a. Upper side of sterile leaflet. b. Upper side of fertile leaflet. c. Underside of sterile subleaflet. d. Underside of fertile subleaflet.

Diagnostic Arrows: 1. Creeping slender rootstock. 2. Widely spaced lower leaflets. 3. Hairy slender stalks. Similar to Woolly Lipfern, but hairy, not woolly, and a more delicate-looking plant.

Laura Louise Foster

SMOOTH LIPFERN (ALABAMA LIPFERN)
Species: *Cheilanthes alabamensis* (Buckl.) Kunze

Style: Small, delicate, smooth-leaved and slightly hairy, black and polished-stemmed lipfern that grows erect from a creeping rootstock.

Ecology: Found in our southwestern area, rare and local in crevices of limestone or calcareous rock pockets or dry rocky bluffs and in limestone outcroppings.

Leaves: 8″± over-all; 1″± wide; semi-evergreen, linear lanceolate; erect, smooth, narrow and pointed at tips; sterile and fertile same.

Leaflets: 20± mostly horizontal pairs, alternate above, almost opposite below; twice-cut, quite pointed tips, particularly fertile ones; very short stems.

Subleaflets: Veins free; fertile, pointed tips; sterile, rounded; broadest at base; variously toothed; eared at top of base.

Axis: Black, polished, smooth; slightly hairy when young.

Stalk: Same length or a little shorter than blade length; black, wiry, thin, brittle, slightly hairy; smooth and polished late in fall and winter.

Rootstock: Brown, scaly, slender, creeping. At ground level often hairy. Produces short rows of leaves in semi-tufts.

Roots: Short, slender, black, spreading and creeping; not numerous; not matted.

Fruitdots: Along margins of subleaflets; continuous; covered by turning over of subleaflets' edges, making a false, firm, and continuous indusium; pale, firm.

Marginalia: a. Upper side of sterile leaflet. b. Underside of sterile subleaflet. c. Underside of fertile subleaflet. d. Underside of fertile leaflet.

Diagnostic Arrows: 1. Tall, slightly hairy, almost smooth stalk. 2. Lance-shaped leaf with horizontal, opposite, and evenly spaced leaflets, which are smooth. 3. Fertile leaflets narrow and pointed when in full fruit. Woolly Lipfern coarse and woolly; Hairy Lipfern hairy and less coarse; Smooth Lipfern smooth and delicate, its black stems and axis distinguishing it from the Woodsias and Bladder Ferns.

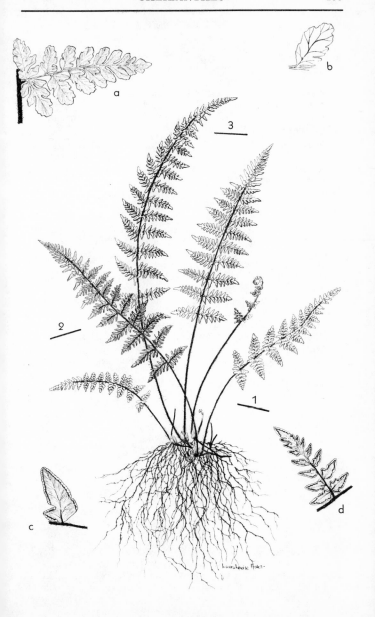

BULBLET FERN
Species: *Cystopteris bulbifera* L. Bernh.

Style: Graceful narrow-leaved tufted fern, usually growing in large masses, long streamer-like fronds hanging down over limestone cliffs, and covering the moist rocks that lie below limestone ledges with various lacy patterns.

Ecology: Delicate, not evergreen; on rocky slopes and steep banks nearly everywhere that limestone rocks occur. Plants in drier localities smaller than those of moist places.

Leaves: 8″± long; 3″± wide; soft pale green. Elongate triangular, often reaching 36″± in length, and known to reach as much as 5′; broadest at base and extended to a long, usually drooping point.

Leaflets: 2″± long. Drooping at ends, and varying from triangular to nearly linear; usually at a slight upward angle to the axis. Alternate, rarely opposite.

Subleaflets: Usually cut to midrib of leaflet; most frequently linear, but very variable in shape, lowest pair of each leaflet conspicuously parallel to axis of leaf.

Axis: Shining yellow, slender.

Stalk: About ⅓ length of leaf; yellow, with a swollen blackish base.

Rootstock: Short (up to 2″± long), slender, slightly horizontal to vertical; black and scaly.

Roots: Black, somewhat irregular in size.

Fruitdots: Few, scattered away from margins. Indusium short, blunt, hoodlike; spores mature in early summer. Bulblets are produced on lower surface of subleaflets; these drop off and germinate into plants.

Marginalia: a. Leaflet with bulblet. b. Fertile subleaflet. c. Bulblet sprouting a young plant. d. Underside of fertile lobe.

Diagnostic Arrows: 1. Long, narrow, and thin leaves. 2. Bulblet on leaflet. 3. Bulblet. Only species of our ferns which has bulblets.

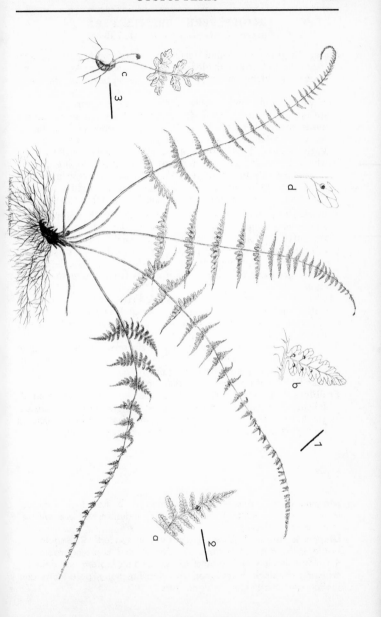

FRAGILE FERN (BRITTLE FERN)
Species: *Cystopteris fragilis* (L.) Bernh.

Style: Bright green small fern, appearing commonly in early spring in crevices of shaded ledges and among rocks, often disappearing during summer droughts. Reappears in the early fall.

Ecology: In rock crevices where there is some moisture, at least in spring; frequently abundant, and forming small mats among moist shaded boulders below ledges; sometimes in rich shaded soil of woodlands and on tree stumps.

Var. *protrusa* Weatherby is a variation, chiefly southward, in which rootstock extends forward beyond developing leaves, sometimes as much as 2″±. Var. *Mackayi* Lawson a variety with very small indusia, and subleaflets only slightly toothed. Chiefly a northern plant, running southward only in mountains.

Leaves: 10″± long; 3″± wide; lanceolate, with pointed tips. These vary a great deal in appearance, depending upon width and cutting of leaflets. Color varies from light to dark green.

Leaflets: Usually about 12 pairs, at right angles or at ascending angle to axis. Cutting of leaflets exceedingly variable, depending upon variations of species. Also varies from young to mature plants.

Stalk: Erect, arched, or prostrate. A little shorter than blade; brittle and easily breaking off, especially near base. Deep brown to black near rootstock, becoming straw-colored or green above; slender, smooth, with only a few scales near base.

Rootstock: Slender, creeping or short, light brown to black, simple or branched; sparsely clothed with brown scales, or masses of brown hairs; old stalk bases prominent.

Roots: Rather numerous heavy black roots.

Fruitdots: Few, scattered. Indusium conspicuous, inflated, delicate hoodlike structure attached at one side of fruitdot. Tends to shrivel up early, and may soon become inconspicuous among fruitdots, so may appear to be entirely lacking.

Marginalia: a. Fertile leaflet, var. *protrusa*. b. Rootstock, var. *protrusa*. c. Fertile leaflet, var. *Mackayi*. d. Indusium, var. *genuina*. e. Indusium, var. *Mackayi*.

Diagnostic Arrows: 1. Lower leaflets widely spaced. 2. Smooth and brittle stalk, dark at bottom. 3. Coarse and creeping rootstock. 4. Smooth leaflets with distinct stems. Smooth Lipfern has delicate creeping rootstock; Blunt-lobed Woodsia has hairy, pale stalks and leaflets are usually hairy with no stems.

HART'S-TONGUE FERN
Species: *Phyllitis Scolopendrium* (L.) Newm.

Style: Glossy, bright green, leathery, evergreen fern with leaves growing upward and outward in circular tufts. Shape of leaf simulates a deer's tongue.

Ecology: Originally extremely rare and local. (From most recent data this fern was found originally only in a few widely scattered and isolated areas — i.e., New Brunswick, two counties in Ontario, two counties in N.Y., and two counties in Tenn. Some of these stations, it is believed, no longer exist. In the last few years, however, many nursery-reared plants, and plants saved from bulldozers, have been introduced into many supposedly suitable places throughout our area.) In shaded, damp, rocky limestone crevices. On high lands where it is cool and moist.

Leaves: 12″ ± long; 2″ ± wide. Dark glossy green above, lighter green beneath; thick, elongated, often with wavy edges; leaf base heart-shaped; tip pointed, often forked; veins free, 2 and 3 times forked; veins' ends distinctly distant from edge of leaf.

Axis: Distinct; yellowish, becoming pale brown at base.

Stalk: Short, thick-furrowed, pale brown; covered with brown scales; old stalks frequently without scales.

Rootstock: Short, upright; hidden by nearly vertical bases of leaves.

Roots: Black, wiry, shallow-creeping; rather sparse.

Fruitdots: Elongate, of varying lengths; in pairs on either side of a vein with indusia opening toward each other.

Marginalia: a. Heart-shaped base of leaf. b. Underside of fertile leaf, showing fruitdot and indusium.

Diagnostic Arrows: 1. Tongue-shaped leaf with wavy edge. 2. Irregularly elongated rows of fruitdots.

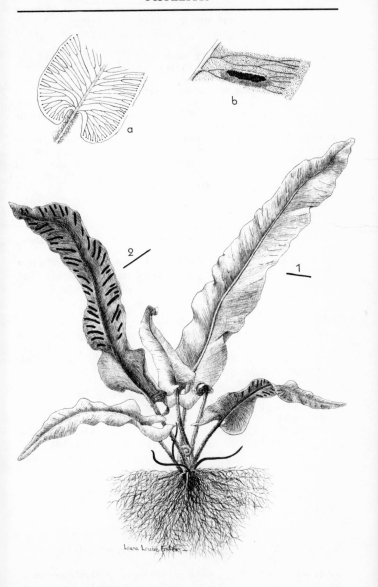

Loura Louise Foster

HARTFORD FERN (CLIMBING FERN)
Species: *Lygodium palmatum* (Bernh.) Sw.

Style: Much like a climbing vine, little like a fern. Long and slender twining stem carries many pairs of little ivy-like leaves, deeply lobed into 5 to 7 blunt-tipped widespread fingers. Plant twines and climbs up and over neighboring twigs, weeds, and even partly up small trees. Fertile leaves, which are much smaller, very deeply cut, and much constricted. They top the "vine" with a pale green feathery crest.

Ecology: In light, moist or wet, acid soil; in semi- or deep shade; in low thickets, open swamps, along banks of streams, in ravines —where mountain laurel grows. Likes a certain amount of sunlight, but must have wet feet. Reported from southern N.H. to eastern N.Y., Ohio, Ky., and south.

Sterile leaves: $2'' \pm$ long; $1\frac{1}{2}'' \pm$ wide; palm-shaped, deeply lobed into 5 to 7 blunt-pointed wide-spreading fingers, margins not toothed. Thin texture, smooth, light green; evergreen until next year's growth. In pairs on separate wiry once-forked stems $1'' \pm$ long.

Fertile leaves: Borne only at top of vine, which is several times branched. Also 5- to 7-fingered, palm-shaped, but much smaller, more deeply cut, and greatly constricted when in full fruit. Fertile leaves not evergreen.

Stalk: $4' \pm$ long; sinuous and branching. Grows individually from rootstock and above ground branches and forks, unlike other ferns. Round, dark, shining black and slightly hairy at base, upper parts brownish or green and slightly flattened, sometimes with edges ridged. Wiry, brittle, and smooth throughout.

Rootstock: Slender, cordlike, black, creeping below surface. Hairy, younger parts covered with bristly red hairs.

Roots: Black, long, slender, branching. Sparsely growing from rootstock.

Fruitdots: Each finger holds 2 rows of $6 \pm$ spore cases. The indusia are overlapping scales which cover the egglike spore cases.

Marginalia: a. Fertile leaflets. b. Sterile leaflets. c. Enlarged section of fertile leaflet.

Diagnostic Arrows: 1. Vine-like growth form. 2. Fertile leaflets at top of "vine." 3. Five-fingered ivy-like sterile leaflet.

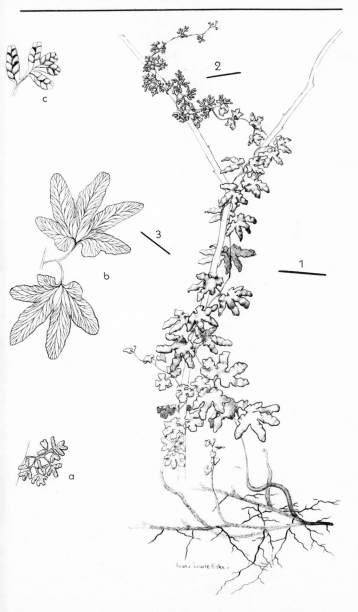

Laura Louise Foster -

CURLY GRASS FERN
Species: *Schizaea pusilla* Pursh

Style: Minute unfernlike plant that looks like its name — curly grass. Almost impossible to find without lying flat on ground, except in winter, when its evergreen, sterile, curling leaves may be distinguished from surrounding dead grasses.

Ecology: For our area to date found only in southern N.J. In wet, very acid soils, sphagnum and cranberry bogs, cedar swamps and under cedar trees, wet sandy soil, dense swamps. Found usually in association with Carolina and Bog Clubmosses and the thread-leaf sundew. Since also found in Nova Scotia and Newfoundland and in similar environment, it is hoped that other stations of this rare fern will be found between the N.J. and Canadian localities.*

Leaves: 2″± long; threadlike, pencil-line wide, wiry, slightly flattened. Sterile leaves coiled and twisted; evergreen. The fertile leaves are slightly longer, quite erect and topped by fertile segments. Their growing form is in tufts direct from the rootstock; no stalks.

Rootstock: Slender, upright.

Roots: Relatively coarse, unbranching, short, sparse, with slender forked tips.

Fruitdots: On tips of fertile leaves in triangular or one-sided, fistlike 5± fingered tiny segments.

---

* In 1960 a large stand of Curly Grass was found near Montauk, Long Island, N.Y. This stand was in a small cranberry bog growing in association with cranberries, sundews, and Marsh St. Johnsworts.

Marginalia: a. Back of fertile leaf. b. Front of fertile leaf and spore cases.

Diagnostic Arrows: 1. Finger-like leaflets holding spore cases. 2. Curling hairlike sterile leaves. 3. Upright fertile leaves topped by triangular fistlike segments.

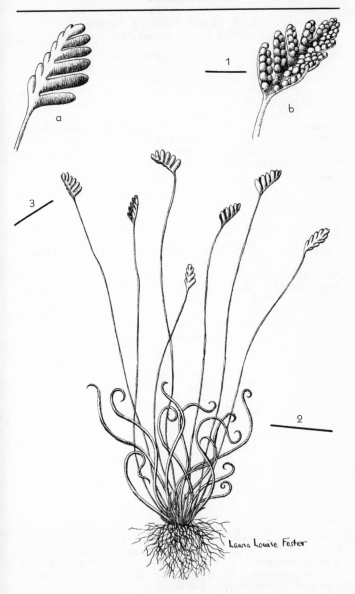

Laura Louise Foster

FILMY FERN (BRISTLE FERN)
Species: *Trichomanes Boschianum* Sturm

Style: Probably daintiest and most delicate of our ferns. Translucent fragile leaves only one cell thick, with no skin, or epidermis, so it can absorb moisture and light more readily in its dim-lighted cavernous habitat. Like a water plant living on land. Leaves often numerous and overlap each other, forming a mass, like a bed of moss.

Ecology: In damp acid grottoes of sandstone cliffs or on rocks and in wet acid pockets in caves well away from direct light. Found in southern Ohio, Ill., Ky., Tenn., W. Va. Very rare in our area, particularly in northern part of range.

Leaves: 6″± tall; 1½″± wide; translucent, light green, evergreen; ovate lance-shaped, one cell thick, like no other of our ferns. Lacy-cut into 6± pairs of leaflets and often cut again into 2± pairs of subleaflets (dried leaves like parchment).

Leaflets: Irregularly cut or lobed, blunt-tipped, often quite flat-tipped.

Stalk: 1½″± long; translucent, green; prominently winged almost to junction with rootstock. Fragile.

Axis: Broadly winged; green.

Rootstock: ¼″± thick; black, wiry, branching and creeping. Covered with tiny roots like hair or wool.

Fruitdots: On 3 or 4 interior lobes of fertile leaflets; tiny green cylindrical masses surrounding and partway up hair tip. Both emerging from the tubular cuplike indusium.

Marginalia: a. Section of rootstock and lower portion of a sterile leaf. b. Fertile leaflet. c. Indusium and fruit and projecting hairlike bristle.
Diagnostic Arrows: 1. Blunt or squared tips of subleaflets. 2. Massed or mosslike growth form. 3. Hairy rootstock. 4. Cuplike indusium on interior lobe of fertile leaflet, with bristle.

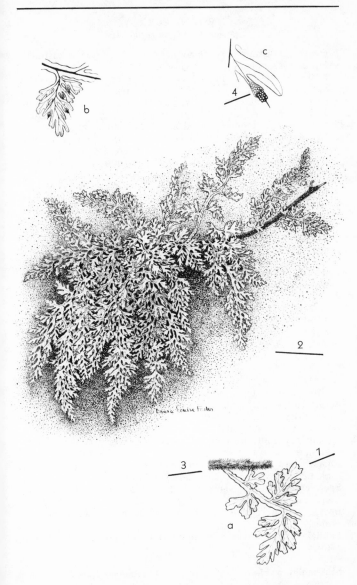

Diana Louise Fisher

ROYAL FERN
Species: *Osmunda regalis* L.

Style: At a distance this fairly common large fern is distinctly
fernlike in appearance, but close up, its widely spaced, oblong
leaflets make it look like a locust tree. By some it is considered
our finest fern; actually it is too coarse really to reflect typical
aesthetic characteristics of ferns, with their lacy, light-filtering,
and delicate growth and form. Royal Fern grows to height of
6′ or more from an elongated rootstock, simulating the ancient
tree ferns. Foliage is translucent pale green where it has sunlight, bright green with reddish stalks where light is less intense.
Variable in size and shape, depending on environment.

Ecology: Habitant of wet lands; along streams, in bogs and lake
fronts, in wet patches, in low thickets, pastures, and meadows.
Will grow happily in water "up to its knees," and in such bogs
will reach height of over 6′ and grow in such profusion as to
simulate tropical jungle growth.

Leaves: Large, semi-coarse, oblong ovate, usually growing erect in
clustered branchlike form. Twice-cut; variable. Fertile leaves
bear light brown, flowerlike spore-bearing leaflets at tips.

Leaflets: Oblong, ascending; 6 or more pairs, not opposite and
widely spaced.

Fertile leaflets: Usually terminal; light brown; densely clustered
and contracted.

Subleaflets: Narrow oblong, ends blunt-tipped or rounded; bases
rounded or cordate; small distinct stems. 8 or more pairs,
widely spread; not opposite. Terminal subleaflets longer,
often semi-eared when next lower subleaflets are contiguous.
Very variable. Veins forked; main vein distinct.

Axis: Quite slender; round; pale pinkish straw color, or greenish,
often blending together.

Stalk: Tall, smooth, almost round; pale straw-colored, reddish at
base; slightly grooved face.

Rootstock: Often 6″ high; semi-erect, covered with old withered
stalks, typically forming a tussock-like base, deeply bedded in
ground.

Roots: Black; many; wiry; growing in all directions deep in ground,
particularly when plant has formed old tussocks.

Spore cases: Naked, short-stalked, in clusters. Longitudinally
opening in halves.

Spores: Green, later brown; contain chlorophyll. Ripe in midsummer.

Fiddleheads: Smooth, wine-colored; fairly stout; prominent in
early spring.

Marginalia: a. Sterile leaflet. b. Sterile subleaflet showing veining.
c. Spore cases and spores. d. Fertile leaflet.

Diagnostic Arrows: 1. Fertile leaflets at top of leaf. 2. Leaflets widely spaced and opposite. 3. Subleaflets narrow oblong, widely spaced, not opposite. When young could possibly be confused with Narrow-leaved Spleenwort.

INTERRUPTED FERN
Species: *Osmunda Claytoniana* L.

Style: Large, coarse fern, arching in growth, with distinct interruptions in center of leaf, which are or were fertile leaflets.
These interruptions make identification easy.

Ecology: Common along roadsides and woodland edges. Rugged
and persistent in almost any kind of soil or location. One of
earliest ferns to appear in spring. Prefers stony, dry soil,
rather than boggy, wet areas preferred by very similar species,
Cinnamon Fern.

Leaves: Large, coarse, oblong oval; broadest at middle; twice-cut;
leaves grow in an arching form from a central crown. Woolly
when first expanded, later smooth throughout. Sterile leaves
distinctly curve outward; fertile leaves more erect, taller, and
more numerous, soon becoming interrupted by 4 or more central
pairs of leaflets bearing spores. All leaves wither early after
frost.

Leaflets: Narrow lance-shaped, broadest at axes, tapering gradually
to blunted tips. Deeply cut into oval, blunt-tipped or rounded,
semi-overlapping lobes. Leaflets ascending, opposite, 18 or
more pairs. Lower leaflets below interruption widely spaced
and often much smaller. Veins forked.

Fertile leaflets: In center part of each fertile leaf are 4 or more
pairs of dark green leaflets, which bear spore cases in dense
cylindrical clusters that later turn to deep dark brown. Ripen
and wither rapidly, leaving interrupted space from early summer
onward.

Axis: Smooth, green; semi-grooved in front.

Stalk: Round, with semi-grooved face; smooth; green; quite stout.
Stalks of fertile leaves much longer and more erect.

Rootstock: Very stout; creeping; stubbly, with old withered,
broken stalks.

Roots: Black, tangled, and thickly matted; grow in all directions;
firmly embedded in ground.

Spore cases: Large, short-stalked; in clusters; green at first,
then dark brown.

Spores: Bright green, short-lived; contain chlorophyll; must
germinate within a few days.

Fiddleheads: Stout; very woolly, brown; among earliest to appear
in spring.

Marginalia: a. Fertile leaflet below sterile leaflet. b. Sterile subleaflets, showing veining and forward-pointing tips. c. Spore cases
and spores.

Diagnostic Arrows: 1. Interruptions. 2. Tall stalks of fertile leaves
with widely spaced lower leaflets. 3. Smaller, arching sterile leaves.
4. Taller and more erect fertile leaves. 5. Overlapping sterile sub-

Laura Louise Foster

leaflets. Combination of these characteristics lacking in similar species:
Cinnamon Fern, Virginia Chain Fern, Ostrich Fern.

CINNAMON FERN
Species: *Osmunda cinnamomea* L.

Style: Large, strong, vigorous, coarse, and very common fern, growing in arching circular clusters as individual plants from sturdy, heavy rootstock covered with thickly matted horsehair-like roots. In late spring golden cinnamon clublike fertile leaves easily distinguish it from other spring plants.

Ecology: Widely spread in areas in damp and waterlogged locations; moist and shady places; along streambanks, or edges of swamps, lakes, and ponds. Together with Interrupted Fern, which enjoys the drier regions, it constitutes most numerous, common, and prominent ferns in our area. Found in almost every swamp in the United States and sometimes so profuse as to form jungle-like areas.

Leaves: 3′± high; large, coarse; twice-cut; lanceolate; growing from central rootstock. In spring covered with scattered tufts of wool. Sterile leaves mostly erect or arching; after first heavy frosts wither and fall off, leaving erect and naked stalks.

Fertile leaves: First to appear, and first to wither; bright green at first, soon turning to lustrous cinnamon-brown. Stiff, erect, club-shaped, narrow, pointed; cut into pairs of leaflets (sporophylls), which are also club-shaped, growing upward, hugging and parallel to main stem.

Leaflets: Narrow lance-shaped; pointed; cut deeply, almost to axes, into oblong lobes with points; not overlapping. 20 or more pairs, nearly opposite. Cinnamon wool tufts at base near axes. Veins forked.

Axis: Smooth, green; semi-grooved in front, with scattered cinnamon wool during early part of the season, often persisting.

Stalk: Round, with semi-grooved face; smooth, green; covered with cinnamon wool at first, often with some wool persisting throughout season. Stalks of fertile leaves die early summer; left as withered entwining stalks covered with light-cinnamon-tan wool, bearing at ends rusty empty fruit cases.

Rootstock: Very stout; stubbly, with old, withered, broken stalks. Creeping, often partially exposing above surface of ground its stiff and bristly growth form. At crown-ends are buds for future years, and at basal ends are old, withered, and decayed parts of rootstocks of past years.

Roots: Strong, wiry, branching off on all sides; matted; very firmly embedded in soil.

Spore cases: Large, short-stalked; in clusters; green at first, then cinnamon.

Spores: Bright green, short-lived; contain chlorophyll; must germinate promptly or die in few days.

Fiddleheads: Large; densely covered with silvery white hairs, turning later to cinnamon-brown as leaves expand.

Marginalia: a. Underside of sterile leaflet.   b. Subleaflets, showing veining.   c. Variation of leaflet form.   d. Fertile leaflet.   e. Spore cases and spores.

Diagnostic Arrows: 1. Woolly tuft at base of leaflet.   2. Clublike fertile leaf.   3. Subleaflets.   Combination of these characteristics lacking in similar species: Interrupted Fern, Virginia Chain Fern, Ostrich Fern.

The Water Ferns

THE Water Ferns, or **Hydropteridales,** are represented in our area by two families, the **Marsileaceae,** with one genus of only one species, *Marsilea quadrifolia* (Water Shamrock), and the **Salviniaceae,** with two genera — *Azolla caroliniana* (Mosquito Fern) and *Salvinia rotundifolia* (Floating-moss Fern). The species of these two families are not indigenous to our area, but were introduced some years ago and have spread to various localities, where they have become quite common. They are small, attractive ferns used in aquaria and garden pools, from which they have undoubtedly escaped and re-established themselves as part of our ecology.

Marsilea quadrifolia, originally from Europe, is found as far north as Massachusetts, where in winter the thermometer is many degrees below zero and the ice many inches thick. *Azolla carolinia* is a native of our southern states, and *Salvinia rotundifolia* is from the tropics. Neither of these two species is very hardy and rarely found existing in the North and middle East for more than a few seasons.

The Water Ferns are usually ranked above the true ferns and considered fern allies, since they differ from the true ferns primarily by having two distinct kinds of spores: the *megaspores,* or large female spores, and the *microspores,* or tiny male spores. (All true ferns have one type of spore.) The spores of the Water Ferns are borne on special stalks and are contained in special capsules, or *sporocarps*. The sporocarps of *Marsilea* contain both the male and female spores, whereas *Azolla* and *Salvinia* have separate sporocarps, one for each of the clusters of spores of each sex.

Genus *Azolla*

see p. 178

There are two genera listed for the family Salviniaceae: the genus *Azolla,* with 6 species, and the genus *Salvinia,* with 10 species. Only one of these 16 species for the family — *Azolla caroliniana* — can be considered well enough established in our area to be illustrated in this *Field Guide. Salvinia rotundifolia* is common in aquariums and sometimes in summer garden pools, but it is so rarely reported from the wild in our area that it is given only a brief description. *Azolla,* however, has spread from the southern states to the middle Atlantic and middle-western states wherever there is not too much intense cold in winter. (I have observed it winter satisfactorily in a pond where, even though there was little ice, the temperature went below 20°F. several times that season.)

Azolla, being a tiny plant with clinging roots, probably is most frequently spread by waterfowl, particularly the wading birds, and is apt to be found in pools or waters where it had not been seen before.

Azolla caroliniana is a minute floating fern that looks like a tiny bit of the tip of an arbor vitae leaf, or like a red or green snowflake. When well established, it spreads in masses over the surface of still ponds and backwaters. Where it is exposed to the most direct rays of the sun, it often turns to an "autumnal red" and grades into a bright green color as it spreads into its preferred shady locations. It is often found in semi-brackish waters, and at low water it clings happily to the muddy banks. It also will creep up the wet mossy banks of ponds for several inches above the water level. The leaves of the *Azolla* are in two rows and two-lobed. They are minute and delicately membranous. They are deeply cleft into pointed oval leaflets that grow from tiny fan-shaped branches, which are of such a fragile nature that disturbances along the surface of the water break off the outer edges or ends, and small fern plants float free. The leaflets grow in *imbricated* rows (layered upon one another). The lower leaflets are below the surface of the water, the upper leaflets float on the surface. From the under-surface of the branches grow the very fine roots. Both the sporo-carps are soft and thin-walled and are usually borne in pairs in the *axils*, or joinings, of the leaves. The sporo-carps consist of one large roundish capsule containing several masses of the tiny microspores, or male spores, and one smaller, somewhat acorn-shaped capsule con-taining only one large female spore. In spring when the spores have ripened, but before fertilization, both kinds break off from their stems and are carried to the surface of the water by masses of tiny spring algae. The capsule containing the micro-spores opens and breaks up into many spherical coherent groups of disc-like structures called *massulae*. The massulae have barb-ended hairlike appendages by which they attach themselves to the female spore for fertilization. The female spore, or megaspore, has a canal at its top leading to the egg. Through this canal the sperm must pass to reach the egg. To assure the sperm's approach-ing the open end of the canal, the megaspore has fine hairlike filaments that float from its top to guide the sperm to the location of the canal. The fertilization process is performed in a proto-plasmic substance that originally surrounded both the micro-spores and the megaspore; this also furthers the necessary proper contacts. When the egg has been fertilized, the holding proto-plasmic substance disintegrates and the egg falls to the pond floor, later to be liberated into a new floating fern.

There is one more fascinating and interesting characteristic of *Azolla* which I must mention here. The sporocarps are outgrowths of the fertile leaves. The leaves grow in the form of an encircling ring which eventually surrounds completely either the micro-spores or the megaspores. Before the growth of the ring has com-pletely encircled the spores, however, a colony of blue-green algae, *Anabaena*, moves into the cavity and establishes itself there until the sporocarp later bursts open. It is rare to find an *Azolla* plant without *Anabaena* as tenant. This is called "shelter association," since the fern shelters the algae with no benefits derived for either, as far as is known today.

Salvinia rotundifolia Willd., a native of South America, is very similar in behavior and ecology to the Mosquito Fern, *Azolla caroliniana*. They are both tiny ferns that float free on the sur-faces of the still, fresh waters of ponds, lakes, canals, dikes, and ditches of the southern areas. The leaves of *Salvinia rotundifolia*, the Floating-moss Fern, are blue-green, almost round, $\frac{3}{8}''\pm$ in diameter, with cordate (heart-shaped) bases and with tiny stems attached to a short, $2''\pm$, little-branched, light brown stalk. The floating leaves are arranged in opposite pairs that are flat to the surface of the water. The pairs are seldom overlapping. Their upper surfaces are completely covered with stiff, tiny, silvery hairs, which apparently resist water and keep these leaves right side up at all times. The Floating-moss Fern has no true roots. The cinnamon brown, feathery or hairy rootlike appendages hanging below the surface leaves and the stalk are seemingly parts of a much divided third leaf that acts as an absorbing body in place of true roots. The sporocarps, in clusters of four or more,

are borne on the undersurfaces of the stalk at the axils, or joinings, of the leaves. Unlike the *Azolla*, the male and female sporocarps (also rarely found) are of the same size and shape. The male sporocarp contains many tiny microspores; the female sporocarp contains only a few larger mega-spores. Like those of *Azolla*, the stalks of *Salvinia* are brittle. They break apart readily and thus establish many free-floating, separate, tiny fern plants that often spread rapidly over a considerable body of water. They can become a nuisance in a small garden pool or in an aquarium.

Genus *Marsilea*

see p. 178

There are more than 50 species of Marsileas throughout the world. Some are aquatic and some are semi-aquatic plants. Only one species, the aquatic *Marsilea quadrifolia*, has been satisfactorily established in our area. This species was first introduced from Europe to this country into Bantam Lake, Litchfield County, Connecticut, in 1862. Since that time, it has multiplied profusely and spread to other New England and middle-western states.

Marsilea quadrifolia grows in still, quiet, fresh waters. Its roots and often its rootstocks are anchored in the muddy bottom. Its sterile leaves, divided into four leaflets like a shamrock, are borne on single slender green stalks of lengths dependent on the mean depth of the water. The leaves usually float on, or just below, the surface of the water, like small pond lilies. (The stalks of some vigorous plants — especially in shallow water — support their leaves well above the surface. The leaves of the *Marsilea* that are out of water frequently fold up at night, opposite pairs of leaflets folding face to face. This also occurs with some of the young submerged leaves.) The stalks that bear the sporocarps sprout from the main stalk a short distance from its base and terminate in one — or more often a pair of — hard-shelled, brown or purplish bean-shaped capsules (sporocarps) consisting of several transverse compartments, each containing a large female spore and many tiny male spores. When the spores are ripe and swollen, the capsule bursts open vertically into two parts, exposing the many compartments, each of which is surrounded by a mucilaginous ring, which in turn expands with the access of water and exudes the spores from their confines, but by its viscosity it holds the female spore long enough for it to be fertilized by one of the many male cells, or sperms.

Genus *Azolla*

MOSQUITO FERN (WATER FERN; CAROLINA POND FERN)
Species: *Azolla caroliniana* Willd.

Style: Minute, free-floating, truly aquatic fern. When well established, grows in sheets across surface of still waters in such dense masses that supposedly smothers mosquito larvae. Tiny layered leaves, which change from red in full sun to bright green in shade, give an iridescent character to colonies of these ferns, similar to that found in fall foliage colorings.

Ecology: Semi-hardy; particularly abundant in still backwaters, ponds, and even in brackish bayous in temperate zones. Readily transplanted by birds from one watery spot to another, where it multiplies, if not killed by extreme cold and ice.

Leaves: $\frac{1}{5}''\pm$ wide; $\frac{1}{4}''\pm$ long; centrally branching, deeply cleft; vary in color from red to bright green.

Leaflets: 2 rows; imbricated, pointed oval; delicately membranous.

Stalk: Tiny, pale brown, brittle.

Roots: Pendent, tiny, few; from axils of stalks.

Fruit: Sporocarps. Megaspore supposedly acorn-shaped; microspores globular. Ripe in spring.

Genus *Marsilea*

WATER SHAMROCK (WATER CLOVER; PEPPERWORT)
Species: *Marsilea quadrifolia* L.

Style: Aquatic fern growing from roots embedded in bottoms of ponds and lakes with leaves floating above or below surface of water. Leaves are usually 4-part like a shamrock. The stems are very slender and often entwined with other water plants.

Ecology: In still bodies of fresh waters, usually in lakes or ponds. Hardy and persistent once established.

Leaves: $\frac{1}{2}''\pm$ across; like a 4-leaved clover; young leaves coiled in bud like a true fern.

Leaflets: 4 equal wedge-shaped petals with rounded outer edges. (Rarely 6-part.) Smooth above and below; young leaves slightly hairy; veins several times forked.

Stalk: Tall, thin, green, tenuous.

Rootstock: Creeping above or below bottoms of ponds or lakes.

Roots: Deeply embedded in pond bottom. Grow from joints of stalks to rootstocks.

Fruit: Sporocarps in singles or pairs near roots; hard-shelled, beanlike in shape; size of peppercorn; young covered with yellowish hairs.

Mosquito Fern

Underside of branch with spore cases

Top view of plant

Water Shamrock

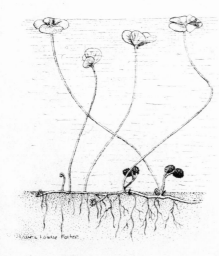

Top view of leaf

Spore cases

The Succulent Ferns

THE **Ophioglossaceae,** or Succulent Ferns, are represented in our area by the two genera, *Ophioglossum* and *Botrychium*, or the Adder's-tongue Ferns and Grape Ferns respectively. Listed for the world are 4 genera of Ophioglossaceae. The genera *Rhizoglossum* and *Helminthostachys* have only one species each, the former occurring in South Africa, the latter in Asia. Of the other two genera: *Ophioglossum* has 54 species world-wide, of which two species are in our area; and *Botrychium* has 36 species world-wide, of which 7 are in our area. (Since the Succulent Ferns are often "embarrassingly transitional" in form, and sometimes in habit, the number of species listed depends on the authority cited and his classifications for species, subspecies, varieties, and forms.)

The Succulent Ferns are not closely related to other ferns, such as the Polypody group (**Polypodiaceae**) and some are of the opinion that they are not true ferns, but they are certainly among the most primitive of ferns. They are perennial, smooth, without scales of any kind, and they have soft and fleshy stems, and roots with no hardened stalk tissues. Although the Rattlesnake Fern may grow a foot or more in height and is a conspicuous plant in the woodlands, many of the species are tiny and difficult to find, since they may be hidden among the vegetation. This is especially true of the common Adder's-tongue, which is often surrounded by grasses. The difficulty lies in finding the first specimen; after that, others are usually easily spotted. On the other hand, Engelmann's Adder's-tongue delights in rocky open places, and is very easily seen. The little Daisyleaf Grape Fern (so named because the leaf resembles that of the feverfew daisy) and the Triangle Grape Fern are likewise often difficult to see in shadow-specked woodlands. The Dwarf Grape Fern seems to be not only scarcer than the others, but most frequently is a tiny plant.

The Succulent Ferns do not have fiddleheads. The young sprout comes through the soil in an erect form, smooth and straight for the Adder's-tongues, and in a bent form for the Grape Ferns. The leaves unfold laterally, producing an erect vernation. Each year new shoots, formed the year before, grow from the common subterranean rootstock. Often three or four buds will be found developing annual sprouts; sometimes two will sprout one year and none the following year. The Succulent Ferns thus appear as isolated plants. The single fleshy stem supports one sterile leaf (or sometimes two in *Ophioglossum Engelmannii*) and one fertile stalk, or *sporophyll*, which bears the spore cases. The gametophytes are tuberous and subterranean, and consequently contain no chlorophyll. They associate with a fungus for their nourishment. Before the plant has been formed, the gametophytes are almost impossible to find, but they are strong and persistent and it is not rare to find the remains of one of them at the rootstock of a mature plant. It is believed that the gametophytes exist underground for some eight or more years. The sporangia, or spore cases, are formed from the main tissue of the fertile stalks. These sporangia are round, naked without a ring (annulus), and when ripe, open by a transverse slit like other primitive ferns.

ADDER'S-TONGUE FERN
Species: *Ophioglossum vulgatum* L.

Style: Small, elusive, unfernlike plant, with simple, narrow, oblong, grass-green single leaf attached halfway up delicate, smooth, and fleshy stalk tipped by fertile spike, which resembles a snake's tongue. Soon withering in midsummer.

Ecology: Damp patches of turf in fields and woodlands. Common throughout area.

Leaf: 4″± long; $\frac{1}{2}$″± wide; oblong, blunt-tipped, smooth, succulent, bright green, often stemmed, ascending or with upper half downcurving. Veins in regular large and small chainlike or netted pattern.

Stalk: 3″± long; fragile, succulent, round, smooth.

Sporophyll: 1$\frac{1}{2}$″± long; narrow, like two rows of beads; pointed tip, on a usually erect stem 1″± above leaf.

Roots: Spreading, smooth, fleshy, 2″± below surface. Bud for next season's plant borne at apex.

LIMESTONE ADDER'S-TONGUE FERN
Species: *Ophioglossum Engelmannii* Prantl

Style: Similar to *O. vulgatum* but shorter, less erect. Leaf, larger in proportion and paler green, is distinctly elliptical, with sharp-pointed tip. Often sends up new leaves in late summer.

Ecology: In limy, gravelly depressions in pastures; often woodlands, sometimes on ledges. Found in our western areas, often in considerable numbers.

Leaf: 3″± long; 1$\frac{1}{2}$″± wide; elliptical, distinctly pointed tip, smooth, succulent, light green, seldom stemmed, upper half downcurving. Veins in irregular large and small netted pattern; the inside pattern the larger, longer, and narrower.

Stalk: 2″± long; fragile, succulent, pale, round, smooth.

Sporophyll: 1$\frac{1}{4}$″± long; narrow pointed tip on a short, usually bent stem.

Roots: Spreading, smooth, fleshy; 2″± below surface. Bud for next year's plant borne at apex.

Marginalia: Adder's-tongue Fern: a. Growth form. b. Sporophyll. Limestone Adder's-tongue Fern: c. Growth form. b. Sporophyll.

Diagnostic Arrows: 1. Blunt-tipped leaf, Adder's-tongue Fern. 2. Pointed-tip leaf, Limestone Adder's-tongue Fern. 3. Unevenly netted veins, Limestone Adder's-tongue Fern. 4. Evenly netted veins, Adder's-tongue Fern.

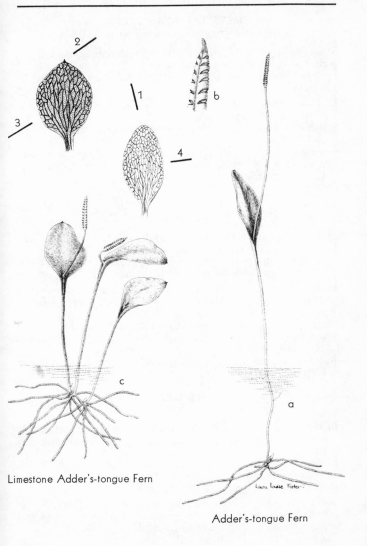

Limestone Adder's-tongue Fern

Adder's-tongue Fern

DAISYLEAF GRAPE FERN
Species: *Botrychium matricariifolium* A. Br.

Style: Slightly larger little fern with pale green daisy-like leaf and clusters of bright yellow spore cases.

Ecology: Found along edges of rich moist woodlands in cooler regions.

Leaf: 1"± long; oblong, twice-cut, in daisyleaf form; variable, erect, often clasping sporophyll.

Stalk: 4"± long; slender, fleshy, small, pale green, fragile; length variable.

Sporophyll: Branched clusters, erect; spore cases yellow, prominent.

Rootstock: Erect; roots smooth, fleshy, numerous, spreading; 2"± below surface.

DWARF GRAPE FERN
Species: *Botrychium simplex* E. Hitchc.

Style: Tiniest and consequently most difficult to find Grape Fern. Leaf is variable, though simply compound.

Ecology: In damp meadows, moist woodlands, and on pasture edges. More common in our northern areas. Rather poor soil.

Leaf: 1½"± long; variable in simple compound form; ascending close to stem, often clasping, with or without stem. Variable as to position on stalk. Smooth, fleshy, pale green.

Stalk: ¾"± long; slender, fleshy, smooth; pale green; fragile.

Sporophyll: Single stalk variable in length; spore case prominent and widely spaced.

Rootstock: Erect; roots smooth, fleshy, few, spreading, deep-set; 2"± below surface.

TRIANGLE GRAPE FERN
Species: *Botrychium lanceolatum* (Gmel.) Rupr.

Style: Slightly larger, darker green little Grape Fern with distinctly triangular leaf high up on stalk. Looks like tiny Rattlesnake Fern.

Ecology: More likely to be in moist, cool, rich, more acid woodlands than two preceding species, which prefer woodland edges and more open spaces, often with Daisyleaf.

Leaf: 1"± long; triangle-shaped, cut into 3 parts with deeply toothed leaf edges. Semi-erect, high up on stalk close to sporophyll; smooth, fleshy, darkish green. Nearly stemless.

Stalk: 3"± long; slender, smooth, pale green.

Sporophyll: Branched, clusters, slightly widespread; spore cases greenish yellow.

Rootstock: Erect; roots smooth, fleshy, numerous; grow in deep-rooted tangled masses.

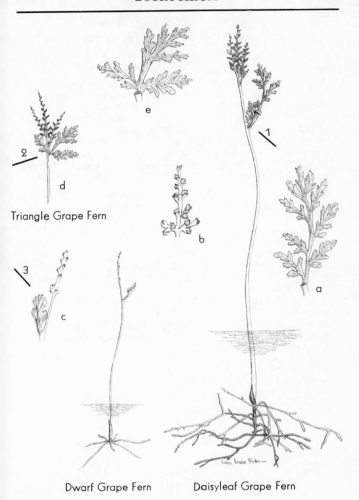

Triangle Grape Fern

Dwarf Grape Fern   Daisyleaf Grape Fern

Marginalia: Daisyleaf Grape Fern: a. Leaf. b. Sporophyll. Dwarf Grape Fern: c. Leaf and sporophyll. Triangle Grape Fern: d. Leaf and sporophyll. e. Leaf enlarged.

Diagnostic Arrows: 1. Leaf close to clustered sporophyll, Daisyleaf Grape Fern. 2. Leaf very close to branched sporophyll, Triangle Grape Fern. 3. Simple leaf and simple unbranched sporophyll, Dwarf Grape Fern.

CUT-LEAVED GRAPE FERN
Species: *Botrychium dissectum* Spreng.

Style: Extremely variable species, of medium size; triangular leaves grow from fertile stalk at or below surface of ground. Appears like two plants. Sterile leaf for typical species is very lacy-cut, the varieties cut into varying degrees of oblong pointed leaflets, subleaflets, and lobes. Sterile leaves late appearing and last through winter and spring, though they turn bronze color with frost. Therefore, partially evergreen.

Ecology: Common throughout area in one form or another. In dry or moist open woodlands, fields, pastures, and sandy areas of pinelands and scrub oaks. Generally impartial to types of soil, if not too hot and arid.

Leaf: 3″± long; triangular, 3 sections; semi-leathery, coarse, fleshy, reflexed, often parallel to soil; thrice-cut and more, very variable; also variable in color, from pale yellow-green to dark blue-green.

Leaflet: Variable, though usually narrow, oblong, and pointed. Margins toothed, serrated, or lacy-cut.

Stalk: Smooth, membranous, light green, fragile. Stalk of leaf 1″± high; stalk of sporophyll 2″±; both fork upward from near ground level.

Sporophyll: On tall erect stalk in branched clusters of light yellow spore cases. Soon ripening and withering.

Rootstock: Erect; roots short, fleshy, numerous, branching; 3″± below surface. Often one root descending deeper and simulating a tap root.

Marginalia: a. Leaflet of *B. dissectum* typical. b. Sporophyll. c. Leaflet, var. *tenuifolium*. d. Leaflet, var. *obliquum*. e. Leaflet, forma *elongatum*. f. Growth form typical.

Diagnostic Arrows: 1. Sterile leaf and stalk branching from main stalk close to surface of soil. 2. Erect and slightly branched sporophyll.

hauna Louise Foster.

MOONWORT (MOONWORT GRAPE FERN)
Species: *Botrychium Lunaria* (L.) Sw.

Style: An exceedingly rare little Succulent Fern. More common in folklore and fable than "in person." Its single leaf divided into 6 or more pairs of half-moon, or fan-shaped, leaflets, which are reputed to tilt to avoid as much direct sun as possible.

Ecology: In dry pastures, meadows, and on hillsides and rocky ledges. Found supposedly only along Canadian border and northward.

Leaf: $2''\pm$ long; $\frac{3}{4}''\pm$ wide; narrow, oblong, rounded at end; erect from about middle of stalk; little or no stem; smooth, fleshy; variable. Not evergreen. Leaf tip slightly bending downward. Divided into nearly opposite pairs of leaflets.

Leaflet: 4 or more pairs of half-moon, or fan-shaped, slightly stemmed leaflets; closely spaced or overlapping at apex. Margins wavy. Often concave.

Stalk: Main stalk $2''\pm$; short, fleshy. Leaf stalk $\frac{1}{4}''\pm$ or almost absent. Sporophyll stalk $4''\pm$; over-all height usually less than $6''$.

Sporophyll: Long, slightly branching clusters start below height of top of leaf. Spores fairly large. Uppermost clusters pendent.

Rootstock: Erect; roots few, short, horizontally-spreading.

Marginalia: a. Sporophyll. b. Fan-shaped leaflet. c. Growth form.
Diagnostic Arrows: 1. Pendent sporophyll. 2. Semi-concave moon-shaped pairs of leaflets.

LEATHERY GRAPE FERN
Species: *Botrychium multifidum* (Gmel.) Rupr.

Style: Largest of the Little Grape Ferns. Very leathery and succulent. Stout and coarse. Rare but well scattered throughout our area with variable forms, depending on their ecology, and intergrading "embarrassingly." In early summer often new and old leaf side by side, both green, old leaf limp and soon withering. Named varieties usually twice the size of the typical.

Ecology: More northern species, especially the typical, which prefers drier, more acid and sandy locations; the varieties — *intermedium* and *oneidense* — prefer moist woodlands, damp fields, and semi-open wet areas.

Leaf: 3″± long and wide; broadly triangular; cut into 3 to 5 sections, with long prominent stems. Reflexed. Heavily fleshy or leathery. Bright green. Leaf and stalk about same length as sporophyll and stalk. Evergreen to extent that old leaf stays green well after new year's leaf is full-grown.

Leaflets: Lowest pairs largest. Subleaflets blunt-tipped or rounded, margins sinuous and/or fine-toothed. Densely clustered and overlapping in typical. Varieties' subleaflets more pointed and more widely spread apart.

Stalk: Medium long; stout, fleshy, semi-erect. The two stalks branch from near ground.

Sporophyll: Wide-spreading and branching; short, prominent, with many spore cases. Develop later than leaves, usually in autumn.

Rootstock: Erect; roots coarse, thick, few, wide-spreading horizontally; 3″± below ground. Look like angleworms.

Marginalia: a. Subleaflet. b. Leaflet. c. Leaflet, var. *oneidense.*
Diagnostic Arrows: 1. Angleworm-like roots. 2. Last year's leaf. 3. Large clustered sporophyll. 4. Triangular leaf and overlapping leaflets. 5. Long prominent stems.

Laura Louise Foster.

RATTLESNAKE FERN
Species: *Botrychium virginianum* (L.) Sw.

Style: Largest, most common, and earliest to appear of Grape
Ferns in our area. Bright green, lacy-cut, horizontal, triangular
leaves rise prominently as individuals above woodland floor or
low undergrowth of thickets. Easily distinguished from other
Grape Ferns by its thin-textured, non-leathery, and lacy-cut
leaf.

Ecology: Throughout our area in rich, moist or dry woodlands,
and wet thickets. Sub-acid soil. In shaded areas — soon
disappears from sunny spots.

Leaf: 10″± long; 12″± wide; triangular; divided into segments
of leaflets on small stems. Membranous; variably though
distinctly lacy-cut. Reflexed to almost horizontal growth.
Bright green.

Leaflet: Oblong to narrow oblong, cut and toothed; semi-blunt
or semi-pointed tips. Variable from plant to plant. Veins
few and simple.

Stalk: Stalk for leaf 12″± long; erect, smooth, fleshy, round;
pink at base. Sporophyll stalk of equal length, more slender;
grows from juncture of leaf and main stalk; soon withering
and disappearing.

Sporophyll: 6 or more simple and tapering, widely spreading
branches. Spore cases distinctly bright yellow. Appears early
summer.

Rootstock: Erect, obscure. Roots fleshy, medium long, stout,
numerous, tangled, horizontally branching and spreading,
2″ or more below surface, with numerous vertical budlike
appendages.

Marginalia: a. Section of sporophyll. b. Subleaflet, var. *intermedium*.
c. Leaflet lobe, showing veins and cuttings. d. Cut form of leaflet.
Diagnostic Arrows: 1. Sporophyll stalk grows from juncture of main
stalk and leaf. 2. Horizontal, coarse, shallow root with vertical budlike growths.

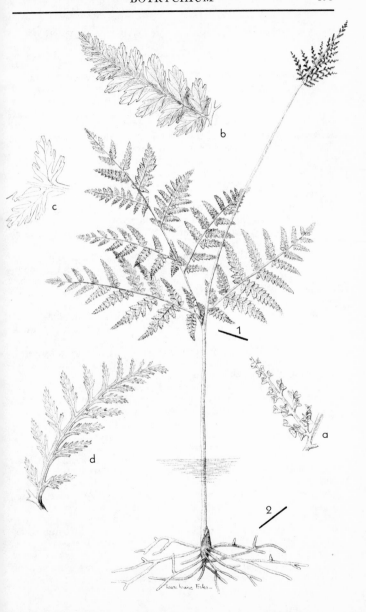

The Horsetails, or Scouring Rushes

THE Horsetails are plants of a single living genus, *Equisetum*, and of the single family **Equisetaceae**, and of the single order **Equisetales**. The Equisetales are considered the most primitive of the Pteridophyta, or fern families, being closely allied to the prehistoric order of the Calamitales, large and abundant treelike plants of the Carboniferous period nearly three hundred million years ago. The Equisetales are the sole living remains of a long line of ancestors. Their history is better known than that of any living order of plants. It is interesting to note that the Calamites were so numerous in early days that their spores left for us the great beds of cannel coal and jet.

The genus *Equisetum* contains about 25 species throughout the world. There are 10 species listed for our area.

The Horsetails are most numerous in the temperate zones, decreasing in numbers toward the poles and toward the equator. They are rare in the Southern Hemisphere, and are supposedly absent in Australia and New Zealand. They are found in loose sandy and gravelly wet soils; in marshes and wet meadows; in the standing waters of rivers, ponds, and lakes; in damp woods; and often along the banks of fast-moving rivers and streams.

Above ground the Horsetails are usually annual, but below ground they are perennial and long-lived. The annual or perennial shoots above ground are seldom more than three feet high, although there is one species in the tropics that reaches thirty feet or more in height. Their growth is distinctly symmetrical in form. The upright stems when branching do so in regular whorls. Their growth form is rarely unbalanced. Both the stems and the branches perform photosynthesis, whereas in most other plants, only the foliage has this function. (In certain Horsetails, i.e., *E. arvense*, the short-lived fertile stems contain no chlorophyll.) The upright stems are cylindrical, bamboo-like, and, for most species, hollow tubes that are interrupted at the nodes. This is also true of the smaller, more slender, and less cylindrical branches. The outsides of both stems and branches are fluted with grooves and ridges with more or less rough surfaces that contain gritty silex particles in forms of rows, rings, bands, teeth, or even rosettes, depending on the species. Below the nodal points a rind, or skin, spreads upward and over the node in the form of a clasping scale, or leaf, called the *leaf-sheath*. This leaf-sheath is cut into numerous sharp-pointed teeth, varying in numbers and shapes for the different species. Where there are branches, they develop from the bases of the leaf-sheaths at the nodes, and the branches in turn have their own *nodes* (bases of sheaths) and *internodes* (distance between nodes) and leaf-sheaths. Branches rarely branch again unless injured, with the exception of the Wood Horsetail, a species in which rebranching is common. The growth form of both stems and branches is always one of the lengthening of the internodes. This is also true for the *rhizomes*, or underground stems.

The insides of the stems and branches are characterized for most species by a large central canal, or *centrum*, which is surrounded by numbers of smaller canals called *vallecular cavities* embedded in the outer tissue under each groove. Alternating with them and between the grooves and under the ridges are tiny longitudinal air tubes, the *carinal canals*. The sizes and shapes of these three kinds of cavities in cross section furnish the key characters used in determining the species.

The underground growth and form of the Horsetails, consisting of the rhizomes and roots, are very similar to the aboveground growth of the stems and branches. The rhizomes, which are from a few inches to many feet underground, are widely spreading for many species. The rhizomes have their nodes and internodes and are fluted with grooves and ridges. They have the equivalents of leaf-sheaths, which are covered thickly with hairs; this is never the case with the aerial leaf-sheaths. The rhizomes have the three types of inner air cavities, and the roots and branchings of the rhizomes sprout in whorls from the bases of the nodal points. The rhizomes of some species develop underground tubers that evidently can supply additional nourishment if necessary.

The Horsetails are *homosporous*, because they have only one kind of spore, but they have two kinds of gametophytes, or prothalli — male and female.

At the top of each fertile stem there is developed a solitary cone, or *strobilus*, with or without a sharp point, and with or without a stem, depending on the species. The strobilus looks like an armored catkin. Its outer surface consists of tightly fitted polygonal scales, usually hexagonal. A stalk connects the center of each scale to the cone's axis and around this stalk and also at right angles to the cone's axis are cylindrical *sporangiophores*, or spore-case-holding appendages with slit sides. When the strobilus is mature, it lengthens slightly and splits the armor into neat individual polygonal pieces, exposing the spores to be spread abroad. (See illustration, page 205, *E. arvense*, for split strobilus.)

The spores of the Horsetails are numerous, round or oval, and minute. They contain chlorophyll and moisture. When ripe, they live only a few days and germinate in a few hours. They are enclosed in four distinct coats.

The outer coat splits into four ribbons, which stay attached to the spore at one spot only. These ribbon-like strips with spatulate tips are called *elaters*. They are extremely *hygroscopic*, or susceptible to moisture. They curl and uncurl around the spore as they become exposed to the atmosphere and their curling and twisting action not only aids in the spores' dissemination, but also in keeping enough of the spores clasped together to insure proximity for the later-developed tiny male and female prothalli to be able to mate in the same tiny bit of moisture.

On germination, the spores throw off their other coats and change from round hard bodies to the soft prothalli, male or female.

The male prothalli are usually numerous, very small, yellowish green, and only slightly lobed or spreading. The less numerous female prothalli are much larger (almost $\frac{1}{2}''$ in size), widely spreading, with many distinct lobes, and dark green in color.

The *antheridia*, or male organs, usually develop first, and each one produces several hundred sperms, which are larger and more numerous than in any of the fern genera. The *antherozoids*, or sperms, have many cilia at their top ends. Their lower ends are flattened and widened into the shape of a paddle, with which they give added impetus to the propulsion of the cilia.

The *archegonia*, or female organs, are formed along the undersides of the edges of the prothalli, usually near the bases of the lobes where the indentations retain moisture. As they develop, they push up and around the edge of the prothallus. The single eggs are embedded quite near the edges, and leading up and out from each egg is a canal that protrudes as a neck to open and receive the sperm from the neighboring prothallus.

Even though it is typical for the Horsetails to have separate male and female prothalli, sometimes prothalli are found to contain both male and female sex organs on the same prothallus.

Far and away the most common Horsetail is the Field Horsetail.

E. arvense. Not only is it extremely common, but it occurs in many forms that often delude us into believing we have found a different species when we first come upon one of the forms unfamiliar to us. Of all the ferns and fern allies found in our area, the Field Horsetail is credited with the largest number of different-named forms, or formae. Maurice Broun in his *Index to North American Ferns* (see Bibliography) lists 13 formae and the one northern variety, *E. arvense* var. *boreale*, with three formae for this variety, giving us a total of 17 named forms for the one species *E. arvense.* Furthermore, these many formae may blend with one another, giving us many more forms probably as yet unnamed. Certainly no other species of our plants has more different-named or unnamed variations from the typical.

DWARF HORSETAIL (DWARF SCOURING RUSH)
Species: *Equisetum scirpoides* Michx.

Style: Smallest living species of Horsetails. Grows in curling, entwining, matted form, like horsehair. Usually well hidden in the tangled grasses or deep mosses with which it grows. Black sharp-pointed cones of the more erect fertile stems often give away its hiding place.

Ecology: Rare, local. In rich moist woods; on wet and springy banks; in gravel borders of ponds, on moist ledges above brooks; on rotting logs and often embedded in moss. A forest species of our cooler areas. Common above Canadian border.

Stems: $6''\pm$ long; $\frac{1}{16}''\pm$ thick; fertile and sterile alike; ascending, prostrate and entwined with one another; 3 broad ridges, deeply concave, give a ridge appearance. Stomata in two rows in each furrow. Sometimes with small irregular branches; evergreen; dark green; fertile stems usually more erect. Sheaths $\frac{1}{6}''$ long with 3 teeth (seldom 4); triangular, sharp-pointed; dark center, light edges. Internodes $\frac{1}{2}''\pm$ apart.

Cavities: No central cavity; 3 large vallecular cavities about middle of stem.

Strobilus: Small, black, stemless cone with a sharp-pointed tip.

Rootstock: Creeping, widely branching; tiny, no more than $\frac{1}{16}''$ thick.

Marginalia: a. Strobilus and sheath. b. Cross section of stem.
Diagnostic Arrows: 1. Curling growth (usually less upright). 2. Three vallecular cavities, but 6 ridges.

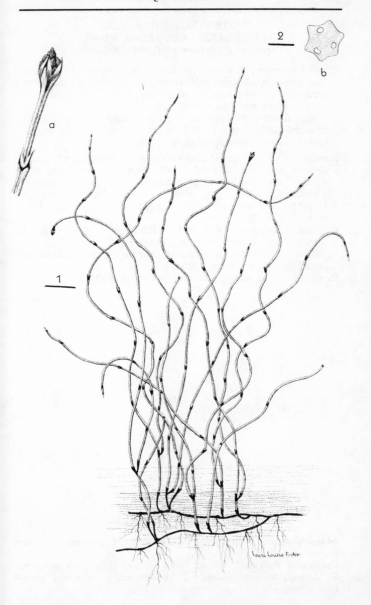

Laura Louise Foster

VARIEGATED HORSETAIL
(VARIEGATED SCOURING RUSH)
Species: *Equisetum variegatum* Schleich.

Style: Evergreen, dark green, slender, seldom branching Horsetail
that grows in twisting, half-recumbent, upcurving tufts from a
semi-exposed rootstock. Called "variegated" because of its
distinct black and white sheaths.

Ecology: A more northern species, frequenting lime outcroppings
in moist sandy slopes, gravelly beaches, meadows, bog margins,
and cool and shaded spots in open woods.

Stems: $15''\pm$ tall; fertile and sterile same length; unbranched;
slender, weak; $\frac{3}{16}''\pm$ thick; dark green with persistent black
sheaths funneling upward; teeth prominent, sharp-pointed,
with distinct white edges. 5 or more ridges, slightly rough, with
broad furrows between, containing two rows of stomata. Internodes $1''\pm$ long.

Cavities: Central cavity $\frac{1}{3}$ or less diameter of stem; vallecular
cavities large, distinct. Carinal canals small.

Strobilus: Short-stemmed, ovoid, abrupt; sharp-pointed tip;
cone larger than diameter of stem.

Rootstock: Near surface; slender; black and creeping.

Marginalia: a. Strobilus and white-margined sheaths. b. Cross
section of stem.
Diagnostic Arrows: 1. Round flattish-topped cone with sharp tip.
2. Variegated-color sheath. 3. Semi-branching or tufted growth
from rootstock.

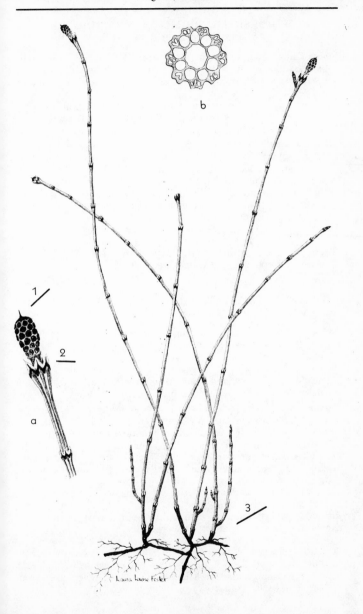

ROUGH HORSETAIL (COMMON SCOURING RUSH)
Species: *Equisetum hiemale* L.

Style: Tall, slender, evergreen, dark green, hollow, rough-surfaced, bamboo-like plant, with ash-gray bands outlined above and below by dark edges. Evergreen thicket-like growth particularly noticeable in winter woods.

Ecology: Common throughout the area, except in pine barrens. Low and wet places in woods, along watercourses, on damp shaded slopes, either sandy, rocky, or grassy.

Stems: Up to 5′± tall; ½″± thick at base. Slender, erect, evergreen, solitary or in clusters, seldom branched. Fertile and sterile stems alike. Rough-surfaced, 30± broad ridges with prominent bands of silex. Sheaths cylindrical, ¼″± wide; tight to stem, green at first, then gray with dark base and top. Teeth sharp-pointed, brown-edged, soon withering. Internodes 4″± long. Stomata in two regular rows in grooves.

Cavities: Central cavity ⅔± diameter of stem. Vallecular channels small.

Strobilus: Short-stemmed, with sharp-pointed tip.

Rootstock: Branching and widely creeping.

SMOOTH HORSETAIL (SMOOTH SCOURING RUSH)
Species: *Equisetum laevigatum* A. Br.

Style: Similar in growth and form to Rough Horsetail but very smooth, very hollow, and paler green and more slender and fragile.

Ecology: In wet clayey and sandy soil. Along waterways, in meadows, pastures, and prairies. Rare and local in East from Massachusetts south. More common in Middle West and West.

Stems: 1′ to 3′ tall; ¼″± thick at base; slender, erect, very hollow, usually not evergreen. Mostly in clusters; seldom branched. Smooth surface, 18± rounded, double-furrowed edges; few and poorly developed bands of silex. Sheaths ⅜″± wide; funnel upward, dark or dark-banded. Teeth with white margins, sharp-pointed, soon withering. Internodes 1¾″± long. Stomata in single rows in furrows.

Cavities: Central cavity very large, ¾± diameter of stem. Vallecular channels small.

Strobilus: Short-stemmed, with and without a sharp tip.

Rootstock: Branching and widely creeping.

Kansas Horsetail, *E. kansanum* Schaffner, similar to a slightly rougher Smooth Horsetail. Its cone has *no pointed tip*, sheaths are less clasping and teeth larger. Rarely, if ever, evergreen. Rare and local in our area from Ohio west.

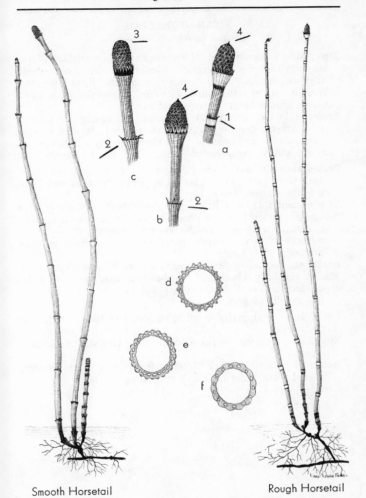

Smooth Horsetail   Rough Horsetail

Marginalia: Strobilus, stem, and sheath: a. Rough Horsetail.   b.
Smooth Horsetail.   c. Kansas Horsetail.   Cross section of stem: d.
Rough Horsetail.   e. Kansas Horsetail.   f. Smooth Horsetail.
Diagnostic Arrows: 1. Clasping sheath, Rough Horsetail.   2. Spread-
ing sheath, Kansas and Smooth Horsetails.   3. Blunt-topped strobilus,
Kansas Horsetail.   4. Sharp-pointed strobilus, Rough and Smooth
Horsetails.

FIELD HORSETAIL
Species: *Equisetum arvense* L.

Style: Most common of our Horsetails and most variable in form. Majority of bushy Horsetails — whether upright or decumbent, small or medium large — prove to be the Field Horsetail. Weedlike in growth, found with and considered as a weed; adapts growth habits to ecology of weeds.

Ecology: Found throughout the area, frequently on railroad embankments growing happily in the cinder beds; also in fields, woods, glades, and waste places. Thrives in any soil, but prefers damp, sandy, semi-shaded areas. Difficult to exterminate.

Fertile stems: 6″± tall; erect; flesh color; stout; succulent; short-lived; often with stubby whorled branches. Sheaths with large, dark and clasping lance-shape teeth.

Sterile stems: 18″± tall; erect or decumbent; solitary or close together; annual; rough surface, silex in dots; 12 or more furrows; stomata in furrows. Sheaths widening upward; brown at top and bottom; free or partly united; deciduous; chaffy margins. Internodes 2″± long.

Branches: Ascending or divergent, seldom rebranching; bushy, solid, regularly whorled; 3- to 4-angled; lower part of sheath pale brown; 3 or 4 sharp-pointed dark-tipped teeth, first internode usually longest.

Cavities: Central cavity small, ¼ diameter of stem. Vallecular cavity large.

Strobilus: 1″± long; on tip of fertile stem; long-stemmed, blunt-tipped.

Rootstock: Slender, dark brown, free-forking and creeping; covered with a brown felt. Often bearing tubers.

Marginalia: a. Fertile stem. b & c. Immature sterile stems. d. Mature sterile stem. e. Bursting mature strobilus. f. Sheath of main stem. g. Sheath of branch. h. Cross section of main stem. i. Sheath and branches.

Diagnostic Arrows: 1. Sheath dark at top and bottom. 2. Branches ascending to make a flat top except for central stem. However, Field Horsetail extremely variable in growth form.

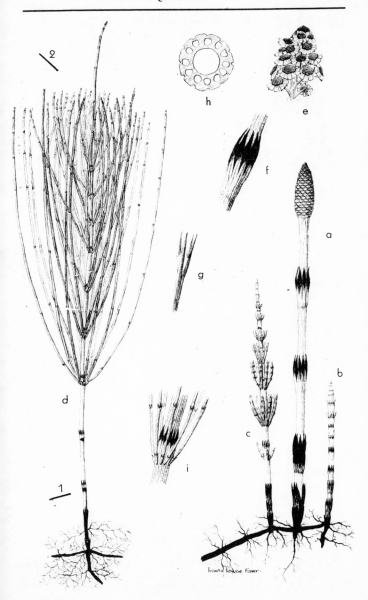

MEADOW HORSETAIL (SHADE HORSETAIL)
Species: *Equisetum pratense* Ehrh.

Style: Fairly rare, coolness- and shade-loving, feathery or spidery-looking Horsetail, with delicate, thin branches that spread horizontally outward in perfect whorls.

Ecology: In humus-rich neutral soil along shaded banks of streams; in cool rocky woods; on slopes of ravines; and sometimes in damp and shaded sandy spots. In our more northern, cooler areas.

Fertile stems: 15″± high; erect; first appear without branches, branching after cones disappear — like flat-topped sterile stems.

Sterile stems: 18″± high; erect; annual; slightly rough. 12 or more ridges, broader than furrows; no spikes on ridges. Stomata in two distinct bands in furrows. Internodes 1″± apart; first internode slightly shorter; sheath ⅓″± wide; cup-shaped; clasping, persistent, saw-like, sharp-pointed teeth, with dark centers and distinct white margins.

Branches: 5″± long; whorled; straight and horizontally spreading; thin, delicate, 3-angled; lowest branches a little shorter, bending below horizontal next to stem, then bending up again. No rebranching. Teeth of branches triangular and clasping.

Cavities: Central cavity ⅓ diameter of stem. Vallecular cavities small.

Strobilus: 1″± long; very long stems, blunt-tipped. Early fruit, rarely fruiting.

Rootstock: Black, slender; horizontally creeping deep in soil. Black, wiry kinky roots.

Marginalia: a. Sterile mature stem. b. Fertile stem with cone. c. Sheath of branch. d. Sheath of sterile stem. e. Sheath of fertile stem. f. Sheath and first sections of branches. g. Cross section of stem.

Diagnostic Arrows: 1. Spidery and delicate growth form; like shady growth form of Field Horsetail, only more delicate. 2. White-margined, dark, clasping teeth of sheath. 3. Long-stemmed strobilus.

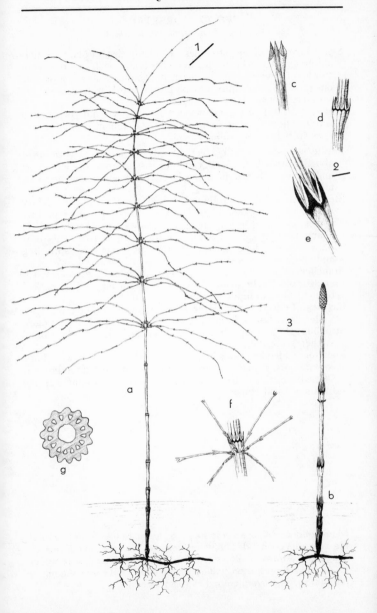

WOOD HORSETAIL
Species: *Equisetum sylvaticum* L.

Style: Loveliest of our fern allies and a truly elegant plant. Emerald-green, with delicate lacy branches that grow from upper two-thirds of stem in well-spaced horizontal whorls, spreading outward and gracefully drooping downward; usually grows as solitary, though closely spaced, little tree.

Ecology: In wet meadows, wooded swamps, around springs and water, where there is some sunlight. Common in our eastern area, in rich, moist, sub-acid soil.

Fertile stems: 8″ ± tall; erect; at first, flesh-colored with small abortive branches. After cone has disappeared, become green and branched like sterile stems, but flat-topped, smaller, and with larger sheaths.

Sterile stems: 18″ ± tall; erect; annual; mostly solitary; slightly rough; quite hollow; 12 ± flat ridges with two rows of tiny spikes; stomata in two rows in furrows. Internodes 1¾″ ± apart; first internode longest; sheath green at base, chestnut-brown above; long, narrow, triangular, irregularly spreading and clasping; persistent.

Branches: 6″ ± wide; numerous; grow in whorls; drooping; 4 ± angled, often rebranching into tiny 3 ± angled, deeply-toothed branchlets. No branches from lower nodes.

Cavities: Central cavity large, more than ½ diameter of stem. Vallecular cavities large, prominent; same number as ridges.

Strobilus: 1″ ± long; blunt, long-stemmed; fruits May–June. Withers, drops off.

Rootstock: Slender, branching, creeping deep in soil; with horizontal roots, which also grow with part of stem underground. Often bears tubers that are large and ovate, not spherical like tubers of Field Horsetail.

Marginalia: a. Mature sterile stem. b. Immature sterile stem. c. Fertile stem with cone. d. Sheath on stem. e. Cross section of stem.
Diagnostic Arrows: 1. Roots growing from stem as well as rootstock. 2. Abortive branches on fruiting fertile stem. 3. Longer sheaths on fertile stem. 4. Diverging and clasping sheaths.

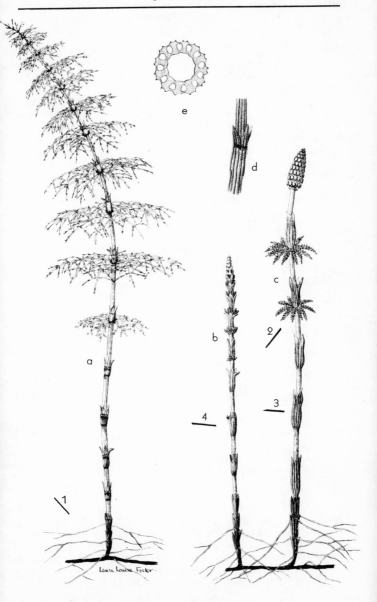

Laura Louise Foster

MARSH HORSETAIL
Species: *Equisetum palustre* L.

Style: Rare and local feathery Horsetail with branches ascending from low down the stem to a flat-topped inverted triangle, from which arises a single erect sterile tip or a shorter tip topped by the fertile cone.

Ecology: Found in our more northern areas, along cold streams, ponds, or shallow waters; in flooded meadows; in wooded swamps. Variable in habit; not often actually in water.

Fertile stems: 18″± high; erect, branched; above rises a short tip of 2 or 3 nodes topped by strobilus.

Sterile stems: 18″± high; erect, with long, thin, tapering tip above flat-topped branches; 8 or more narrow ridges sharply elevated and rounded; stomata in single wide band in furrow. Sheaths loose, enlarging upward, 5± toothed; longer than broad; dark with whitish, rough margins; lance-shaped; pointed, persistent. Internodes about 1″± apart.

Branches: Short, ascending, often so numerous as to hide internodes; flat-topped growth, fairly slender; 5± angled. Unbranched, smooth.

Cavities: Central cavity small, $\frac{1}{6}$ diameter of stem; under grooves. Vallecular cavities large, about same size as central cavities.

Strobilus: 1″± long; blunt-tipped; large, on slender medium-short stem.

Rootstock: Slender, solid, dark; deeply creeping and branching with dark and clasping sheaths.

Marginalia: a. Strobilus with stem less than average short, also white marginal teeth of sheath. b. Joint of side branch. c. Sheath and base of branches on main stem. d. Cross section of stem.

Diagnostic Arrows: 1. Ascending flat-topped branches, one with sterile tip and one with strobilus tip. 2. Central cavity small and vallecular cavity large, both about same size.

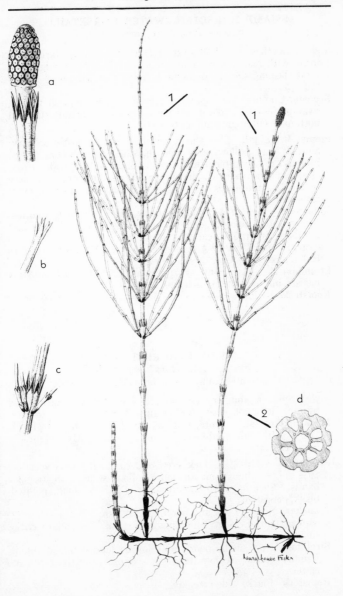

SWAMP HORSETAIL (WATER HORSETAIL)
Species: *Equisetum fluviatile* L.

Style: Smoothest and hollowest of Horsetails. Very variable in form, with many, few, or no branches. Many flat ridges and tight-clasping sheaths distinguish it from similar Shore Horsetail.

Ecology: Common throughout northern area in sluggish waters, swamps, ponds, and ditches where there are muddy-surfaced bottoms. Often growing deep in still waters.

Stems: 36″± tall; ¼″± thick; all alike, erect, mostly solitary; annual; very hollow, very smooth. 20± flat obscure ridges. Stomata in broad band in furrows. Sheaths ⅓″± wide, green, clasping; teeth narrow, sharp-pointed, dark brown, very close to stem. Internodes 2″± apart. Branching after strobilus is formed.

Branches: ½″± long; ascending, usually halfway up stem; whorled, 6± ridged; smooth, hollow, slender, variable in length and number. Internode nearest stem short.

Cavities: Central cavity ⅘ diameter of stem. Vallecular cavities lacking except at base or when dry.

Strobilus: 1″± long; blunt, short-stemmed. (Forma *polystachyum* has strobili on some branch tips.)

Rootstock: Reddish, hollow, same size as stems, wide-creeping.

SHORE HORSETAIL
Species: *Equisetum litorale* Kühl.
(often considered hybrid *E. fluviatile* × *E. arvense*)

Style: Smaller, thinner, less smooth, less hollow, more ridged Swamp Horsetail, with whiplike tips. Very variable in form.

Ecology: Wet sandy shore, rare and local in North and Middle West. Although usually sterile, spreads abundantly and rapidly by rootstocks.

Stems: 24″± tall; ¼″± thick; erect or decumbent. Very variable; 10± ridges, almost smooth, quite hollow; stomata in irregular bands. Sheaths widening upward. Teeth ⅓″ long, pointed, black, persistent.

Branches: None, or few and irregular; 4± ridges; 4± teeth.

Cavities: Central cavity ¾± diameter of stem. Vallecular cavities small.

Strobilus: Very small, poorly developed, long-stemmed, blunt. Usually sterile, seldom bursting. Spores abortive with no elaters.

Rootstock: Black, wide-creeping.

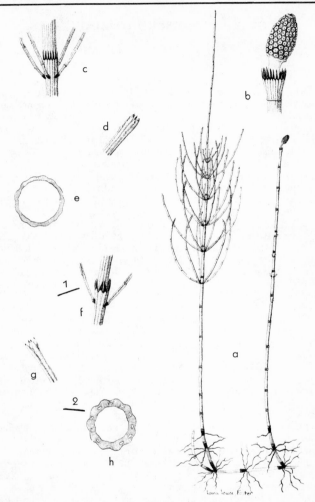

Marginalia: Swamp Horsetail: a. Sterile and fertile stems. b. Strobilus. c. Sheath of main stem. d. Sheath of branch. e. Cross section of stem. Shore Horsetail: f. Sheath of main stem. g. Sheath of branch. h. Cross section of stem.

Diagnostic Arrows: 1. Divergent teeth of Shore Horsetail; fewer and larger than in Swamp Horsetail. 2. Smaller central cavity of Shore Horsetail; fewer and deeper ridges.

The Clubmosses, Ground Pines, or Running Pines

THE Clubmosses are the best known of the fern allies. They belong to the order **Lycopodiales,** and together with the **Selaginellales,** or Spikemosses (see page 234), they constitute the only two living orders in the class **Lycopodiinae.** (Often the Spikemosses are grouped under the order Lycopodiales and not given their own order, Selaginellales; but since the Spikemosses are all *heterosporous*, or have two kinds of spores — male and female — and the Clubmosses are all *homosporous*, or have only one type of spore — neither male nor female — it seems better to assign these two fern allies to separate orders, Selaginellales and Lycopodiales respectively.)

The fossil history of the Clubmosses supposedly dates them back to the Paleozoic Era, more than three hundred million years ago. They are the only common living offspring of the ancient Clubmoss trees, which, together with the giant Horsetail trees and the extinct Lepidodendrons and Sigillarias, made ferneries into vast forest jungles, so vast in fact that the beds they laid down — primarily by their tiny spores — resulted in the geological seams from which we have mined for centuries our coal, our cannel coal, and our jet.

The order Lycopodiales has one family, **Lycopodiaceae,** with two genera. The genus *Phylloglossum* has only one species, which is supposedly restricted to Australia, New Zealand, and Tasmania. The other genus, *Lycopodium*, has more than 100 species found throughout the world. Those in the tropics are commonly epiphytic, and those in the temperate and northern zones are usually terrestrial. For our area there are listed 11 species, all terrestrial.

The Clubmosses are small, usually fully evergreen, perennial plants of upright or trailing or creeping growth. Their many crowded, small leaves are all simple — never divided — stemless, and usually of uniform size. For most of the species they are arranged in rows, or *ranks*, from 4 to 16 around the erect or creeping stem in spirals, whorls, or opposite in overlapping or divergent growth forms. They are invariably narrow and pointed. (The leaves of some species are not only acutely pointed, but have one prominently projecting bristly hair tip to each leaf.) The Clubmosses are unique in the plant world by having *xylem* (wood tissue) and *phloem* (conducting canals) in alternate bands within the cylinders of *both* their stems and roots, whereas such structure for all other plants varies for roots and stems.

The most prolific method for the propagating of Clubmosses is by running (they are often known as Running Pines) and sometimes even by leaping. (See Foxtail Clubmoss, page 224.) Each year the rootstock gets longer. The plant grows along, either above or below the ground. Its growth of former years withers and dies, but as it grows and spreads faster than it dies, colonies increase rapidly for most of the species.

Some species have an additional method of propagation. This is by bulblets, or plantlets, which appear at the bases of the upper leaves, and when fully developed they fall to the ground and start a new plant. (See *L. Selago*, and *L. lucidulum*, page 218.)

All the Clubmosses, however, reproduce by spores. In the supposedly more ancient species, the spore cases are borne near the bases of the upper leaves. For the majority of species found in our area, they are borne above the top leaves in cones, or strobili, with or without stems, depending on the species. The spores are numerous, tiny, almost microscopic in size, semi-kidney-shaped, and yellow in color. They ripen in late summer or early fall and are produced in enormous quantities. Of all the fern allies and of all the ferns, and probably of all the seeds of plants, the spores of the Clubmosses were involved in the greatest number of fields of early commerce. They are so minute and uniform in size that they were at one time used for microscopic measurements; as they are water-repellent and dustlike, they were used for soothing powders for chafes and wounds. Enormous quantities of them were used for coating pills. And as they give off a flash explosion when ignited, they were used for fireworks, and particularly and extensively for photographic flashes. In addition to these spore uses, the stems and leaves of certain species were used for mordants in dying woolens, and the leaves and stems of other species were used for emetics and even poisons.

The spore cases when ripe open with a transverse slit and the powdery spores are widely dispersed by the smallest current of air. The gametophytes formed by the spores are equally minute. For some species the spores seem to burrow deeply below the surface of the ground, for others only moderately so, and some develop on the surface. The microscopic size and the elusive habits of the gametophytes of the Clubmosses make them almost impossible to find and, consequently, to study. Those that are subterranean are *saprophytic*, or develop by getting sustenance from fungi. They contain no chlorophyll. (Those that are semi-surface are supposed to contain chlorophyll.) It is believed the spore takes seven or more years to develop the gametophyte and that another ten or more years are required before the gametophyte develops the new young plant above the ground, making a life cycle of almost twenty years from spore to gametophyte and to the plant again.

The gametophytes of those species that have been studied are like minute rounded tubers with tiny rhizome-like roots at their bottoms and semi-overlapping celled lobes on their tops. The lobes on the inner circle encase the antheridia, or male organs, while

the lobes on the outer circle encase the archegonia, or female organs. The eggs of the female organs are embedded in a narrow short-necked funnel, and the microscopic, numerous biciliate sperms are developed in cavities under the edges of the lobes adjacent to the lobes that house the female organ and the egg. This close juxtaposition of the male and female must be essential for the tiny gametophyte of the Clubmoss, because in the majority of cases they are subterranean, a condition that would predispose little or no moisture in which the sperm can move.

Many of the species of the Lycopodiums are frequently referred to as Ground Pines. They all look as though they were close relatives to the pines, hemlocks, and cedars. The small leaves of all the species have a distinct resemblance to pine and hemlock needles or cedar sprigs. The fact that they are often referred to as pines and cedars is due not only to their shiny pine-green and evergreen leaves but also to the fact that most of them are often found in the woodlands and forests where their lofty associates, the coniferous trees, abound. Running Pine is also a name frequently given to them, since the most common species of Clubmosses are those which are running or widely creeping and spreading over the forest floor. Because "Ground" and "Running" Pines or Cedars are names used extensively for the Clubmosses, we find considerable confusion in the common names for the different species both here and abroad. The name Ground Pine is used to denote the species *Lycopodium obscurum*, *L. tristachyum*, *L. complanatum*, and sometimes for other species as well. The name Running Pine is applied to *L. clavatum*, *L. complanatum*, *L. lucidulum*; Running Moss is used for *L. clavatum*; and Running Cedar for *L. complanatum*.

The same common or colloquial name is often applied to two or more different species. Therefore it seems better to use those common names that are translations of their Latin names, such as the following:

Alpine or Mountain Clubmoss for *L. alpinum*

Carolina Clubmoss for *L. carolinianum*, also known as Slender Clubmoss, because of its very slender upright stem

Foxtail Clubmoss for *L. alopecuroides* (like a fox's tail)

Savin-leaved Clubmoss (named after sabin or savin, names for junipers or cedars) for *L. sabinifolium*; also known as Cedar-like Clubmoss

Fir Clubmoss, Little, Mountain, Cliff, or Rock Clubmoss, which looks like the little rock-loving Selaginellas, for *L. Selago* (*Selago* was the original generic name for all Lycopodiums)

Bog or Marsh Clubmoss for *L. inundatum*

Ground Cedar or Three-branched Ground Pine for *L. tristachyum* (three-branched)

Tree Clubmoss for *L. obscurum* var. *dendroideum* (like a tree); also called Ground Pine or Round-branched Ground Pine

Shining Clubmoss for *L. lucidulum* (shining); also called Trailing Evergreen Clubmoss

Stiff, Bristly, or Interrupted Clubmoss for *L. annotinum* (*annotinus* meaning "belonging to the year," or "with annual constrictions")

Running Pine, Running Cedar, or Ground Cedar for *L. complanatum* (flattened); also known as Christmas Green and Trailing Evergreen

Staghorn Clubmoss, with many names, such as Wolf's Claw, Foxtail Clubmoss, Robin Hood's Hatband, Forks and Knives — all of which refer to the clublike upright and often forked growth form — for *L. clavatum* (*clava* means "club"); additional names are Common Clubmoss, Running Clubmoss, Running Pine, and Running Moss.

The Clubmosses are very difficult to transplant. Transplanting is not recommended, therefore, for any of the species except the Bog Clubmoss, which seems to do fairly well if kept in a boggy, cool, and shaded acid soil.

FIR CLUBMOSS
(MOUNTAIN CLUBMOSS; LITTLE CLUBMOSS)
Species: *Lycopodium Selago* L.

Style: Small, evergreen, dull yellow-green plant growing in tight flat-topped tufts, stems covered with scale-like, tiny leaves closely pressed together. Branches without cones.

Ecology: On cool damp shaded ledges in mountainous regions.

Stems: 4″± long; single or branched; all stems about same height; upcurving from an imperceptible horizontal stem.

Leaves: ⅛″± long; 8-ranked; narrow, smooth sides; sharp-pointed tips; rounded at bases.

Sporophyll: Same as leaves; sometimes with bulblets. Spore cases kidney-shaped; yellow; borne in axils of upper leaves. Sides of spores concave.

Var. *patens* (Lloyd's Clubmoss): grows in less regular tufts; stems show annual indentations; leaves more spreading. Usually found in drier and more southern regions.

SHINING CLUBMOSS
Species: *Lycopodium lucidulum* Michx.

Style: Medium-sized, bright shining green, evergreen, bristly-leaved plant, growing in fairly loose tufts, sometimes forming "fairy rings." Without cones.

Ecology: In shady spots along streambanks in cool moist woods; in rich and acid soil throughout the area.

Stems: 6″± long; single and branching; growing up from short, obliquely rising horizontal stem. Erect stems thickly covered with bristly leaves; often indentation formed by smaller leaves, denoting start of annual growth.

Leaves: ⅜″± long; 6-ranked; narrow lance-shaped; edges slightly toothed; top leaves ascending, lower leaves irregularly spreading or reflexed.

Sporophyll: Like slightly smaller leaves; often with bulblets. Spore cases kidney-shaped; prominent; orange-yellow; borne in axils of upper leaves. Sides of spores concave.

Both *L. Selago* and var. *patens* also produce bulblets in axils of upper leaves, a common form of propagation, especially for *patens*.

Marginalia: Fir Clubmoss: a. Growth form. b. Fruiting tip. c. Sporophyll with spore case. Shining Clubmoss: d. Growth form. e. Fruiting tip. f. Sporophyll with spore case. Lloyd's Clubmoss: g. Fruiting tip. h. Sporophyll with spore case. i. Bulblet.

Diagnostic Arrows: 1. Unbranched or once-branched upright stems forming flat-topped growth form for the Fir Clubmoss. 2. Leaves of

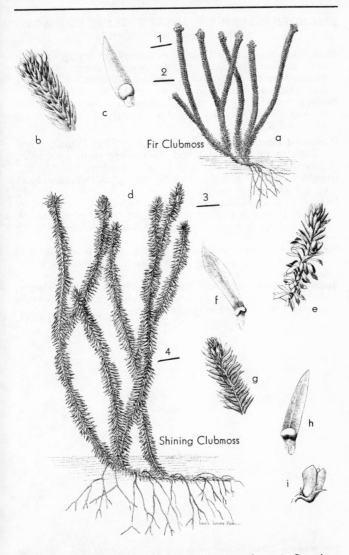

Fir Clubmoss pointing upward and pressed together.   3. Branching upright stems of Shining Clubmoss with uneven growth form.   4. Annual interruption, Shining Clubmoss.

STAGHORN CLUBMOSS (WOLF'S CLAW CLUBMOSS)
Species: *Lycopodium clavatum* L.

Style: This densely leaved Clubmoss has upright branching stems
that simulate deer horns or wolf claws. Its evergreen trailing
branches were widely used for Christmas decorations, hence it
is no longer a common plant in most areas.

Ecology: Found in northern parts of our area; in open wooded
thickets; along rocky slopes; and particularly in pine woodlands
where soil is loose and acid.

Horizontal stems: Surface-running; semi-arching; branching and
interlacing for many feet and often many yards; rooting at
intervals; densely covered with leaves; evergreen.

Upright stems: 10″± high. Densely leafy; branching into forks
of varying heights; evergreen.

Leaves: ⅓″± long; 10-ranked; narrow, tapering upward to tiny
hairlike tip and downward to quite narrow base; edges toothed,
rough. Leaves usually ascending, sometimes spreading or
deflexed.

Strobilus: 3″± long; cylindrical; one or more; branching from
slender stems 6″± long; with sparse, yellowish, scale-like
leaflets.

Sporophyll: Yellow-tan; scale-like; triangular ovate, with abrupt,
sharp, and hairlike tip; sides irregularly and prominently
toothed. Spore case kidney-shaped.

Marginalia: a. Sterile leaf with hair tip. b. Fertile leaf with spore
case.
Diagnostic Arrows: 1. 3 or more strobili on long stem. 2. Leaves
pointing upward.

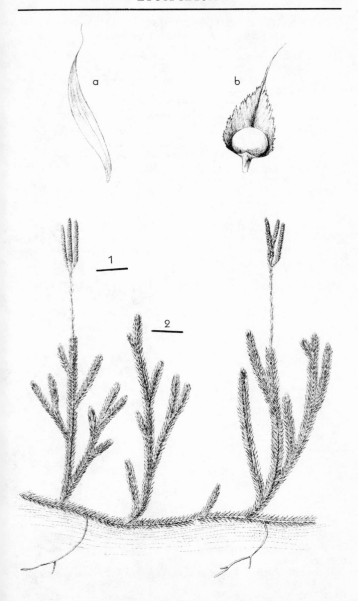

STIFF CLUBMOSS (BRISTLY CLUBMOSS)
Species: *Lycopodium annotinum* L.

Style: Stiff and prickly, light to dark green, evergreen Clubmoss that looks like a smaller, more delicate, paler, duller green Shining Clubmoss with small individual short-stemmed cones. Leaves seldom ascending.

Ecology: Found in moist woods and in cool, damp, and shaded thickets of our more northern areas.

Horizontal stems: Surface-running, often below surface debris; branching, sparsely leaved, rooting at intervals.

Upright stems: 6″± long; single, or once- or twice-branched; not uniform in height; bristly-leaved; often with indentations formed by smaller leaves making start of annual growth.

Leaves: ⅓″± long; 8-ranked; semi-whorled; narrow lance-shaped, with very sharp pointed tip and a narrowed base; edges often slightly toothed.

Strobilus: Slim and pointed; 1½″± long; yellowish; short stems.

Sporophyll: Yellow-tan; triangular ovate with abrupt, sharp-pointed tip, edges irregularly and prominently toothed. Spore case kidney-shaped.

Var. *acrifolium* Fern.: leaves slightly toothed, spreading or ascending.

Var. *pungens* Desv.: leaves not toothed, ascending or appressed.

Marginalia: a. Sterile leaf (typical), toothed edges.   b. Sterile leaf of var. *pungens*, showing lack of teeth on edges.   c. Fertile leaf with spore case.

Diagnostic Arrows: 1. Strobilus and no stem.   2. Leaves spreading. 3. Annual interruption.

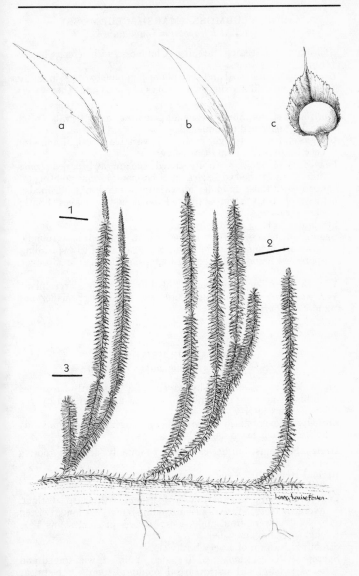

BOG CLUBMOSS (MARSH CLUBMOSS)
Species: *Lycopodium inundatum* L.

Style: Small, creeping, arching Clubmoss with erect, bushy-topped fertile stems.

Ecology: Found in cool and shaded bogs; in pine barrens; in sandy, damp, and acid marshes; along edges of ponds and other watery spots.

Horizontal stems: Surface-creeping; rooting at intervals; often arching; flattened on undersides.

Upright stems: $8'' \pm$ high; erect; few; variable in height and size; very bushy tops. Only tips evergreen.

Leaves: $\frac{1}{4}'' \pm$ long; 8- to 10-ranked; narrow awl-shaped; sometimes with toothed edges; leaves of horizontal stems pointing upward, with those on underside twisting around to point up also; leaves of upright stems appressed and ascending; leaves of bushy tips spreading.

Strobilus: In form of a bushy top.

Sporophyll: Green; sharply pointed; slightly curved; base rounded with narrow joining to the stem; appressed to widely spreading. Spore case round; yellow; in bushy tops. Sides of spores convex.

Var. *Bigelovii* Tuckerm.: bushy tails less spreading; larger plant.

Var. *elongatum* Chapm.: bushy tails very spreading; smaller and more southern plant.

FOXTAIL CLUBMOSS
Species: *Lycopodium alopecuroides* L.

Style: Semi-evergreen, bushy-leaved and distinctly foxtailed Clubmoss growing in arching form. Easily recognized by yellowness in winter.

Ecology: A lover of acid spots; sphagnum bogs; piny, damp, sandy hollows in our more southerly areas.

Horizontal stems: Surface-creeping; commonly arching; rooting at tips.

Upright stems: $10'' \pm$ high; erect; seldom forked; densely leaved; deciduous; very bushy.

Leaves: Many-ranked; narrow, awl-shaped, with sharp, distinct, divergent teeth. Leaves of horizontal stems $\frac{1}{4}'' \pm$ long, twisted to point upward from undersides. Leaves of erect stems $\frac{3}{8}'' \pm$ long, spreading, crowded.

Strobilus: In form of a very bushy tip.

Sporophyll: Green, long, awl-like, sharp-pointed, widespread and round at base, with narrow basal joining to stem; toothed near base. Spore case yellow; ovoid, in bushy tops.

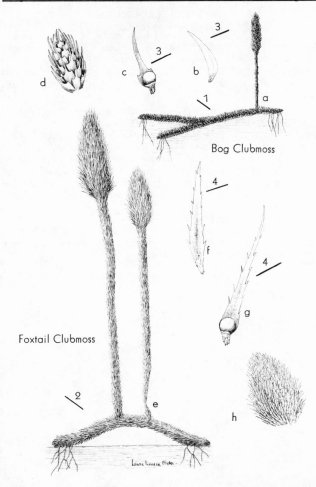

Bog Clubmoss

Foxtail Clubmoss

Laura Louise Foster

Marginalia: Bog Clubmoss: a. Growth form. b. Leaf. c. Sporophyll with spore case. d. Enlargement of bushy tip. Foxtail Clubmoss: e. Growth form. f. Leaf. g. Sporophyll with spore case. h. Enlargement of bushy tip.

Diagnostic Arrows: 1. Horizontal stem of Bog Clubmoss flat to ground. 2. Horizontal stem of Foxtail Clubmoss arching. 3. Leaves of Bog Clubmoss seldom and slightly toothed. 4. Leaves of Foxtail Clubmoss with distinctly toothed edges.

CAROLINA CLUBMOSS
Species: *Lycopodium carolinianum* L.

Style: Our smallest and most easily recognized Clubmoss. Almost naked, slim, erect fertile stem topped by small tight cone.

Ecology: Found along the southerly coastal plains in damp and sandy spots; wooded bogs; pine barrens; and in open, grassy, sandy, moist places.

Horizontal stems: Surface-creeping and branching; short; flat on ground and rooting frequently; deciduous.

Upright stems: $2\frac{1}{2}''\pm$ high; erect; remotely leaved; round; slim, with slightly thicker cone of tightly appressed leaves.

Leaves: $\frac{1}{3}''\pm$ long; 6-ranked; leaves of two upper ranks broad lance-shaped, spreading, sharp-pointed, entire; leaves of 4 lower ranks smaller, narrow lance-shaped, erect; leaves of erect stem $\frac{1}{8}'' \pm$ long; scale-like, narrow lance-shaped, pointed, and tightly appressed.

Strobilus: Single cone-like tips, $\frac{3}{8}''\pm$ long, sharp.

Sporophyll: Yellow-green; rounded, kidney-shaped with abruptly pointed tip and narrow basal lip; edges slightly rough. Spore case kidney-shaped. Sides of spores convex.

Marginalia: a. Sporophyll with spore case. b. Leaf of erect stem. c. Leaf of horizontal stem. d. Enlargement of tip.

Diagnostic Arrows: 1. Tall slender, almost naked upright stem. 2. Bristly leaved and frequently horizontal-rooting stem.

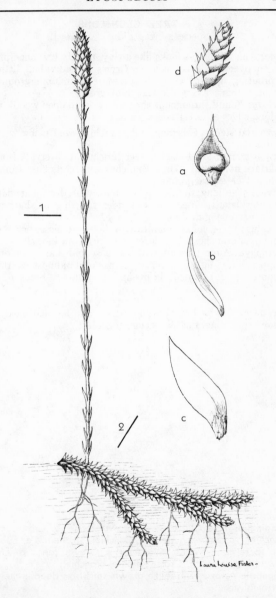

1

2

d

a

b

c

Laura Louise Foster

TREE CLUBMOSS
Species: *Lycopodium obscurum* L.

Style: This Clubmoss looks like a tiny, thickly branched pine tree with oversized erect cones. Grows as individual little trees sprouting upward every 6″ or more from underground horizontal stem. Evergreen and shiny green.

Ecology: Found throughout the area in damp open woods, usually along edges of forest bogs.

Horizontal stems: Creeping and branching well below surface of ground.

Upright stems: 12″± high; erect; arising at intervals from subsurface horizontal stem. Branches and rebranches from single stem 2″± above ground.

Leaves: ¼″± long; 6- to 8-ranked; numerous, divergent, flattened, narrow lance-shaped; smooth sides tapering to sharp-pointed tips, narrowing at bases.

Strobilus: 1½″± long; cylindrical; yellow; stemless; borne on tips of upper branches; often dozen or more on one branch.

Sporophyll: Almost round, with flat base and sharply pointed tip; upper sides slightly notched; translucent; almost overlapping. Spore cases rounded, bean-shaped; yellow. Sides of spores convex.

Var. *dendroideum:* branches more erect and less flattened; leaves more spreading, finer, less close together.

Marginalia: Tree Clubmoss: a. Growth form. b. Cross section of branchlet. c. Enlarged view of branchlet. d. Leaf. e. Sporophyll with spore case. Var. *dendroideum:* f. Growth form. g. Enlarged view of branchlet. h. Cross section of branchlet.

Diagnostic Arrow: 1. Treelike growth form from deep-in-the-ground horizontal stem.

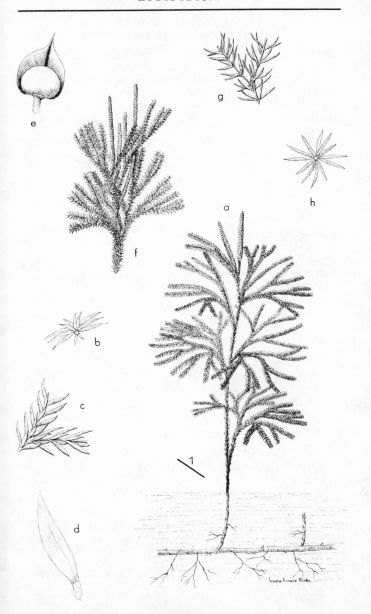

luna louise Foster

GROUND CEDAR (GROUND PINE)
Species: *Lycopodium tristachyum* Pursh

Style: Small, upright; grows like tiny evergreen trees topped by thin-stemmed candelabra of cones. Leaves spread in well-balanced, rounded or flat-topped upright fans. Blue-green.

Ecology: Widely scattered in our cooler areas in dry, sandy, shaded woodlands, or open pastures.

Horizontal stems: Deeply subterranean, widely creeping, almost naked.

Upright stems: $12''\pm$ high; erect, treelike, branched and rebranched into fairly uniformly fan-shaped lower branches, with upper branches usually flat-topped. Bluish green; evergreen.

Leaves: Tiny, 4-ranked, grown together for about half their length; sharply pointed, lance-shaped. Upper leaves with tips pointing up and in; side leaves about same size and shape; bottom leaves much smaller.

Strobilus: $2\frac{1}{2}''\pm$ long; blunt-tipped, cylindrical, borne on $3\frac{1}{2}''\pm$ slender stems branching into candelabra of 3 or 4 cones. Leaves of stems sparse, scale-like, spreading.

Sporophyll: Light yellow, semi-deltoid, abrupt at base, with long, sharp, pointed tip at top; edges rough and chaffy. Spore case almost round. Sides of spores convex.

Marginalia: a. Upper surface of branchlet. b. Undersurface of branchlet. c. Sporophyll with spore case.

Diagnostic Arrows: 1. Flat-topped growth form. 2. Candelabra usually of 4 cones.

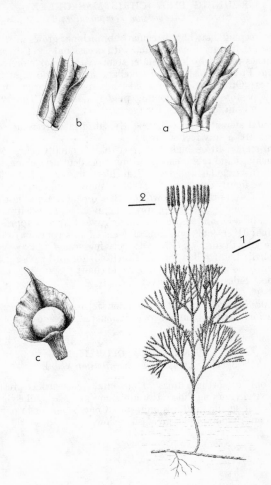

RUNNING PINE (CHRISTMAS GREEN)
Species: *Lycopodium complanatum* L.

Style: Creeping, crawling, irregularly branching; grows in tangled masses that spread over ground with occasional erect divergent branches topped by long slender stems with one or more cones.

Ecology: Prefers moist shaded woodland areas, as do most Clubmosses. Often found on exposed sandy roadsides, or in thickets, or in pasture edges adjoining pine woodlands. The typical plant only in far North. Evergreen.

Horizontal stems: Surface- or slightly subsurface-creeping, covering an area many feet square.

Upright stems: $10''\pm$ high; less erect than Ground Cedar. Many branchings and rebranchings, forming pendent or arching, semi-rounded irregular tangles. Branchlets flattened, with lower surface slightly concave. Stems often show annual constrictions.

Leaves: Tiny, 4-ranked, grown together for more than half their length. Side leaves sharp, spreading, pointed, and deltoid; top leaves broader and appressed; underleaves tiny and appressed.

Strobilus: $2\frac{1}{2}''\pm$ long, on stems of $3''\pm$. 1 to 4 cones in candelabrum growth form. Stems with very few scale-like leaves.

Sporophyll: Light yellow, orbicular deltoid, abrupt at base; sharp, abruptly pointed tip; edges rough and chaffy. Spore case almost round. Sides of spores convex.

Var. *flabelliforme* Fern.: our common form. Surface-creeping; branchlets without annual constrictions; less cool areas.

SAVIN-LEAVED CLUBMOSS
Species: *Lycopodium sabinifolium* Willd.

Found only in northern areas. Horizontal stems surface-creeping, like those of Running Pine. Upright stems and leaves like Ground Cedar's but smaller and less uniform. Cones single or in pairs on $2''\pm$ stems. Sporophylls greenish yellow.

Marginalia: Running Pine: a. Upper surface of branchlet. b. Undersurface of branchlet. c. Sporophyll with spore case; similar for Savin-leaved Clubmoss. Savin-leaved Clubmoss: d. Undersurface of branchlet, showing even leaves. e. Upper surface of branchlet again showing even leaves.

Diagnostic Arrows: Running Pine: 1. Straggly growth form. 2. Candelabra of 2 or 3 cones.

The Selaginellas, or Spikemosses

THE order of Spikemosses, or **Selaginellales,** is represented in our area by one family, the **Selaginellaceae,** with one genus, *Selaginella*. Two species of this genus are common: *Selaginella rupestris*, or the Rock Spikemoss, and *S. apoda*, or the Meadow Spikemoss. Both are found generally throughout our area. *S. selaginoides* is rare and reported only from those regions close to the Canadian border. This species is similar to *S. rupestris* in growth and form. It is a larger plant, but grows in smaller mats, or colonies. Its leaves are much narrower and all of the same shape, with distinctly spiny margins but without a bristle tip. The fertile tips are more rounded than 4-angled, with slightly larger loose-spreading leaves. The megaspore is pale yellow. *S. selaginoides* prefers moist grassy lands, as does the Bog Clubmoss, *L. inundatum*, to which it bears considerable resemblance except for its much smaller size.

There are over 800 species of the genus *Selaginella*. The great majority of them are found in the tropics and are semi-prostrate or creeping plants, similar in growth and form to *Selaginella apoda* and resembling in many ways the damp-loving mosses, hepatics or liverworts, with which they are often confused. This group of Selaginellas is broadly referred to as the Creeping Selaginellas.

On the other hand the Stiff, or Rock, Selaginellas, similar to *S. rupestris*, are species that prefer drier, higher, more rocky, and less tropical regions. Even though the Stiff Spikemosses are found around the world, there are not more than a few dozen species known to exist as of today's count. These Stiff Spikemosses are also very frequently overlooked and bypassed as another stiff True Moss, whereas they actually resemble closely a diminutive *Lycopodium Selago*. (*Selaginella* means "little Selago," and *Selago* is an early name for *Lycopodium*.) The Stiff Spikemosses usually appear to be pale gray-green. The tiny hairlike spines on the margins of the leaves, plus the usual white-topped bristle tips (which in turn have minute bristles on their margins), give the plant, together with its growth and form, a misty gray-green color.

 The Selaginellas, like some of the Lycopodiums, bear their spores in the axils at the bases of the leaves at the ends of the fertile spikes, or stalks. These sporophylls, or fertile tips, are distinctly quadrangular in *S. rupestris*, and semi-quadrangular in *S. apoda*. Unlike the Lycopodiums, however, the *Selaginellas have two types of spores*: the microspores, or male spores, and the megaspores, or female spores. These two types of spores are contained in separate spore cases, or spo-

rangia. The male spores are usually above those cases containing the female spores. The microspores are like orange dust. The megaspores are light yellow or dead-white in color, and usually consist of 4 rather large pitted or ridged, round pyramidal spores. When the two types of spores germinate, they produce separate gametophytes. The male gametophyte, which is extremely small, consists usually of a single antheridium, or male organ, and the female gametophyte, which is much larger, though still minute, consists of a mass of green tissue with several archegonia, or female organs. Both develop before they leave their spore cases and even adhere to the spores after leaving the spore cases. When the female gametophytes are nearly fully developed, the spore cases crack open, exposing the eggs to fertilization. The fertilized egg directly produces a new plant.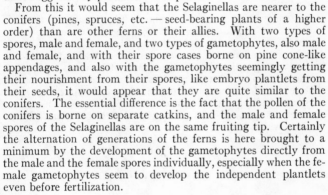

From this it would seem that the Selaginellas are nearer to the conifers (pines, spruces, etc. — seed-bearing plants of a higher order) than are other ferns or allies. With two types of spores, male and female, and two types of gametophytes, also male and female, and with their spore cases borne on pine cone-like appendages, and also with the gametophytes seemingly getting their nourishment from their spores, like embryo plantlets from their seeds, it would appear that they are quite similar to the conifers. The essential difference is the fact that the pollen of the conifers is borne on separate catkins, and the male and female spores of the Selaginellas are on the same fruiting tip. Certainly the alternation of generations of the ferns is here brought to a minimum by the development of the gametophytes directly from the male and the female spores individually, especially when the female gametophytes seem to develop the independent plantlets even before fertilization.

MEADOW SPIKEMOSS
Species: *Selaginella apoda* (L.) Spring

Style: Delicate, weak, evergreen, pale yellow-green, flat-growing and creeping plant that forms an open tracery mat of tiny, translucent, acutely pointed, flat leaves and tiny, pale green, threadlike, branching stems. Often mistaken for moss.

Ecology: Fairly common habitant of muddy or damp limy soil; in meadows and open swamps; along streambanks; in pastures; and often in damp patches in lawns. Characteristically tropical but evergreen if given some protection.

Stems: Creeping and lying close to ground; very slender; spreading alternately and branching, forming flat mats. Roots slender, spreading and forking from all parts of stems.

Leaves: Of two sizes: larger, $\frac{1}{8}''\pm$ long; smaller, $\frac{1}{16}''\pm$ long. Yellow-green, acute ovate, unequal-sided, broadest toward tip of stem. Very thin, membranous; margins finely toothed; distinct midrib; no bristles; leaves arranged alternately on stem at right angles on all 4 sides; top and bottom leaves appressed and pointing forward and about $\frac{1}{2}$ size of lateral leaves.

Fruit: Fruiting spikes $\frac{1}{2}''\pm$ long at ends of branches, half erect; obscurely 4-angled leaves in 4 rows of equal size, bearing separate spore cases for microspores and megaspores in upper and lower axils of fruiting leaves, respectively. Spore cases open transversely at apex. Usually paler green than rest of plant. Megaspores white.

Marginalia: a. Growth form. b. Section of plant. c. Leaf. d. Fruiting tip.

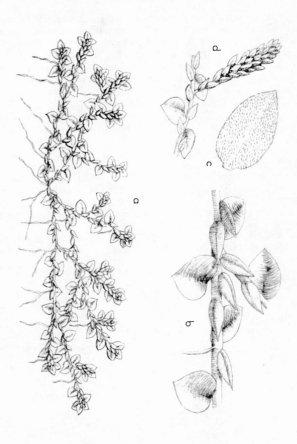

ROCK SPIKEMOSS
Species: *Selaginella rupestris* (L.) Spring

Style: Small, gray-green, evergreen, tough and rigid mosslike plant; often grows as creeping and spreading intertwining community into dense mat several feet square. Gray-green color and semi-prostrate growth distinguish it from true mosses.

Ecology: In thin dry soil on tops of rocks and dry ledges of granite or gneiss; on mossy rocks; gravelly slopes, or semi-moist sand hills; and in other exposed dry and thin-soiled locations.

Stems: $2''\pm$ long; runners fork upward into tufts of $1''\pm$. Stems completely covered by appressed and overlapping leaves, except at fertile tips. Roots slender, branching mostly from tufted stems.

Leaves: Sterile leaves $\frac{1}{8}''\pm$ long; narrow lanceolate, convex, with deeply grooved keel. Leaves densely appressed, margins prominently spiny; each leaf tip with long pointed bristle. Fertile leaves broader at base, pointed ovate, margins very spiny, with less of a bristle at tip. Arranged in 4 ranks of closely overlapping leaves containing at their bases the spore cases. Leaves stay deflexed after spores have fallen.

Fruit: Fruiting spikes $\frac{1}{3}''\pm$ long at ends of branches; erect; distinctly 4-sided. Leaves slightly spreading. Megaspores yellow.

Marginalia: a. Growth form. b. Sterile tips. c. Fruiting tip. d. Fruiting leaf. e. Sterile leaf.

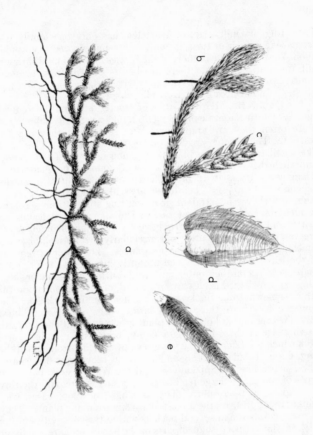

The Quillworts

THE order of Quillworts, or **Isoetales,** has only one family, the **Isoetaceae,** which in turn has only one genus, *Isoetes*, containing about 70 species. One or more of the species may be found throughout the world wherever there are bodies of still fresh or semi-brackish waters, such as backwaters, river edges, ponds, lakes, or ditches. In our area there are 10 listed species.

The Quillworts, Merlin's Grass, or Isoetes, are small, perennial, summer-fruiting aquatic plants. Often they are totally submerged, quite often they are amphibious, and sometimes they are terrestrial. The Isoetes are unfernlike in appearance. They look like small tufts of chive plants, or young onions. Their slender unbranched leaves are awl-shaped, with rounded or quadrate or triangular surfaces, with or without stomata, or breathing cells, depending on species. Their leaves are seldom more than 12 inches high, and they grow straight or in twisting spirals from a central swollen rosette-like base, or *corm*. The slim pointed leaves are brittle and for their main parts have 4 vertical air channels which are interrupted frequently and irregularly by horizontal walls, which give the leaves jointed appearances. The lower extremities of the leaves flatten and widen abruptly into spatulate or spoon shapes, convex on their outer sides, and concave on the inner sides. These spoon-shaped leaves are *imbricated*, or layered one upon the other, somewhat like the leaves of the head of an artichoke. The youngest leaves are those on the inside. The outside and oldest leaves wither and fall off as the plant grows outward and upward. At the base of these leaves is a fleshy, brownish, roundish corm from which the 12 or more leaves grow upward, and from which the long, fleshy, tubular, forking and abundant roots grow downward. The Isoetes, like the Spikemosses and the Water Ferns, have two types of spores, the large female spore, or megaspore, and the tiny male spore, or microspore. The sporangia, or spore cases, containing the spores, are the largest of any known living plant. They

are borne in several pockets within the concavities of the lower spoon-shaped parts of the leaves, and are wholly or partly covered by a *velum*, or an indusium, formed by a thin leaf tissue. Above the spore case is a small triangular ligule of obscure function.

The innermost, or newest, leaves are usually sterile. The next outermost leaves usually have embedded in them 4 or more pockets containing the microspores, and the outside leaves contain in their pockets the megaspores; or — as is more common — the two types of spores are borne in the middle and outer leaves, based on the alternating cycle of the leaves' growths. Sometimes in some species the two types of spores are found intermingled in a single pocket, or spore case. The megaspores are numerous, 100 or more to a spore case. They are chalky white, crusted with silica, and are tetrahedral in shape. On the upper surface of each megaspore are three equidistant longitudinal lines meeting at an apex, called *commissural ridges*. The areas between the ridges are of four general types of surfaces: (1) *Reticulate*, or pitted; (2) *Tuberculate*, or pebbled; (3) *Echinate*, or prickly; and (4) *Cristate*, or crested. It is the markings and characters of these surfaces, or areas, which are used to diagnose the different species.

The microspores are minute, grayish, powdery, usually oval in shape, and with smooth or slightly roughened surfaces. They are extremely numerous. In some species several hundred thousand microspores are contained in one spore case.

Both the male and the female spores produce their own gametophytes, or prothalli. The male gametophyte usually produces 4 *spermatozoids*, which are tiny and slender with two long cilia, or hairlike appendages, at either end, by which they propel themselves. The female gametophyte is a round, many-celled structure on top of which there are one or more shallow channels from which project little funnel-like necks. Embedded in the gametophyte at the base of the funnels are the single eggs. The necks open when the eggs are ready for fertilization and close after the entry of the spermatozoid. The young plants develop directly from the fertilized egg within the archegonium in the female gametophyte.

Even though several species of the Quillwort family are found generally throughout the world and in most of our own watery areas, this family of the fern allies is to most people, and even to those interested in ferns, the least familiar of all the families of the Pteridophyta. Generally very little research work has been done with them. The treatment given them in the majority of guide books is scanty and often cursory. Because they are so similar in habit, growth, and form to some common and numerous aquatic and amphibious grasses, they are not only frequently overlooked, but are also hard to find when they are intermingled with the grasses. Furthermore, as the majority of the species are usually submerged, they are often inaccessible and a special expedition may have to be made to collect them. When they are once found a further difficulty arises, since the great similarity in growth and form and ecological preferences of most of the species of Quillworts makes it necessary to diagnose the characters of the megaspores to recognize properly the species found. Even though the megaspores can be seen with the naked eye as tiny saltlike granules, the characteristic surface areas for identification can only be seen with the aid of a binocular microscope — impractical to use in the field.

BRAUN'S QUILLWORT AND MEGASPORES OF OTHER SPECIES

Braun's Quillwort: *Isoetes echinospora* Durieu (var. *Braunii*, var. *muricata*, var. *robusta*)

   9″ ± tall; submerged along shores of ponds and lakes, N.J. northward. Megaspores echinate; distinct ridges.
   a. Inside view of lower leaf, showing spore case, indusium, ligule, air channels. b. Cross section of lower part of leaf. c. Cross section of leaf. d. Megaspore.

e. **Eaton's Quillwort:** *Isoetes Eatonii* Dodge (var. *Gravesii*, var. *canadensis*)
   20″ ± tall; submerged in mudflats of rivers and tidal shores, N.J. northward. Megaspores cristate; small distinct ridges.

f. **Virginia Quillwort:** *Isoetes virginica* Pfeiffer
   12″ ± tall; slender, delicate, amphibious. In occasional or temporary waters. Local to Va. Megaspores echinate; irregular ridges.

g. **Lake Quillwort:** *Isoetes macrospora* Durieu (var. *hieroglyphica*, var. *Dodgei*, var. *lacustris*)
   8″ ± tall; deeply submerged in still waters, Va. northward. Megaspores reticulate; distinct ridges.

h. **Black-based Quillwort:** *Isoetes melanopoda* Gay & Durieu
   12″ ± tall; ponds, wet thickets, puddles, N.J. westward. Megaspores tuberculate; distinct ridges.

i. **Riverbank Quillwort:** *Isoetes riparia* Engelm. (var. *Amesii*, var. *Robbinsii*, var. *reticulata*)
   12″ ± tall; muddy or sandy riverbanks and tidal shores, N.J. northward. Megaspores semi-cristate; distinct ridges; both aspects varying for different varieties.

j. **Butler's Quillwort:** *Isoetes Butleri* Engelm.
   4″ tall; terrestrial; barrens, ledges, flats, Tenn. westward. Megaspores tuberculate; distinct ridges.

k. **Engelmann's Quillwort:** *Isoetes Engelmannii* A. Br.
   24″ ± tall, with broad 1″-base; amphibious; throughout the area. Megaspores reticulate; deeply pitted; low ridges.

l. **Pitted Quillwort:** *Isoetes foveolata* A. A. Eaton
   20″ ± tall; amphibious, almost terrestrial. Conn. to N.H. Local. Megaspores reticulate; distinct ridges.

m. **Tuckerman's Quillwort:** *Isoetes Tuckermanii* A. Br.
   15″ ± tall; slender; deeply submerged in quiet waters, Conn. northward. Megaspores cristate and reticulate; distinct ridges.

Diagnostic Arrows: 1. Spiral-like growth from bulbous base. 2. Externally visible spore cases.

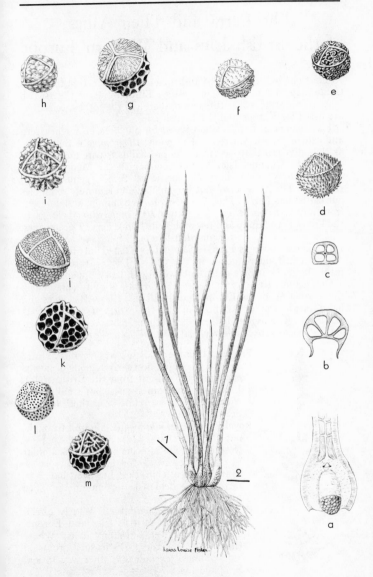

The Ferns and Their Allies
of the British Isles and Western Europe

ALMOST one half of the ferns and their allies described in this *Field Guide* may also be found in western Europe and/or the British Isles. This group constitutes more than half the total species that are listed for Europe and the British Isles.

Five genera of ferns are not listed for our area in northeastern and central North America. The genus *Anogramma* is referred to as the only fern that is annual (its prothallus is perennial). It is rare in the Channel Islands, but common in the Mediterranean area. It looks somewhat like our Rock Brake, genus *Cryptogramma*. The genus *Blechnum* is common, and remotely resembles our Christmas Fern. The genus *Ceterach* is common, and different from any fern we have. The genus *Hymenophyllum* belongs to the Filmy Fern family and resembles our Filmy Fern, *Trichomanes*. The genus *Notholaena* is somewhat like our Lipferns, *Cheilanthes*.

One genus of Water Fern — *Salvinia* — is listed only for Europe, or as an introduced genus in the British Isles. It resembles a rather large, light blue-green duckweed with hairy upper surfaces.

One genus of the fern allies — *Pilularia* — is quite common in the warmer regions of Europe and the British Isles. Its leaves and habitats are similar to those of the Quillworts, *Isoetes*, but its leaves grow individually from a creeping rootstock with short-stalked sporocarps, as in our Water Clover *Marsilea*.

Fragrant Cliff Fern, *Dryopteris fragrans*. Rare and only in most northerly regions of northern Europe. Absent from the British Isles. Like the American species, but smaller and with even more close together leaflets. See page 62.

Royal Fern, *Osmunda regalis*. Found throughout British Isles and northern parts of western Europe in ecological regions similar to those described for American species. Many years of collecting, however, have unfortunately depleted its numbers. See page 168.

Bracken, *Pteridium aquilinum*. Widely spread throughout both British Isles and Europe, except in limy, wet, and sunny areas. Where there is some shade grows in such profusion as to almost exclude all other vegetation. See page 134.

Maidenhair Fern, *Adiantum Capillus-Veneris* (our Venus Maidenhair Fern). Local and rare. Found in damper and warmer parts of western Europe and in more southerly coastal areas of British Isles. See page 142.

Hart's-tongue Fern, *Phyllitis Scolopendrium.* Rare in the most northerly areas, but extremely common in shaded rocky regions, particularly on stone walls and old masonry. Differs from rare American species mainly by veins being nearer leaves' margins. See page 160.

Ostrich Fern, *Matteuccia Struthiopteris.* Found in the cooler latitudes of northern Europe, local and quite rare. Absent from British Isles except as an introduced species. See page 118.

Lady Fern, *Athyrium Filix-femina.* Common throughout British Isles and Europe except along east coast of England. Inhabits same types of areas as American species. See page 110.

Fragile Fern, *Cystopteris fragilis.* Common fern in both Europe and British Isles in mountainous, shaded, cool regions. One of most widespread ferns throughout the world. See page 158.

Rusty Woodsia, *Woodsia ilvensis.* Very rare except in the high mountainous areas on exposed rocks. Habitat and behavior very similar to American species, but less abundant. See page 146.

Alpine Woodsia, *Woodsia alpina.* Very rare, found only in the highest, most mountainous areas of northern Scotland, the northern Alps, and up to Arctic Circle. See page 148.

Male Fern, *Dryopteris Filix-mas.* Hardy, common throughout the area, with many forms and varieties (some of which have recently been given the rank of species). See page 66.

Crested Buckler Fern or **Crested Fern,** *Dryopteris cristata.* Found throughout the area in damp woods. Absent from higher and colder regions. Local and rare in some regions. See page 74.

Narrow Buckler Fern is our Spinulose Woodfern, *Dryopteris spinulosa.* **Broad Buckler**

Fern is our Mountain Woodfern, *D. austriaca*. Both common throughout area; Broad Buckler particularly so. See page 68.

Braun's Holly Fern, *Polystichum Braunii.* Absent from British Isles, but found in northern areas of western Europe. (See Check-list, page 272, for other species of genus *Polystichum* which are common.) See page 128.

Marsh Fern, *Thelypteris palustris.* Like our Marsh Fern, common throughout the area, though it does not form as large colonies nor is it as widespread as our species. See page 84.

Beech Fern, *Thelypteris Phegopteris.* Common throughout the area in cool and damp regions similar to those inhabited by our Long or Narrow Beech Fern. See page 82.

Oak Fern, *Gymnocarpium Dryopteris.* Throughout British Isles and western Europe, but absent from lime areas, warmer regions, and rare in Ireland. Not as common as North American species in our area. See page 78.

Limestone Fern or **Robert's Fern,** *Gymnocarpium Robertianum.* Rare and local in the limestone regions. More common in British Isles and Europe and found at less high altitudes than is American species. See page 49.

Polypody Fern, *Polypodium vulgare.* Common throughout the British Isles and Europe. Found in same types of locations as our American species. See page 130.

Maidenhair Spleenwort, *Asplenium Trichomanes.* Common throughout the area. In southern Europe as well. This and Rustyback Fern, *Ceterach officinarum*, are the two most abundant small rock ferns. See page 94.

Wall Rue, *Asplenium Ruta-muraria.* Very common little rock fern in the British Isles and Europe. In old masonry, in and around stone walls, as well as on limestone cliffs. See page 100.

Green Spleenwort, *Asplenium viride.* In high rocky, hilly, and mountainous areas where it is cool and shaded. More abundant and a

larger plant generally than our American
species. See page 98.

Parsley Fern, *Cryptogramma crispa.* This rare
and northern species with us is found
throughout the higher, more acid, and mountainous areas of the British Isles and northern
Europe. It is rare, but more common than
in the northeastern United States. See
page 57.

WATER FERNS

Mosquito Ferns, *Azolla caroliniana* and *A.
filiculoides,* found in still waters and ditches
occasionally throughout British Isles and
Europe. Both species were introduced from
America. See page 178.

Water Shamrock, *Marsilea quadrifolia.* From
Central Europe and has been introduced into
the British Isles and northeast United States.
See page 178.

SUCCULENT FERNS

Adder's-tongue Fern, *Ophioglossum vulgatum.*
Common throughout British Isles and western Europe in same ecological regions as our
species. See page 182.

Moonwort, *Botrychium Lunaria.* Local and
rare throughout British Isles and Europe.
Other Botrychiums — *lanceolatum,* *matricariifolium,* *multifidum,* *simplex,* and *virginianum* — absent now from British Isles,
but found sparingly in central, western, and
northern Europe. See page 188.

FERN ALLIES

Quillworts, *Isoetes echinospora.* Widely distributed throughout British Isles and Europe.
I. lacustris, our *macrospora,* quite widespread, and *I. hystrix* are found in British
Isles. Highly probable that other species
of the Quillworts are to be found in Europe
and the British Isles. See pages 240-43.

Scouring Rushes (Horsetails), *Equisetum hiemale* and *E. variegatum.* Common in British
Isles and Europe. *E. scirpoides* found in
northeastern Europe and Asia. See pages
198, 200, 202.

Field Horsetails, *Equisetum arvense*, Meadow Horsetail, *E. pratense*, and Wood Horsetail, *E. sylvaticum*, all found in British Isles and western Europe. See pages 204, 206, 208.

Marsh Horsetails, *Equisetum palustre*, Swamp Horsetail, *E. fluviatile*, and Shore Horsetail, *E. × litorale*, all found in British Isles and western Europe. See pages 210 and 212.

Fir Clubmoss, *Lycopodium Selago.* Found throughout mountainous areas of British Isles and Europe. See page 218.

Staghorn Clubmoss, *Lycopodium clavatum*, and **Stiff Clubmoss,** *L. annotinum*, both found in British Isles and Europe. Staghorn Clubmoss quite common. Stiff Clubmoss rare and local. See pages 220 and 222.

Bog Clubmoss, *Lycopodium inundatum.* Found in British Isles and Europe, in marshy areas. Very rare or absent in northern areas and rare and local elsewhere. See page 224.

Running Pine, *Lycopodium complanatum.* Supposedly not found in British Isles, but found in mountainous areas of temperate zone in Europe. See page 232.

Spikemoss. The only spikemoss that occurs in our area and in the British Isles and western Europe is the Northern Spikemoss, *Selaginella selaginoides.* This species is only briefly described because it is rare and local to the most northerly tips of our area. However, in the British Isles and Europe it is rather common in the damp grassy or mossy grounds of the mountainous regions throughout the areas. See page 234.

Ferns in the Flower Garden

BY H. LINCOLN FOSTER

IN TEXTURE, color, and shape, ferns proclaim themselves as the perfection of green leaf forms. Where we find them in nature they are so thoroughly a muted part of the total landscape that we accept them without special note. Ferns remain so much a part of the world of nature that they are not suited to the formal gardens with border perennials. They belong in the company of spring bulbs and those flowering plants that still wear some of the air of their original wildness.

Used thus in conjunction with early bulbs and spring flowers, ferns can fill the shaded corners beneath a flowering tree or in the flowerbed on the shady side of the house. The first uncurling fiddleheads neatly accompany the early rush of blossoming wild flowers and such bulbs as daffodils, jonquils, and narcissuses. When the flowers fade and their foliage begins to wilt, then the expanding fern fronds provide fresh and continual greenness.

Except for a few rock-dwelling species, ferns generally ask for a situation in the garden where the soil is not scorched by the sun. They demand a light soil rich in humus, the kind that takes nature years to make in the woods. This soil can be provided in the garden by the incorporation of generous amounts of commercial peat. In such a soil ferns of many sizes and kinds will grow happily together; but some, because of their texture and form and habit of growth, are more desirable than others in a garden.

The Woodferns of the genus *Dryopteris*, with their ranges of sizes and leaf shapes, offer perhaps the most attractive and adaptable of all the ferns. There is not an unpleasing species in the group. They all grow from a central crown and hold their freshness throughout the summer. The largest is the magnificent Goldie's Fern, which may grow to a full four feet in rich soil, with broad firm-textured leaves whose color grades from the deepest green near the stem to a golden green at the tips of the leaflets. Like other Woodferns, their strong stalks are decorated with golden-brown scales. Of similar effect but of lesser stature are the Clinton's Fern, the Marginal Woodfern, the Male Fern, and the Crested Fern.

For a more lacy effect the Spinulose Woodferns are ideal, and the Boott's Fern combines the fine cutting of the Spinulose Woodferns and the more erect and stiffer grace of its ancestor the Crested Fern. Of easy culture in rich, moist, shaded gardens, the Woodferns of the genus *Dryopteris* provide in variety and neatness almost all one could ask for in the garden.

Another with its own special charm is the Lady Fern, which is easily managed and is suitable for growing among herbaceous backgrounds. However, it has an unhappy tendency to become somewhat tattered rather early. This is also true of the graceful and light Silvery Spleenwort.

For contrast of shape and texture there is perhaps no fern to equal the Maidenhair. From the magic of early unwrapping of the frond in spring to the full swirling design of the mature leaf, the Maidenhair asserts its loveliness amid the delicate flowers of spring or the lushness of summer In rich soil and shade a clump of Maidenhair will increase its compact growth sometimes to the point of needing restraint. You can easily bring the rootmass in bounds by slicing off with a spade as much of the clump as you wish, thus furnishing the start of further clumps for other locations.

The Christmas Fern, with its many leaf forms, and Braun's Holly Fern supply narrow upright accents. The former is perhaps the most adaptable and suitable of all ferns for growing with flowering plants. The brilliance of its greenness, the neatness of its upright habit, and the overwintering sturdiness of the fronds make it an ideal addition to the garden. The only drawback is a tendency for the heavy fronds of last year to become untidy and smothering in spring before the new fronds have taken over. Where the old fronds smother spring plants or look unsightly, they can be snipped away as early in spring as you wish, with no damage to the plant.

Braun's Holly Fern has much the same kind of erect grace as the Christmas Fern but it is more demanding in cultural requirements. It has to have rather deep shade and a constant supply of moisture, as is suggested by the fact that this fern is rarely found in nature except in a cool climate near flowing water. When its needs can be met, however, the cuttings of the fronds and the golden-brown scaliness of the stalks make this a distinctive treasure.

Where woodland gardens are extensive and a large coverage of fern foliage is desirable, the large Osmundas may be used for massive effect, and the Beech and Oak Ferns for lovely carpetings.

The Bracken, Sensitive, Ostrich, and Hayscented Ferns are to be avoided because they increase too rapidly and are almost impossible to eradicate, once established.

The small rock-dwelling ferns are not included here because generally they do not take kindly to the flat ground conditions of herbaceous gardens, though frequently they may be added to those gardens where rocks and ledges are features of the landscape. The culture of these ferns is considered below, however, under the heading "The Fern Garden."

FERNS AS UNDERPLANTING

Ferns can be freely used to great advantage in association with a variety of shrubs and beneath many trees. If planted thickly ferns make a handsome ground cover and, because of their light rooting, do not take away needed moisture from the shrubs or trees. In this kind of site even the more invasive ferns may be used for a rapid-growing, dense ground cover. The form and texture of ferns tend to minimize the legginess of many shrubs, and pleasing effects may be achieved by choosing the leaf shapes of ferns for complement and contrast to the growth habit of the woody plants. The solid formality of heavy-leaved rhododendrons and laurel is remarkably lightened by an underplanting of Maidenhair or Beech Ferns.

THE FERN GARDEN

As a special field of horticulture a garden exclusively of ferns presents a wonderful challenge to skill in soil culture and landscape design. For the devotee there is such a wealth of varied charm among the ferns in species and varieties that a whole garden may be devoted solely to their growth. In a comparatively small garden an amazing number of species may be grown. Here the great clumpy Osmundas and the greedy spreading Sensitive and Hay-scented Ferns have no place, but even these may be restrained with a barrier of rockwork or metal edging sunk in the ground.

The general site of the fern garden should include some sloping ground, some dense shade, some light shade, and an open, partly sunny location. All these, however, must be either naturally moist or situated where the area may be watered artificially. An open, moisture-retaining soil is so important to all ferns that it is worth while to provide the whole area with a good basic soil before small pockets of special conditions are developed. A heavy clay soil or a dry sandy soil must be transformed by the incorporation of humus. This can be done by making leaf compost or by purchasing peat.

Because ferns are so closely associated in our minds with the natural beauty of wilderness and woods, it is generally advisable to make every effort to provide a setting of informal naturalness. The inclusion of some large stones and an unevenness of soil levels will help to provide such setting in the absence of a natural site. Shade provided by deep-rooted trees or shrubs that will not rob all the moisture from the ground is ideal. The shade on the north side of a building or along a wall provides a good site, if a somewhat unnatural one. Many fern enthusiasts have found that the shade provided by a vine-covered arbor or shade-house is easily effected and controlled for density.

No single planting formula can be given. Each garden will suggest its own treatment and every gardener will express his own whims. If the fern garden as a whole can be broken up by natural features or by paths into a number of separate sections, each part may then provide a site of special conditions or for the grouping of special genera. It is generally advisable to make an over-all plan in advance, taking into consideration the total effect by studying heights, texture, and cultural requirements. Such a plan will, however, probably be rather frequently modified by the demands of the site, the supply of plants, or the changing interests of the gardener. There lies the charm of fern gardening.

To meet the special needs of various ferns the best plan is to study a few sites where ferns are flourishing in natural settings and then try to reproduce those conditions in the garden. For the general run of Woodferns this is comparatively simple. It is mostly the small rock-loving ferns that pose the problems. Some of these are found almost exclusively on acid rocks, others exclusively on limy rocks, and some are rather indifferent, so long as the material is porous and moisture-providing. In fact this last condition of a friendly, root-welcoming sort of rock, full of fissures or pockets, seems most important of all. In such pockets there is slowly built up a mixture of small rock particles and the humus of decaying vegetation. Such a soil, placed in the cracks between moisture-holding rocks that are built up one on another to suggest a natural ledge and placed in such a location as to furnish free circulation of air, but out of the glare of the sun, will offer a home for small Aspleniums, Woodsias, Cliffbrakes, and Lipferns. In the absence of suitable natural stones, old bricks set endwise into a sloping bank, with a sandy humus filling the cracks between, may give them an ideal home.

COLLECTING AND PROPAGATING

Many of the common ferns are found in such abundance in nature that they may be collected without danger of destroying the site. The more rare ferns, like the Male Fern and Goldie's Fern and Braun's Holly Fern, and certain of the uncommon rock ferns, should not be collected in the wild. The very fact that they are rare suggests that they do not multiply quickly in nature and every effort should be made to conserve them in those places that furnish the kind of special conditions they require. It means also that these conditions are difficult to reproduce in most gardens.

The common ferns can be transplanted almost any time of year as long as their roots are not permitted to dry out before replanting. It is safest to dig a good ball of soil with each plant in order not to destroy the fine hairlike roots so essential for keeping fronds fresh and flourishing. A stout spade with a sharp blade for cutting foreign roots is essential for taking up an adequate ball with large ferns like Osmundas or a good-sized mat for the running ferns. For smaller varieties a strong butcher knife with which to cut a neat circle about the plant is sufficient. For those ferns growing in crevices of rock a sharp knife and much patience and skill are required to get the full root system without injuring it.

The mat-forming ferns can be multiplied by dividing them into pieces, as long as there is some underground rootstock and the growing tip is not destroyed. Crown growers may be divided in the spring with a strong knife, and frequently small offsets can be pulled away from the side of the crown. This should be done with the whole plant dug out of the ground and the soil washed from the roots, so that the fine rootlets can be teased apart without damaging them.

When first transplanted all ferns require frequent watering until they become established, to prevent excessive wilting.

The best way to acquire a supply of the rarer species or to get a large number of the commoner ones without too much hard work is to grow them from spores. The spores of all the species can be treated alike until they have reached size enough to be put in the garden as promising young plants. A single frond, or even a small piece of frond with ripe spores, will furnish as many spores as anyone would wish to handle. Place the frond in a cellophane wrapper. As it withers the spores will fall out as an infinitely fine dust.

Every grower has his own favorite growing medium and favorite container, but essentially the method is always the same. For the amateur who wishes only a few plants of a species, a small clay flowerpot or a covered plastic refrigerator dish makes the handiest container. This should be cleaned with boiling water, or a weak solution of potassium permanganate. Fill the container with a soil mixture, one part each of sand, peat, and loam. It is best to sterilize this soil with steam or boiling water before filling the containers. The soil will then not carry competing weed seeds or foreign spores of mosses and fungi. It is a wise precaution to pour over the soil in the container enough boiling water to soak through. When this has cooled sow the spores on the surface as thinly as possible. Cover the pot with a piece of glass, or place the cover securely on the plastic dish. This will keep the soil from drying out. Place the containers in a warm room out of the direct sun. If pots are used it may be necessary to stand them in a dish of water to prevent drying.

Small green discs of the prothalli will appear from two weeks to two months or more. Later these will send up the tiny erect fernlike plants, the sporophytes. These will begin to make roots and may be transplanted into individual pots of new soil or in flats. When first transplanted they should be kept covered, as they have been up to this point, in order to keep in the moisture. Gradually give them more air, to toughen them up for use in the garden.

Our native ferns are not recommended for house plants. However, the little ferns like the Aspleniums can be successfully kept alive several years or more in a well-balanced and carefully tended terrarium.

The Ferns and Their Allies in the Past

BY THEODOR JUST

Chief Curator, Department of Botany, Chicago Natural History Museum

THE ORIGIN of life is shrouded in mystery. Nothing is known about the time when the first plants appeared and what they looked like, or the fortuitous circumstances that made their appearance possible. Most likely a long series of preliminary events was required before living matter (protoplasm) with all its chemical and structural complexity could be formed. Certainly these primitive plants were able to react to their environment, manufacture their own food, and reproduce their own kind. It has been estimated that photosynthesis, the process by which green plants make their own food with the aid of energy derived from sunlight, may have appeared over a billion years ago.

The first plant fossils are found in rocks of Pre-Cambrian age, considerably over 500 million years old. Since these fossils are not well preserved, little can be learned from them regarding their structure and functions. They have, however, been referred to the blue-green algae and bacteria, the simplest known living plants. But with the beginning of the Paleozoic Era, about 500 million years ago, new plant forms appear in the geological record. First came the unicellular motile types, or flagellates, later followed by other algae, especially green algae and possible forerunners of brown and red algae. Most of these settled as vast sediments that left extensive geological formations as records of their activity. All of them were aquatic.

The appearance of land plants, particularly vascular plants, in the Upper Silurian and Lower Devonian Periods, about 300 million years ago, represents the second major step in the geological history of the Plant Kingdom. The presence of vascular tissue enabled these plants to invade land and maintain themselves there. The early land plants (genus *Psilophyton*) were first described from Canadian deposits but have since been found in many other parts of the world, especially in the United States, and in northern and western Europe. Fairly simple in structure, some early vascular plants were made up of a creeping underground stem from which arose the small green, leafless, erect parts that branched sparingly and carried spore cases at their tips. The best-preserved representatives of this group were found in the famous Rhynie chert of Scotland, and referred to the genus *Rhynia*. Their internal structure is actually better known than that of many living plants. Forked branching, so characteristic of the veins of our living ferns, was typical of these early vascular plants (Psilophytales). Others, more complex, were elaborately branched and bore leaves.

Along with the psilophytes occurred forerunners of the major groups of vascular plants. For instance, the earliest ferns known existed in the Devonian, but have long been extinct. They are often grouped together as Coenopteridineae. An outstanding example is the Devonian fern genus *Archaeopteris*, used as an index fossil of the Upper Devonian strata of the eastern United States and Canada. These plants produced large fronds three feet or more in length, were probably shrubby, and grew along streams. The compound fronds resembled those of many modern ferns, but produced sporangia of two kinds on special fertile pinnae. *Archaeopteris* may possibly be a link between psilophytes and seed ferns.

The early pteridophyte floras of the Devonian and Lower Carboniferous Periods were rather uniform; the floras of the Upper Carboniferous (Pennsylvanian) and Permian Periods, some 200 million years ago, show definite differences in composition. Thus it is possible to distinguish four major floral provinces, namely: (1) the Euramerican Permo-Carboniferous flora, extending from the eastern United States across Europe to the Ural Mountains and Iran (for reconstruction see pp. 258–59); (2) the Angara, or Siberian, flora, ranging from the Ural Mountains across Siberia to the Pacific coast of Asia; (3) the Cathaysia flora, ranging from China (Shansi Province) and Korea to the East Indies (Sumatra), New Guinea, and western North America as far as Colorado, Oklahoma, and Texas, where it bordered on the Euramerican flora (these three provinces apparently enjoyed a relatively warm climate and are characterized by the rain-forest coal flora); (4) the Glossopteris flora, by comparison, made up the cool-climate rain forest found throughout Gondwanaland, the southern land mass that included large sections of central and southern South America, central and southern Africa, Australia, Antarctica, and India south of the Himalayan arch. This province is named after the most common fossils — tongue-shaped leaves with reticulate venation — that may belong to a separate group of gymnosperms (cycads, conifers, etc.).

Our knowledge of fossil floras is based on fossils of different states of preservation. Leaves and other flat parts are often found as mere impressions, with practically no organic material left. If, on the other hand, some organic material remains — usually in a carbonized state — these fossils are called compressions. Some of the finest compressions, from the world-famous Mazon Creek area of northern Illinois, are of middle Pennsylvanian age and are preserved in sandstone nodules that easily split open to show the fossil and its counterpart. Hundreds of species of fern-like parts have been recorded from these nodules. Other fossils are so well preserved that their internal structure can be studied in detail, and mostly represent small pieces of roots, stems, stalks, seeds, sporangia, cones, and spores. Coal-balls furnish most of these petrified fossils. Over 150 species have so far been found in American material. Coal itself may contain numerous spores, which can be isolated and used for correlation of coal seams over large areas.

Consequently, many fossil plants are known only from one organ or from several parts that have been identified as belonging to the same species. Reconstruction of fossil plants is an arduous and difficult task, depending partly on lucky finds and definitely on extensive and detailed study of every clue offered by the all too often fragmentary material. The scene of a swamp forest of the great coal age shown on pages 258–59 reflects, therefore, the combined efforts and knowledge of generations of students of fossil plants as seen and executed with the skill and techniques of the best artist-preparators.

This exhibit contains life-size models of the fossil members or forerunners of most modern groups of vascular plants. Of the 22 species of plants shown, a dozen represent large treelike clubmosses, two belong to horsetails, and three are ferns. The remainder are seed ferns and one represents the extinct group of conifer-like trees, the *Cordaites*. The treelike clubmosses, sometimes attaining 100 feet in height and over 5 feet in diameter, are remarkable for the fact that the woody portion of the stem is relatively small, whereas the bulk of the trunk is made up of bark. The surfaces of these trunks show characteristic markings indicating the position of leaves (leaf cushions and leaf scars). In *Lepidodendron* (scale trees) the leaf cushions are rhombic in shape, so densely packed as to form an armor, and indicative of the spiral arrangement of leaves. By comparison, Sigillarias were so named because of the seal-like impressions of their persistent leaf scars, usually arranged in vertical rows on the smooth or ribbed stem. The horsetails are represented by two members, one a slender herb with small wedge-shaped leaves, belonging to the genus *Sphenophyllum*, and the other a large treelike calamite (genus *Calamites*), whose whorled leaves are usually treated as the genus *Annularia*. Unlike the treelike clubmosses, these giants reached the height of some bamboos, which they resembled by their cylindrical reedlike stems, whose interiors are often preserved as casts with characteristic markings that reflect the interior structure of calamite stems. Most calamites were profusely and regularly branched, and thus were bushy in appearance. Fossil ferns are represented by tree ferns, the stems of which belong to the now completely extinct genus *Psaronius*. Those shown in the illustration bore leaves, belonging to the genus *Pecopteris*, in straight rows, as shown by the arrangement of leaf scars. Other members of this genus with leaf scars in the modern spiral arrangement have also been found.

Unlike their descendants, fossil clubmosses, horsetails, and ferns grew to be the size of great trees and were important members of Paleozoic forests. Today the small size of the plants and small number of species belonging to these groups limit them to the layer of herbaceous plants. Yet, fossils resembling the modern genus *Equisetum* have been found from the Carboniferous Period on and have been referred to the genus *Equisetites*. Therefore, the latter represents one of the oldest stocks of vascular plants. The majority of fernlike leaves so characteristic of this age has been shown to belong to a group of extinct seed plants, the seed ferns or pteridosperms.

Many of the early ferns have since become extinct and are today represented only by the Ophioglossales and Marattiales, but most of the ferns living during the great coal age and subsequent periods belong to eusporangiate groups. By comparison, more than 90 per cent of living fern genera are of the leptosporangiate types that became prominent during later geological periods, namely the Mesozoic and Cenozoic Eras. Thus families like the Osmundaceae, Schizaeaceae, Gleicheniaceae, and others appeared early during Mesozoic times (Triassic and Jurassic), whereas Polypodiaceae, Cyatheaceae, and others appeared during the Cretaceous period before the beginning of the Cenozoic Era. Thus the majority of our living ferns appeared after the great coal age, particularly during the last 100 million years or so. Their rapid development and expansion parallel therefore in large measure the expansion of flowering plants. Although it is customary to refer to the great coal age as the age of ferns (and their allies), it is clear that at present the leptosporangiate groups are the more successful ferns.

A LIFE–SIZE RESTORATION OF A SWAMP FOREST OF THE COAL AGE

Ernest R. Graham Hall, Chicago Natural History Museum

About 240 million years ago, ancestors of our modern horsetails, clubmosses, ferns, and cone-bearing trees grew together in vast swamps with the now extinct seed ferns, many of them attaining the size of forest trees. Their remains accumulated to form thick mats of plant debris. Covered and compressed by sediments, while being changed chemically, these immense deposits of the vegetation of the past became the coal beds of today.

The two tall trunks in the left foreground, the large trunks in the middle and left background, and the fallen log across the center of the picture, together with the large pine-like leaves and cones in the upper left-hand corner, all represent fossil **clubmosses** of the genus *Sigillaria*.

The symmetrical tree with whorled branches and leaves in the right-hand foreground is a fossil **horsetail** of the genus *Calamites*. The small plants in front of the fallen log are fossil **horsetails** of the genus *Sphenophyllum*, whose whorled leaves are wedge-shaped.

The dark slender trunk left of the center is the stem of a fossil **fern** belonging to the genus *Caulopteris*.

The fernlike fronds behind the second tree in the left foreground represent the genus *Neuropteris* of the now extinct seed ferns. The nutlike structures hanging from the tips of the leaves are the seeds.

This life-size restoration includes some fossil animals of extraordinary dimensions, the roach (*Archeoblattina beecheri*) being 6 inches long and the dragonfly in the center (*Meganeura monyi*) having a wing spread of 36 inches.

This exhibit is scientifically the most accurate and grand display of fossil plants in any museum in the world.

Bibliography,
Check-Lists, and Index

Bibliography

General

Birdseye, Clarence and Eleanor G. *Growing Woodland Plants.* New York: Oxford University Press, 1951.

Bower, Frederick O. *The Ferns (Filicales) Treated Comparatively with a View to Their Natural Classification.* Cambridge, Eng.: Cambridge University Press, 1923–28. 3 v.

Broun, Maurice (ed.). *Index to North American Ferns.* Orleans, Mass.: Published by the compiler, 1938.

Christensen, Carl. *Index Filicum.* Copenhagen: H. Hagerup, 1906. Supplements 1913, 1917, 1934.

Clute, Willard Nelson. *The Fern Allies of North America North of Mexico.* New York: Frederick A. Stokes Co., 1905.

——. *Our Ferns: Their Haunts, Habits and Folklore,* 2nd ed. New York: Frederick A. Stokes Co., 1938.

Copeland, Edwin Bingham. *Genera Filicum, the Genera of Ferns.* Waltham, Mass.: Chronica Botanica Co., 1947.

Durand, Herbert. *Wild Flowers and Ferns in Their Homes and in Our Gardens.* New York: G. P. Putnam's Sons, 1925.

Eaton, D. C. *Ferns of North America.* Salem, Mass.: S. E. Cassino, 1879–80. 2 v.

Fernald, Merritt Lyndon. *Gray's Manual of Botany . . . A Handbook of the Flowering Plants and Ferns of the Central and Northeastern United States and Adjacent Canada,* 8th ed. New York: American Book Co., 1950.

Gleason, Henry A. *The New Britton and Brown Illustrated Flora of the Northeastern United States and Adjacent Canada.* New York: New York Botanical Garden, 1952. 3 v.

Lawrence, George H. M. *Taxonomy of Vascular Plants.* New York: Macmillan Co., 1951.

Manton, I. *Problems of Cytology and Evolution in the Pteridophyta.* Cambridge, Eng.: Cambridge University Press, 1950.

Marie-Victorin, Frère. *Les Lycopodinées du Quebec et leurs formes minueres.* Montreal: University of Montreal, 1925.

Roberts, Edith A., and Julia R. Lawrence. *American Ferns: How to Know, Grow and Use Them.* New York: Macmillan Co., 1935.

Slosson, Margaret. *How Ferns Grow.* New York: Henry Holt & Co., 1906.

Verdoorn, Frans, in collaboration with others. *Manual of Pteridology.* The Hague: Martinus Nijhoff, 1938.

Waters, Campbell E. *Ferns: A Manual for the Northeastern States with Analytical Keys Based on the Stalks and on the Fructification.* New York: Henry Holt & Co., 1903.

Wherry, Edgar T. *Guide to Eastern Ferns*, 2nd ed. Philadelphia: University of Pennsylvania Press, 1948.

Wiley, Farida A. *Ferns of Northeastern United States.* New York: American Museum of Natural History, 1936, revised 1948.

Articles

Benedict, R. C. "Ferns As House Plants," *American Fern Journal,* **12**:77–92 (1922).

——. "Problems in the Study of the Spinulose Ferns," *American Fern Journal,* **14**:69–74 (1924).

Blake, S. F. *State and Local Fern Floras of the United States.* Reprinted from *American Fern Journal,* **40**:148–65 (1950).

Manton, I., and S. Walker. *Cytology of the Dryopteris spinulosa Complex in Eastern North America.* Reprinted from *Nature,* **171**:1116 (June 20, 1953).

Maxon, W. R. "Ferns As a Hobby," *National Geographic Magazine,* **47**:541–86 (1925).

Svenson, H. K. "The New World Species of Azolla," *American Fern Journal,* **34**:69–84 (1944).

Fern Books or Lists for Specific States and Localities Covered in This Field Guide

The counts of Ferns and Fern Allies given below are based on S. F. Blake's "State and Local Fern Flora of the United States," *American Fern Journal,* **40**:148–65 (1950). These counts are approximate. Since 1950 new species have been discovered; and some species have been deducted from Blake's list because they were wrongly classified as species or wrongly identified.

MAINE 50 Ferns 27 Allies
Ogden, Edith Bolan. *The Ferns of Maine.* Reprinted from the *Maine Bulletin,* **51**, No. 3 (October 1948), at the University Press, Orono, Maine.

NEW HAMPSHIRE 47 Ferns 27 Allies
Scamman, Edith. *Ferns and Fern Allies of New Hampshire,* Bulletin No. 2, New Hampshire Academy of Science, Durham, N.H., 1947. Printed by Smith & Town, Berlin, N.H.

VERMONT 53 Ferns 28 Allies
Flynn, Nellie F. *Flora of Burlington and Vicinity: A List of the Fern and Seed Plants Growing without Cultivation.* Burlington, Vt.: Botanical Laboratories, University of Vermont, 1935.

MASSACHUSETTS 50 Ferns 26 Allies
Dame, L. L., and F. S. Collins. *Flora of Middlesex County, Massachusetts.* Malden, Mass.: Middlesex Institute, 1888.

Hoffmann, Ralph. "The Flora of Berkshire County, Massachusetts," *Proceedings of The Boston Society of Natural History*, **36,** No. 5:171–382 (1922).

Robinson, John. *The Flora of Essex County, Massachusetts.* Salem, Mass.: Essex Institute, 1880.

RHODE ISLAND 42 Ferns 15 Allies

Wright, Kenneth E., and Dorothy L. Crandall. "Rhode Island Ferns," *Torreya*, **41**:73–75 (May–June 1941).

CONNECTICUT 51 Ferns 26 Allies

Graves, Charles Burr, and others. *Catalogue of the Flowering Plants and Ferns of Connecticut.* State of Connecticut, State Geological and Natural History Survey Bulletin No. 14 and Supplement No. 48 of 1930.

NEW YORK 62 Ferns 31 Allies

Small, John Kunkel. *Ferns of the Vicinity of New York.* Lancaster, Pa.: Science Press Printing Co., 1935.

NEW JERSEY 53 Ferns 25 Allies

Chrysler, M. A., and J. L. Edwards. *The Ferns of New Jersey, Including the Fern Allies.* New Brunswick, N.J.: Rutgers University Press, 1947.

PENNSYLVANIA 56 Ferns 22 Allies

Canan, Elsie Deane. *A Key to the Ferns of Pennsylvania.* Lancaster, Pa.: Science Press Printing Co., 1946.

Clute, Willard N. *The Ferns and Fern Allies of the Upper Susquehanna Valley.* Binghamton, N.Y.: W. N. Clute & Co., 1898.

INDIANA 34 Ferns 17 Allies

Deam, Charles C. *Flora of Indiana.* Indianapolis, 1940.

Friesner, Ray C. *Key to Genera of Indiana Ferns and Fern Allies.* Butler University Botanical Studies **1**:55–60. Indianapolis, 1929.

ILLINOIS 48 Ferns 14 Allies

Jones, George Neville. *Flora of Illinois, Containing Keys for Identification of the Flowering Plants and Ferns.* The American Midland Naturalist Monograph No. 5, 2nd ed. Notre Dame, Ind.: University of Notre Dame Press, 1950.

OHIO 52 Ferns 22 Allies

Hopkins, L. S. "The Fern Flora of Ohio," *Fern Bulletin*, **15**:1–13 (1907).

Schaffner, John H. *Revised Catalog of Ohio Vascular Plants.* Columbus, O.: Ohio State University, 1932.

MICHIGAN 55 Ferns 26 Allies

Billington, Cecil. *Ferns of Michigan.* Cranbrook Institute of Science, Bulletin No. 32. Bloomfield Hills, Mich., 1952.

WISCONSIN 52 Ferns 25 Allies
Tryon, R. M., Jr., and others. *The Ferns and Fern Allies of Wisconsin,* 2nd ed. Madison, Wisc.: University of Wisconsin Press, 1953.

KENTUCKY 45 Ferns 8 Allies
Williamson, John. *Ferns of Kentucky.* Louisville, Ky.: John P. Morton & Co., 1878.

VIRGINIA 58 Ferns 19 Allies
Massey, A. B. *The Ferns and Fern Allies of Virginia.* Bulletin of the Virginia Polytechnic Institute, 37, No. 7 (May 1944).

WEST VIRGINIA 53 Ferns 15 Allies
Strausbaugh, P. D., and Earl L. Core. *Flora of West Virginia* (Pt. 1). West Virginia University Bulletin, Ser. 52, No. 12-2. Morgantown, W. Va., 1952.

MARYLAND 54 Ferns 20 Allies
DELAWARE 34 Ferns 17 Allies
DISTRICT OF COLUMBIA 40 Ferns 13 Allies
Reed, Clyde F. *The Ferns and Fern-Allies of Maryland and Delaware, Including District of Columbia.* Baltimore, Md.: Reed Herbarium, 1953.

CANADA
Marie-Victorin, Frère. *Flore laurentienne.* Montreal: Les Frères des Ecoles Chrétiennes, 1947.
Eifert, Virginia S., and Bruce Metcalfe. *Native Ferns.* Toronto: Canadian Nature Magazine, 1946.

NEW ENGLAND
Dodge, Raynal. *The Ferns and Fern Allies of New England.* Binghamton, N.Y.: W. N. Clute & Co., 1896.
Eastman, Helen. *New England Ferns and Their Common Allies.* Boston: Houghton Mifflin & Co., 1904.

For Localities Adjacent to Those Covered in This Field Guide

GEORGIA 45 Ferns 15 Allies
McVaugh, Rogers, and Joseph H. Pyron. *Ferns of Georgia.* Athens, Ga.: University of Georgia Press, 1951.

TENNESSEE 50 Ferns 11 Allies
Shaver, Jesse M. *Ferns of Tennessee with the Allies Excluded.* Nashville: George Peabody College for Teachers, 1954.

MINNESOTA 47 Ferns 25 Allies
Tryon, Rolla M., Jr. *The Ferns and Fern Allies of Minnesota.* Minneapolis: University of Minnesota Press, 1954.

SOUTHEASTERN UNITED STATES

Small, John Kunkel. *Ferns of the Southeastern States*. Lancaster, Pa.: Science Press Printing Co., 1938.

British Isles and Western Europe

FOR CONTEMPORARY TEXT AND ILLUSTRATIONS

Ceruti, Arturo. *Botanica Illustrata*. Turin: Chiantore, 1946.

Clapham, A. R., and others. *Flora of the British Isles*. Cambridge, Eng.: Cambridge University Press, 1952.

Hyde, A. A., and A. E. Wade. *Welsh Ferns*. Cardiff: National Museum of Wales, 1948.

Hylander, Nils. *Nordisk Karlvaxtflora*. Uppsala: Almqvist and Wiksell, 1953.

Mansfeld, R. "Verzeichnis der Farn und Blütenpflanzen des Deutsches Reiches," *Ber. Deutsch. Bot. Ges.*, **58** (1940).

Step, Edward. *Wayside and Woodland Ferns*. London and New York: Frederick Warne, 1949.

Stokes, W. J. *The Observer's Book of British Ferns*. London and New York: Frederick Warne, 1950.

FOR ILLUSTRATIONS AND NOT NECESSARILY FOR TEXT

Britten, James. *European Ferns*. London, Paris, New York: Cassell, Pitter, Galpin & Co., *ca*. 1900.

Moore, Thomas. *The Ferns of Great Britain and Ireland*. London: Bradberry & Evans, 1855. Nature-printed.

Sowerby, John E. *British Wild Flowers*. London: John Van Voorst, 1876.

More Recent Fern Publications

Cody, W. J. *Ferns of the Ottawa District*. Ottawa, Ont.: Canada Department of Agriculture, 1956.

Jermy, A. C. *A Revised Preliminary Census List of British Pteridophytes*. Supplement to *British Fern Gazette*, Vol. 9, Pt.1. London: British Museum for British Pteridological Society, 1960.

Taylor, P. G. *British Ferns and Mosses*. London: Eyre and Spottiswoode, 1960. The Kew Series.

Vannorsdall, Harry H. *Ferns of Ohio*. Wilmington, O.: Published by the Author, 1956.

Wherry, Edgar T. *The Fern Guide: Northeastern and Midland U.S. and Adjacent Canada*. New York: Doubleday & Co., Inc., 1961.

Check-List for Northeastern and Central North America

THIS list of the ferns and their allies may be used to record the species you have found. Blank spaces are provided for hybrids, varieties, or forms found and identified.

........ADIANTUM CAPILLUS-
       VENERIS
........ADIANTUM PEDATUM
........ADIANTUM ....
........ADIANTUM ....

........ASPLENIUM BRADLEYI
........ASPLENIUM MONTANUM
........ASPLENIUM PINNATIFIDUM
........ASPLENIUM PLATYNEURON
........ASPLENIUM RESILIENS
........ASPLENIUM RUTA-MURARIA
........ASPLENIUM TRICHOMANES
........ASPLENIUM VIRIDE
........ASPLENIUM ✕ GRAVESII
........ASPLENIUM ✕ KENTUCKIENSE
........ASPLENIUM ✕ TRUDELLI
........ASPLENIUM.....................

........ASPLENOSORUS EBENOIDES

........ATHYRIUM FELIX-FEMINA
........ATHYRIUM PYCNOCARPON
........ATHYRIUM
       THELYPTEROIDES
........ATHYRIUM ....
........ATHYRIUM ....
........ATHYRIUM ....
........ATHYRIUM ....

........AZOLLA CAROLINIANA
........AZOLLA ....

........BOTRYCHIUM DISSECTUM
........BOTRYCHIUM
       LANCEOLATUM
........BOTRYCHIUM LUNARIA
........BOTRYCHIUM
       MATRICARIIFOLIUM
........BOTRYCHIUM MULTIFIDUM
........BOTRYCHIUM SIMPLEX
........BOTRYCHIUM VIRGINIANUM
........BOTRYCHIUM ....
........BOTRYCHIUM ....
........BOTRYCHIUM ....
........BOTRYCHIUM ....

........CAMPTOSORUS
       RHIZOPHYLLUS
........CAMPTOSORUS ....

........CHEILANTHES
       ALABAMENSIS
........CHEILANTHES FEEI
........CHEILANTHES TOMENTOSA
........CHEILANTHES LANOSA
........CHEILANTHES.....................

........CRYPTOGRAMMA CRISPA
........CRYPTOGRAMMA STELLERI

........CYSTOPTERIS BULBIFERA
........CYSTOPTERIS FRAGILIS
........CYSTOPTERIS ....
........CYSTOPTERIS ....
........CYSTOPTERIS ....

........DENNSTAEDTIA
   PUNCTILOBULA
........DENNSTAEDTIA ....

........DRYOPTERIS AUSTRIACA
........DRYOPTERIS X BOOTTII
........DRYOPTERIS CLINTONIANA
........DRYOPTERIS CRISTATA
........DRYOPTERIS FILIX-MAS
........DRYOPTERIS FRAGRANS
........DRYOPTERIS FRUCTUOSA
........DRYOPTERIS GOLDIANA
........DRYOPTERIS INTERMEDIA
........DRYOPTERIS MARGINALIS
........DRYOPTERIS SPINULOSA
........DRYOPTERIS ....
........DRYOPTERIS ....
........DRYOPTERIS ....

........EQUISETUM ARVENSE
........EQUISETUM FLUVIATILE
........EQUISETUM HIEMALE
........EQUISETUM KANSANUM
........EQUISETUM LAEVIGATUM
........EQUISETUM LITORALE
........EQUISETUM PALUSTRE
........EQUISETUM PRATENSE
........EQUISETUM SCIRPOIDES
........EQUISETUM SYLVATICUM
........EQUISETUM VARIEGATUM

........GYMNOCARPIUM
   DRYOPTERIS
........GYMNOCARPIUM
   ROBERTIANUM

........ISOETES BUTLERI
........ISOETES EATONII
........ISOETES ECHINOSPORA
........ISOETES ENGELMANNII
........ISOETES FOVEOLATA
........ISOETES MACROSPORA
........ISOETES MELANOPODA

........ISOETES RIPARIA
........ISOETES TUCKERMANII
........ISOETES VIRGINICA
........ISOETES ....

........LYCOPODIUM
   ALOPECUROIDES
........LYCOPODIUM ANNOTINUM
........LYCOPODIUM
   CAROLINIANUM
........LYCOPODIUM CLAVATUM
........LYCOPODIUM
   COMPLANATUM
........LYCOPODIUM INUNDATUM
........LYCOPODIUM LUCIDULUM
........LYCOPODIUM OBSCURUM
........LYCOPODIUM SABINIFOLIUM
........LYCOPODIUM SELAGO
........LYCOPODIUM TRISTACHYUM
........LYCOPODIUM ....
........LYCOPODIUM ....
........LYCOPODIUM ....
........LYCOPODIUM ....

........LYGODIUM PALMATUM

........MARSILEA QUADRIFOLIA
........MARSILEA ....

........MATTEUCCIA
   STRUTHIOPTERIS

........ONOCLEA SENSIBILIS
........ONOCLEA ....

........OPHIOGLOSSUM
   ENGELMANNII
........OPHIOGLOSSUM VULGATUM
........OPHIOGLOSSUM ....

........OSMUNDA CINNAMOMEA
........OSMUNDA CLAYTONIANA
........OSMUNDA REGALIS

Check-List for the British Isles and Western Europe

IN THE following list those species marked with an asterisk are described in this *Field Guide*. Those marked with a (B) are supposedly found in the British Isles and not in western Europe, while those marked with an (E) are supposedly found in Europe and not in the British Isles. (See Bibliography for recommended handbooks for those species not occurring in northeastern and central North America.)

........ADIANTIUM CAPILLUS-
  VENERIS*

........ANOGRAMMA LEPTOPHYLLA

........ASPLENIUM ADIANTUM-
  NIGRUM
........ASPLENIUM FONTANUM (E)
........ASPLENIUM MARINUM (B)
........ASPLENIUM OBOVATUM
........ASPLENIUM
  RUTA-MURARIA*
........ASPLENIUM
  SEPTENTRIONALE
........ASPLENIUM TRICHOMANES*
........ASPLENIUM VIRIDE*
........ASPLENIUM............................
........ASPLENIUM............................
........ASPLENIUM............................

........ATHYRIUM ALPESTRE
........ATHYRIUM FILIX-FEMINA*
........ATHYRIUM ....

........AZOLLA CAROLINIANA*
........AZOLLA FILICULOIDES (B)

........BLECHNUM SPICANT

........BOTRYCHIUM
  LANCEOLATUM* (E)
........BOTRYCHIUM LUNARIA*
........BOTRYCHIUM
  MATRICARIIFOLIUM* (E)
........BOTRYCHIUM
  MULTIFIDUM* (E)
........BOTRYCHIUM SIMPLEX* (E)
........BOTRYCHIUM
  VIRGINIANUM*

........CETERACH OFFICINARUM

........CRYPTOGRAMMA CRISPA*

........CYSTOPTERIS FRAGILIS*
........CYSTOPTERIS MONTANA
........CYSTOPTERIS ....
........CYSTOPTERIS ....

........DRYOPTERIS
  ABBREVIATA (B)
........DRYOPTERIS AEMULA
........DRYOPTERIS AUSTRIACA*
........DRYOPTERIS BORRERI
........DRYOPTERIS CRISTATA*
........DRYOPTERIS FILIX-MAS*
........DRYOPTERIS FRAGRANS* (E)

........DRYOPTERIS SPINULOSA*
........DRYOPTERIS VILLARSII
........DRYOPTERIS ....
........DRYOPTERIS ....

........EQUISETUM ARVENSE*
........EQUISETUM FLUVIATILE*
........EQUISETUM HIEMALE*
........EQUISETUM × LITORALE*
........EQUISETUM PALUSTRE*
........EQUISETUM PRATENSE*
........EQUISETUM RAMOSISSIMUM
........EQUISETUM
         SCIRPOIDES* (E)
........EQUISETUM SYLVATICUM*
........EQUISETUM TELMATEIA
........EQUISETUM × TRACHYODON
........EQUISETUM VARIEGATUM*
........EQUISETUM....................
........EQUISETUM....................
........EQUISETUM....................

........GYMNOCARPIUM
         DRYOPTERIS*
........GYMNOCARPIUM
         ROBERTIANUM*

........HYMENOPHYLLUM
         TUNBRIGENSE
........HYMENOPHYLLUM
         WILSONI

........ISOETES ECHINOSPORA*
........ISOETES HYSTRIX (B)
........ISOETES LACUSTRIS*
........ISOETES ....
........ISOETES ....

........LYCOPODIUM ALPINUM
........LYCOPODIUM ANNOTINUM*
........LYCOPODIUM CLAVATUM*
........LYCOPODIUM
         COMPLANATUM* (E)

........LYCOPODIUM INUNDATUM*
........LYCOPODIUM SELAGO*
........LYCOPODIUM....................

........MARSILEA QUADRIFOLIA*

........MATTEUCCIA
         STRUTHIOPTERIS* (E)

........NOTHOLAENA
         MARANTAE (E)
........NOTHOLAENA ....

........OPHIOGLOSSUM
         LUSITANICUM (B)
........OPHIOGLOSSUM VULGATUM*
........OPHIOGLOSSUM....................

........OSMUNDA REGALIS*

........PHYLLITIS
         SCOLOPENDRIUM*
........PHYLLITIS....................
........PHYLLITIS....................
........PHYLLITIS....................

........PILULARIA GLOBULIFERA

........POLYPODIUM VULGARE*
........POLYPODIUM....................
........POLYPODIUM....................
........POLYPODIUM....................

........POLYSTICHUM
         BRAUNII* (E)
........POLYSTICHUM LOBATUM
........POLYSTICHUM LONCHITIS
........POLYSTICHUM SETIFERUM
........POLYSTICHUM....................
........POLYSTICHUM....................

........PTERIDIUM AQUILINUM*

Index

Bold-face type indicates the main descriptive section.